Messages in Trial Markers:
The Youngest Resistance Fighter

By

Kendrick Kirk

ISBN:0615534600
978-0-615-53460-2

wkenkirk@gmail.com

To Dallas and Barbara:
May we always remember the
price of our freedom and those
who paid it.

Kendrick Kirk

The President
OF THE UNITED STATES OF AMERICA
has directed me to express to

JEAN-JACQUES AUDUC

the gratitude and appreciation of the
American people for gallant service
in assisting the escape of Allied
soldiers from the enemy

DWIGHT D. EISENHOWER
General of the Army
Commanding General United States Forces European Theater

LE GÉNÉRAL DE GAULLE 2.2.60

Merci de votre
témoignage !

G. de Gaulle.

Monsieur et Madame J.J. AUDUC.
2 rue du Tourniquet.
Le Mans. (Sarthe)

President Charles de Gaulle thanks Jean-Jacques Auduc for his war efforts.

Medals awarded to Jean-Jacques Auduc

| Croix du | Volunteer | Resistance |
| Combattant | Combattant | Medal |

| Legion of | Croix de | U. S. Medal |
| Honor | Guerre | of Freedom |

CONTENTS

INTRODUCTION

The Auduc family, from Le Mans, is one of the most decorated French families, in appreciation for their contributions to the French Resistance during World War II. Jean-Jacques Auduc became the youngest recipient of the Croix de Guerre (Cross of War) for his Resistance contributions as a 12 year old. His father, Alfred, was inspirational through the undaunted spirit that led him to continue to conduct sabotage even while imprisoned in a Nazi concentration camp. It is interesting to study how Alfred's courage and audacity evolved from his resolve to fight the German occupation with every resource he could muster. Renée, Jean-Jacques' clever mother, became one of the highest ranking female officers in the FFC, the Free French forces. Even his grandmother Marie assisted their Resistance network in remarkable ways. Several other members of this courageous family contributed to their network and some paid a dear price. This is the story of a courageous and inspiring family which was awarded 7 Croix de Guerres, 4 Legion of Honors, 3 U. S. Medals of Freedom and numerous other recognitions. A part of their story was briefly told in the July 7, 2003, edition of *The New York Times*.

To understand how they were impacted by the war, their lives before and after World War II are related. The stories of those who interacted with the Auduc's, molding and transforming their activities, are also told. The person having the most profound influence was the organizer of their network, André Dubois, an SOE agent who, until his capture, was one of the most important radio operators in the French Resistance and was thus one of the most important Resistance fighters. Of similar importance to the Auduc network was American Captain Fred Floege, a member of the OSS on loan to Britain's SOE.

The exploits of Britain's Special Operations Executive (SOE) agents in France during World War II are documented in many books and movies. Not long after the end of the war, these SOE agents first wrote their memoirs and then, discovering the considerable interest that existed in their stories, published their manuscripts. Their and others' stories did little, though, to clear the fog around the operations carried out by the SOE, while some raised serious questions about the efficacy of this necessarily secretive, clandestine organization. This controversy was one factor in the British government's decision to charge University of Manchester professor Michael R. D. Foot to write his definitive history of the SOE, published in 1966, as "SOE in France". Professor Foot was given access to secret files, files that were not made public until 1993. Herein explains a significant part of the serious omissions, as previous publications were drawn from participants' memories formed from a notably limited perspective. Even after Foot's treatise, a serious gap remains in our knowledge of the workings of the SOE in France concerning the activities of French Resistants. This gap is partly due to a fire that destroyed an estimated 60% of SOE's files, among them some of Section F's files on French activities and agents. Five key Cabinet documents were deliberately destroyed as late as January, 1993, for "political expedience". Professor Foot also contributed to the dearth of information on French agents, overlooking the many contributions of French nationals in Section F, to the point where the French translated the title of his book to: "The English in the SOE".

SOE agents in France were either French nationals attached to the RF section of the SOE under General de Gaulle or English nationals and expatriates, even French nationals, who comprised the British run F section under Colonel Maurice Buckmaster. Most of the books published by the former F section agents were in English. The focus of these books was on the activities of the agent/writer and their interactions within the SOE. Rarely does one find a story that satisfies our interest in the trials and the contributions of the French

Resistants, the very ones who quite frequently enabled the SOE agents to carry out their missions. There are memoirs from the French Resistants, but most have not been translated into English. These memoirs often fail to provide insights into their day to day lives in the Resistance. Moreover, these memoirs were written not long after the war and cannot reveal the impact of the war over the course of their lives, lives that were forever scarred by the war.

Several British and American films have been produced on the French Resistance. Some of these films were regrettably shot with low budgets and were crudely made. Sadly, it often seemed necessary to the producers to have a love story at the center of the plot, reducing what might have been devoted to the real lives and activities of the Resistants. Neither manuscripts nor films have provided a true representation of how the French Resistance was organized or how membership in a network changed Resistants' lives forever.

Curious isn't it that the most romantic period of modern history is missing a chapter? Romantic is used in the sense of the ultimate evil being fought by the simplest and noblest of peoples, the ultimate good. There is no detraction from our undying gratitude to our fighting men and women in uniform to draw attention to the valor of the Resistance fighters who often risked much more than their own lives to fight tyranny and with limited means and training.

This is why the extended story of Jean-Jacques Auduc, his courageous family and their fellow Resistance members adds to our understanding. Jean-Jacques was just a lad when he was involved in the Resistance (a word capitalized in this book out of respect). Now in his eighties, he is one of the very few remaining Resistance members. Because his story is being told at his advanced age, 66 years after the war's end, we are shown how the scars of war often never heal.

Through the memoirs of Jean-Jacques' father, Alfred Auduc, we learn to what extremes French Resistance members would go to free their beloved country from Nazi oppression. We are pained by the price they paid. It surprises us to learn that although Alfred hated the Nazis, he formed friendships with certain German officers and drew a definitive line between Nazis and other Germans.

Perhaps it was providential that the author purchased a property southwest of Le Mans, France, in December of 2005. Only a few months later, my wife Claire and I were called on by two men from an organization named "Association des Anciens Combattants Franco-Américains". The two men were Mr. Jean-Claude Faribault and Mr. Jean-Jacques Auduc. They wished for us to join their Association and to participate in the VE Day ceremonies on May 8, 2006. As their Association honors the memories of the French and Americans who sacrificed to liberate France, we considered it a privilege to join. On VE Day, five WWII U.S. military vehicles, wonderfully restored and cared for by their French owners, arrived to escort us in the front seat of a command car to the square in Malicorne-sur-Sarthe, where the ceremonies were to commence. Following a parade, speeches and the laying of wreaths, we gathered in the Salle de Fêtes for our noon meal. It was moving to see that American flags and banners were draped from every rafter and on every wall. As the luncheon ended, a queue formed in front of me with attendees shaking my hand to say "Merci pour vos pères et oncles", wishing they could directly thank those liberating American soldiers for their freedom.

The older generation in France remembers well the Allies' sacrifices for their freedom. Their ceremonies stretch across the former occupied France with tens of thousands paying homage on numerous occasions. Sadly, it is rare to see participants less than age fifty and we must anticipate that such remembrances have their own lifespans.

In 2007, I invited my high school classmates from Marietta, Georgia, to tour France from my property. Twenty classmates and fifteen of their spouses joined me. I asked Jean-Jacques to tell his stories to our group. Hearing him became the most memorable moment of our group's time together. As Claire and I learned more about his family's involvement in the Resistance, we developed a passion to record their history. Even though a few memoirs had been written by members of his Resistance network, our task was challenging. These memoirs were in French, so Claire would translate as I typed and reworded them into English. Their stories were sometimes conflicting, as several were penned some twenty years following the events. There were omissions, misspellings and false conclusions that begged for resolution. Perhaps the greatest challenge was maintaining a logical flow and timeline among the several memoirs. No matter how difficult the writing of this history has been, ours has always been a work of admiration and love.

There is no intent to inflame feelings against the German people or their country by the telling of how the French were mistreated. Genocides have been perpetrated throughout human history and have notably occurred since the fall of the Axis powers. The flaw that possessed Germans to commit atrocities exists in all humankind and continues to plague the world today. Let the reader consider the German brutality as an insight into the darkest recesses of humankind rather than as an indictment of that country and its people.

This manuscript represents a combination of the memoirs and interviews of several of the participants in the Hercule Sacristain Buckmaster Resistance network. The writer chose not to resolve the duplication in events as related by different participants in order to present unabridged versions of the various memoirs. The writer feels that history is best served through such preservation. It is hoped that the reader will not be confused in spite of these minor redundancies. My objective will be met should the reader become enlightened and this history be preserved.

We whose fathers and mothers, uncles and aunts, grandparents and all who sacrificed so much for our freedom and the liberation of oppressed peoples must not forget the price paid for our freedom and those who paid it.

CHAPTER 1   What Price Freedom?

"At age eleven I became a courier of clandestine messages for the French Resistance; at age twelve I performed acts of sabotage and espionage. Was I frightened? Not then. Not until the Gestapo arrested my father and mother, then pursued me as I fled from one Paris safe house to another. Cold, hungry, alone, scared and disoriented, I would fall asleep praying not to wake up. At the beginning I was not aware of how dangerous my parents' activities were, but they had taught me to be clever enough to not be caught. Their lessons served me well as I gave the Gestapo the slip time after time."

These were the thoughts of Jean-Jacques Auduc as he reflected on his family' and his Resistance friends' miserable Christmas Eve, 1943, one of the coldest in memory. Good that he did not know how his father and mother were spending their Christmas Eves. The Gestapo had arrested them on November 2, taking them to Angers where they were tortured terribly, but to no avail. This same Eve, father Alfred Auduc had been chained to a doghouse and made to bark at every German passing by, fearful that he might not survive that evening's cold. Renée, bruised and battered, spent the evening in her freezing cell, wondering whether her husband was still alive and if her son had avoided capture. Why had the Auduc's become so committed as Resistants? For most the price of freedom is an academic or intellectual question. Alfred and Renée Auduc understood unequivocally that they, their family and their beloved France must breathe the air of freedom whatever the consequences. What commitment did it take for them to join the Resistance and put their lives continually at risk? What greater commitment was made when they coaxed other family members, their priest, their doctor and other friends to join the Resistance? And Alfred's sixty-six year old mother? And Jean-Jacques, their eleven year old son? These others did not need much coaxing; they were prepared to support Alfred's initiatives whatever it cost. And cost it did.

Some Anglophiles maintain an image of the French as poor soldiers who buckled readily under the German blitzkrieg. That the French are as brave and hard fighting as any countries' soldiers was proven time after time during The Great War. It was proven again in World War II in ways we are poorly informed of, when some 212,000 French soldiers were killed and close to 1.8 million became POWs. Allied soldiers from World War II are held in high esteem; we know of their willingness to die for their comrades if not for their country. But, a soldier's duty places only his own life at risk, whereas, each member of the Resistance risked the lives of other family members and close friends with each action undertaken. Because of this, Resistants often worked alone with no one else knowing about their activities. In the case of the Auduc's, most of their large family became Resistants, becoming even more exposed to arrest, torture, detention in horrible concentration camps and death.

Alfred Auduc was a passionate man; it was one of his many strengths. What he witnessed at the start of World War II near the border between France and Belgium inflamed his passions. He saw a German fighter strafe and bomb a column of children and nuns, children the ages of his own and nuns like the ones who served his village. After the plane had left, Alfred walked among the dead and wounded, crushed by his incapacity to offer aid. Nothing he heard or saw afterwards made him more resolute than he became at that moment: his life became dedicated to stopping the German war machine. But, what could one man do after German soldiers took tightfisted control of his country?

The Auduc family fought with every means at their disposal in their occupied country and after the war they became one of France's most honored families. Although they did not participate in any spectacular operations, the sum of their contributions was notable and representative of what most Resistance networks, or "réseau", contributed. As a family, the Auduc's was perhaps the only one where three generations received the Croix de Guerre from France and commendations from General Dwight D. Eisenhower. Alfred and Renée received the U. S. Medal of Freedom and from France the Legion of Honor, the Medal of the Resistance, the Medal of Volunteer Combatants and the Medal of Concentration Camp Prisoners.

On June 13, 1945, Jean-Jacques became the youngest French Resistance fighter to receive the Croix de Guerre, with silver gilt star, for his actions on September 21, 1943, when he was 12 years, 2 months and 12 days old. The Croix de Guerre is the only French recognition that is not applied for. Shortly thereafter, on February 13, 1946, General de Gaulle placed his name in the 'Ordre de la Nation' (list of people who served their country in a remarkable way).

Jean-Jacques later, in 1988, received France's highest recognition: the Legion of Honor. The story behind his belated receipt of this honor provides an insight into the political thinking of Charles de Gaulle. Jean-Jacques was recommended for this award soon after the end of the war in 1945. De Gaulle denied him the award because Jean-Jacques had worked for a 'foreign power', that being the United Kingdom, as he worked under the direction of the English controlled Section F of the SOE and not the Section RF that de Gaulle led. One of de Gaulle's fiercest opponents, Francois Mitterand, the socialist President who changed sides as easily as a weather cock, personally presented the Legion of Honor medal to Jean-Jacques. That the award was not given for 43 years was a grave injustice.

Jean-Jacques especially treasures having received the **Medal of Freedom** from General Dwight D. Eisenhower. He remarked: "These recognitions mean much to me and I am forever proud of my family's contributions to the liberation of our country. But, oh my, the cost! I lost my mother; my father became like an empty shell. I lost the opportunity for an education. I was cold, hungry and scared for several of my formative years. My home and everything in it was rendered useless. I never had a chance for a career.

Like most of my countrymen, many of whom suffered similar fates, I acquired a great admiration for our liberators: the Americans, the Canadians and the English. It is to you that I relate my family's story, for you must know that we French fought and sacrificed for our country, as you did, to free Europe from Hitler's tyranny. We needed you desperately. You did not disappoint."

Alfred Auduc was born on June 2, 1902, in Cérans-Foulletourte in France's Sarthe department, where Le Mans is the prefecture (capital). He was the third of eleven children of a farming family. Alfred was short, but well-muscled from hard work. He received little formal education. Instead of attending school, from age six he was contracted for one year at a time to a farmer, from St. John's Day, June 24, to the next St. John's Day. Families with a lot of mouths to feed like Alfred's had to utilize every means and lads were marketable resources. Similar to his dad, Jean-Jacques' father-in-law was rented to a farmer at age seven. These contracts were renewable. Life for the "rented" lads was harsh. Sleeping quarters were in the stables with the animals and meals consisted of soup and a potato for lunch while dinner was potato salad and an apple.

No matter how unhappy a lad became, he could not break his contract.

Consequently, Alfred had no formal education, but learned to be a mechanic. At age 15 he became a blacksmith against his father's wishes. A rep from McCormick noticed he was skillful and hired Alfred at the beginning of mechanized farm equipment. In his spare time, he taught himself to read and write. With his earnings, and partly to impress the ladies, he purchased a U. S. made Indian motorcycle, one which gave him the skill that later molded his army service. This adventuresome lad learned of an opportunity to work in Canada, so he made the arrangements and purchased his ticket. Only, at this same time he met Renée and love conquered that ambition. All was not bliss; however, as noted on their marriage certificate, Alfred's mother did not attend their wedding in opposition to her son's marrying someone from a poor family

Alfred left McCormick to start his own business building well derricks based on ideas he had gleamed from reading magazines and his study of automobile axels. Within five years he had invented a wind powered turbine for bringing up water. He encased the mechanism to keep the parts well-oiled and protected from the elements. The device was advanced enough to receive a patent, only he had no knowledge of such. Unfortunately, the windmill device was too new to be insurable. A strong storm destroyed several of his windmill turbines and Alfred, showing the integrity that was to later set him apart, paid for the repairs, rendering himself bankrupt.

In 1939, when the war broke out, the army drafted him into an engineering division. As a liaison agent, he made many trips on his Army motorcycle between the Belgium border and Normandy. On June 22, 1940, he was captured in Angers and became a POW. Alfred escaped in early July, and was then demobilized. He found a job selling fruit and vegetables. He even made deliveries to the German Kommandantur in Le Mans, using a little delivery van that worked on a gasoline engine that could also run on gas. One had to flip a switch to alternate from the efficient but less powerful gas to the more powerful gasoline prior to encountering a hill. Alfred's trade with the Germans allowed him to gain the Germans' trust, and through them to have a driving permit and gasoline tickets, which were very rare at the time.

Renée Auduc was the daughter of Fernand Angeard and Marie Mallet. She was born in Le Mans on November 16, 1908. Renée received a good high school education and earned several degrees, including ones in typing, shorthand and as an accountant secretary. This is how she became M. Brière's first secretary. M. Brière was the founder of the "Société des Agriculteurs" (*Farmers' Assn*) His office was at 30 rue Paul Ligneul in Le Mans. Among her duties was wearing pads on her shoes so that she could buff the waxed wooden floors as she walked around the office. Her position was to later prove invaluable for the Resistance as it allowed her to gain access to many offices and their important legal stamps essential for forging documents. Renée was to become one of the most decorated ladies in the Resistance.

On August 14, 1930, Alfred and Renée married. They had two sons: Jean-Jacques, born July 9, 1931, and Michel, who was born on August 23, 1939, a mere eleven days before war was declared.

"Messages in Handlebars" is the previously untold, true story of this typical Resistance network organized from London.

Here is a chart of the main people involved in the history of this network:

The Hercule Sacristain Buckmaster Network of the British Special Operations Executive (the "SOE")
Organizers: Frenchman André Dubois (code name "Hercule") of the SOE and American Captain Fred Floege ("Paul", whose mission was coded "Sacristain") of the OSS who became an SOE agent
Heads of Operations: Alfred Auduc and Renée Auduc
Other Prominent Members of this Resistance Network:
Jean-Jacques Auduc, son of Alfred and Renée of Le Mans
Roger Auduc, brother of Alfred, of Cérans-Foulletourte
Marie Auduc, mother of Alfred, of Cérans-Foulletourte, Andre Auduc and Eduoard Auduc
Father Julien Lelièvre, the Auduc family's priest
Dr. Richard Grunberg of Le Mans
Downed American Airmen the Network Rescued:
Sgt. David Butcher of the B-17 "Lakanuki", from Ferguson, Missouri
Sgt. Edward F. Chonskie of the B-17 "The Mugger", from Shenandoah, Pennsylvania
S/Sgt. Albert V. Carroll of the B-17 "The Mugger"
S/Sgt. John Zioance of the B-17 "The Mugger"

Lost American Airmen Whose Graves were Protected:
Lt. Robert S. O'Connor of the B-17 "The Mugger", from Milwaukee, Wisconsin, awarded the Air Medal with 3 Oak Leaf Clusters and the Purple Heart
Lt. Richard W. Peterson of the B-17 "The Mugger", from Denver, Colorado
The nine airmen who perished in the B-17, the Lakanuki, on July 4, 1943
Other SOE agents who interacted with this network:
Gabriel Chartrand from Montreal, Quebec
John Kenneth (Ken) Macalister of Guelph, Ontario

CHAPTER 2   Grandmother Was Our Bastion

Family was the center of life in rural France and in no one's more than the Auduc's. The Catholic Church was in firm control then and their lives were regimented, disciplined and conservative. This is not to say life was all stark or uninteresting, they just didn't have much time for fun.

Marie-Augustine Auduc was born April 4, 1877. She was what the French call "le sel de la terre" meaning "the salt of the earth". Jean-Jacques called her Mémé; he adored her. She conceived 11 children, losing 5 due to childhood diseases and at childbirth in those years when doctors were scarce and medicines were not to be found. Her eldest died at age 20 from the Spanish flu. Her farm in Cérans-Foulletourte, some 20 miles south southwest of Le Mans, played a prominent role in the Auduc family's lives and became an important location for their Resistance network.

Very intelligent, she was self-taught, becoming an accomplished cook on her own. Marie learned from nuns such nursing skills as giving shots and using suction cups. She served as a nurse to her family and her villagers. Growing up on a rural farm, she had taught herself to read and write. She was a capable person, as clever as anyone, who performed varied tasks to support her family. Catering was one of these since she was such an excellent cook. She often catered weddings, but having no car, she sometimes walked 5 or 6 kilometers to and from the event. Occasionally, the families would "forget" to pay her, but she did not complain about this or really about any hardship. When needed, she helped out at the small hotel in Cérans-Foulletourte.

Marie was a petite lady of some 45 kilograms. She wore only black garments as was the custom for "older" ladies of the time and "older" meant from age 45 onwards. She made candies for her family flavored with violet petals in the middle. With her great energy, Marie ran her little farm consisting of a nice garden and several animals such as rabbits, a goat and one pig each year. A neighbor also raised a pig each year and the two pigs were slaughtered as far apart in time as possible and then shared by the two families. The slaughter of the pig was an important event which brought families together. Every edible portion of the pig was used: the feet, the ears, the kidneys, the intestines, even the blood was used for blood sausage.

Before the war, life at "La Bouguelière", the ancient name of her farm, was already rudimentary. Mémé had no electricity until well after the war, something that during the war probably saved her life. Heating came from a wood burning stove and a large fireplace that easily took logs one meter long. These heating sources put so much smoke into the room that the door had to be left cracked, even in mid-winter, allowing clever little wrens to fly in for warming. The room was lit by burning carbure and water (carbure is a carbon compound and is the basis for the English word "carburetor"); only this light carried the risk of exploding if dropped. So, a hand lamp called a "Pigeon", invented by Frenchman Charles Pigeon, which burned the vapors of petroleum distillates, was used when moving around the house. A fine marketer, Pigeon offered 5 free liters of kerosene with the purchase of one of his copper lamps. Only, soon no one had kerosene or gasoline even for their Pigeon lamp. To do his homework, Jean-Jacques would sit with his back to the fireplace and read by the light of the fire.

In wartime, Mémé made the family clothes from raw wool that she yarned. Her socks were so scratchy they could barely be worn. She also made sweaters that were prized for their warmth, but one smelled like a sheep when wearing them.

During the war, the Germans allowed the French to send one package a month to a detainee. During the Great War these packages of clothes and food sustained the French POW's. Mémé energetically prepared packages for her two sons, Alfred and Roger, when they were in concentration camps. Their entire family sacrificed to fill these packages with the most pleasurable items possible like food and warm clothes they would have prized for themselves. Being well aware of her altruism, her priest visited her regularly and helped her with contributions. After the war, they were dismayed to learn that none of their packages made it through German hands.

The French were also allowed to send one letter per month to a detainee, but it had to be written in German, which most did not know. Of course, this was so the letter could be readily censored. Mémé found an Alsatian who she paid to translate her letters into German. It was later learned that all of their letters had been opened by the Germans.

Marie passed away in 1960 at age 83 from Alzheimer's, which had made her aggressive during her last years, something her grandson Michel found especially difficult as Marie had raised him and the two had been adoringly close.

Mémé's farmhouse, La Bouguelière, had a fascinating history. In olden days, only the wealthy possessed gold or silver coins. Trades were based on locally established measures such as the septier which the Auduc's region used, a measure of about 48 quarts of grain. Before Gutenberg's press allowed standardization, words were spelled phonetically based on regional dialects. The measure septier was spelled in other regions as "setier, cestier, sester, setiere, sextiere, sextier, sextere, sestier, sestiere, sestaire, sesterot, sesterium, septier, septarius and septerium", from its Latin origin "sextarius".

The farm's first recorded sale was in 1460, when it was purchased for seven septiers of rye, one mine of buckwheat, one mine of oats and a one year old pig, where two mines equaled one septier. La Bouglière was sold again in 1643 and the name was changed to "La Bouguelière". It was sold again in 1823, along with the owner's bench in the church. The closer a bench was to the pulpit, the more its prestige and its worth. Then, in 1890, Jean-Jacques' great grandfather, Jean Baptiste, purchased it and it remains in the Auduc family today.

An ancient record of La Bouguelière shows the owner's debts amounting to: 24 boisseaux of rye and six soles of cens to the Parish. To the owner of the château of Foulletourte, the renters owed 60 boisseaux of rye, six sols of cens, 12 sols of buckwheat and a pig valued at nine silver coins. In 1607, the property was valued as follows: the house, gardens, and fields were worth 57 journeaux, the vineyards at 45 quartiers and the woods were worth 4 journeaux. Tax records show that in 1643 the owner declared he had a house with fireplace and oven; not every house had such conveniences.

Grandmother Auduc was a good cook and Jean-Jacques loved her baked tomatoes stuffed with sausage. He looked forward to each Thursday when there was no school and his family visited grandmother and grandfather in the countryside. But, they had grandfather's favorite, veal casserole, so often he began to hate it.

'Granmama' would prepare pears by beating them flat and then drying them in her wood burning stove (she had no electricity). The dried, flattened pears were put into a jar, covered with Calvados, an apple brandy, and placed into her cellar for about two years. They were delicious. Those days, for breakfast, Jean-Jacques had bread, butter and a chocolate cereal drink named Banania, still a popular breakfast drink for French children.

Jean-Jacques received his strong Christian faith from his grandmother. His parents did not regularly attend mass, but he went with his grandmother and became head of the boys' choir which afforded him the wearing of a purple robe. During mass, it became his duty to clap to indicate when the congregation should stand or kneel. It was amusing that those old ladies who chastised him for stealing cherries now knelt before him on his command.

Jean-Jacques' middle name is Fernand, that of his grandfather's on his mother's side, as had been the family tradition for generations. Both grandfathers had served in the

Great War. One was in the 18th Dragon Regiment; the other was in the infantry where he was exposed to mustard gas. Jean-Jacques heard the stories of their painful wartime experiences, as well as of the wondrous arrival of the Allied soldiers who came to help and also paid a high price. Their stories were both frightening and exciting for a young lad. The grandpas claimed that the horrible butchery of World War I would never be repeated. And yet, only 22 years later they were proved terribly wrong.

Grandfather Auduc passed away when Jean-Jacques was four and he never really knew his grandfather. He left Jean-Jacques his clarinet, which he was given later, only Jean-Jacques had a tin ear and despised the lessons, so the clarinet was given to his cousin. Instead, his mother enrolled him in dance classes, which he also disliked.

The doctor for grandmother Auduc's village was an Armenian who had fled the Turkish holocaust. Dr. Dertad Essayan was adored by his villagers. He was Jean-Jacques's godfather and was kind and generous to him. One of his gifts was a wooden horse covered with horsehide which Jean-Jacques rode pretending to be an American cowboy. Another gift was the bicycle which he later used to transport clandestine messages. One of the inhabitants of Le Mans was a millionaire. When Jean-Jacques met him, he noticed the spats on the man's shoes, wondering what they were as they looked so out of place. The millionaire was ugly and arrogant with others, so he decided he did not want to be a millionaire. He was abundantly true to his pledge!

CHAPTER 3   Lovely Lives Lose Their Vitality

A Brief on the Causes of World War II and Some Misconceptions

Like any great event in history, volumes have been written on this subject and admittedly what is discussed herein is a quick review, hopefully including a few lesser known determinants.

Germany's victory in the Franco-Prussian War of 1870/71 is a much more important event in world history than is usually conceded. For one, it forged the formerly independent Germanic states into the German Empire. Second, Germany demanded Alsace and the northern portion of Lorraine (the Moselle) following its victory. This loss of its territory forged France into a belligerent posture towards Germany which contributed to the lack of progress towards normal relations and became a root cause of The Great War. Excessive demands from one nation or group of nations upon another leads to future destabilization. Cliché's such as "you reap what you sow" and "history repeats itself" may be derived from such ill-advised retributions.

Another determinant of World War II was Germany's movement to the political right, in reaction to her arch enemy's movement to the left. Russia's Bolshevik revolution fostered political realignments in several European countries. Political realignment was also fostered by the Great Depression, which had devastating effects on an already dire German economy and in many countries resulted in political polarization. The German stage was set for the emergence of a political leader from the right who appealed to the German sense of loss and fear of her neighbors. She wished for a leader who would address the threat posed by communism, atone for her punitive treatment following The Great War and offer solutions to Germany's economic woes.

Adolf Hitler never achieved a majority of the votes in a national election. In the critical elections of 1932, his National Socialist Party won only 30.2% of the primary vote and in the

15

runoff elections, 36.7%. After it came to power, the most votes the Nazi Party ever received was 17.3 million in March of 1933, 43.9% of the votes cast, when Germany's population numbered some 66 million. The failures of two prior Chancellors appointed by President von Hindenberg opened the door to the unpopular Corporal Hitler. Through simplistic intimidation Hitler was able to push his National Socialist party ahead of all others, forcing the aging President von Hindenberg to appoint him as Chancellor in January, 1933. Hitler acted quickly to establish concentration camps, initially for his political opponents, opening Dachau in March of 1933. When Hindenberg died on August 2, 1934, Hitler had the office of president made dormant and took power as the Chancellor and Furher. Following Hitler's rise to power, Germany initiated actions to undo the most onerous provision of the Treaty of Versailles: her loss of territory.

After The Great War, French psyche favored a time of healing following its near fatal wounds, while Germany was obsessed with recovering her enormous losses caused by the reparations demanded in the Treaty of Versailles. This dichotomy may be readily understood. French casualties had exceeded 6 million out of a population of 39.6 million and almost the entire devastation of the Western Front was within its borders. Her economy was flattened. As France received reparations; she craved for peace. The United Kingdom's casualties were about half of France's, still staggering numbers. Germany suffered one million more casualties than did France out of its much larger population of 64.9 million. Her healing could not take place because of the excessive reparations demanded of her. Germany's unreasonable treatment by the victors in WW I became a major determinant of WW II.

France in the 1920's and the first half of the 1930's retained aspects of its feudal society, only, by this period serfs and some peasants had become factory workers. The great chasm between the aristocracy and the working class remained. Factory laborers faced long hours of toil for subsistence wages. They were given no vacations, only the mandatory religious holidays.

France was a politically divided and unstable country when she declared war on Germany in September of 1939. The elections of 1936 had brought to power the **Popular Front** (*Front populaire*), which was an alliance of left wing movements including the French Communist Party (the "PCF"), the French Section of the Workers' International (the "SFIO") and the Radical and Socialist Party. The new government was first headed by SFIO leader Léon Blum, a Jew, and composed entirely of Radical-Socialist and SFIO ministers. Within two years, the government was led by three presidents: Blum; Camille Chautemps, a Radical; and Edouard Daladier, another Radical. Through the 1936 Matignon Accords, the Popular Front introduced new labor laws creating the right to strike; collective bargaining; 2 weeks of paid vacation every year; a 40 hour work week (outside of overtime); and, raised wages by 15% for the lowest-paid workers. The government sought to carry out its reforms as rapidly as possible. On 11 June, the Chamber of Deputies approved the Matignon Accords by a majority of 528 to 7. The Senate voted in favor of these laws within a week.

The Popular Front fell out of power in June of 1937 and dissolved itself in the autumn of 1938, confronted by internal dissensions related to the Spanish Civil War of 1936–1939, to opposition from the right and to the persistent effects of the Great Depression.

The Popular Front had been supported, without participation, by the French Communist Party, which did not provide any of its ministers. This was also France's first cabinet to include female ministers, three, even though French women would not acquire the right to vote until July of 1944, when General Charles de Gaulle granted such rights while Paris was under

Nazi control. De Gaulle had been recognized by the Allies as the head of a provisional French government domiciled in London. One must wonder whether the savvy General was paving the way to his presidency.

The communist party gained in strength from these successes in changing labor laws. Some who were fearful of the National Socialists (Nazi's) in Germany and fascists in Italy gravitated towards the communist party. Concurrently, many French became more and more staunchly anti-communist. The Spanish civil war of 1936 to 1939 profoundly divided French sympathies as it was a struggle of polar opposites: Fascists versus communists. With refugees from both camps streaming into France, sympathies were inflamed. France at the outbreak of the World War II was a deeply divided country, one virtually without leadership. She had every reason to fear war with Germany.

During the early 1930's Germany began the takeover of adjoining territories that it had lost. The Allies' response was to grant Germany one appeasement after another. "Peace at all costs" was consummated when British PM Neville Chamberlain met Adolf Hitler in Munich and signed the Munich Pact on September 29, 1938.

In spite of the Munich Pact, Germany invaded Poland on September 1, 1939. France and England responded two days later with declarations of war against Germany. France had begun mobilization on August 26 and on September 7 attacked the Rhine Valley with eleven divisions along a 32 kilometer front (the "Saar Offensive"). Finding no opposition and deserted villages, the advance was still too slow and their tactical systems too inflexible for an advance deeper than 8 kilometers by September 17. This poor showing, combined with the certain fall of Poland, convinced French command to withdraw its troops to the Maginot Line. Thereafter came a seven month period of tense inactivity, known as the "Phony War", and of no hostilities, leading some to believe that war between the powers could still be avoided. And what to fear, the French had been told their armed forces were invincible, something their sheer numbers might suggest. The antiquity of her armaments suggested otherwise.

Caught in the Onslaught

Jean-Jacques was first impacted by the war in 1939 when his teacher was called up, but it was only a few weeks until a retiree took his place. Following France's capitulation in 1940, a P.O.W. swap allowed his teacher to return. The Germans had offered to release one French P.O.W. for every four Frenchmen who were willing to work in German factories. The P.O.W.'s released were doctors, teachers, managers and others who were not useful in German factories and were needed in France to maintain as much semblance of the status quo as possible. At first, Germany offered French workers a decent salary and allowed them to return to France for their vacations under a program named the "Service du Travail Obligatoire" or "STO". In spite of this exceptional accommodation and the appeal for the French to make a "patriotic gesture", few accepted the German offer. Many young Frenchmen instead fled south to join the Maquis. (**Note 3-1**)

In 1942, Jean-Jacques was a student at Ecole Marceau in Le Mans. Due to the number of teachers who were at the time POWs, there were forty or more students per class. Older retired teachers were called in, as well as some of the teachers' wives. As a deterrent against Allied bombs, the Germans had thought it smart to install anti-aircraft batteries on the flat roof of Jean-Jacques's school. As a result, the students were subjected to one alert after another and each time they would go to the shelter in a completely disorganized manner. More often than not, school functioned every other day.

His parents feared that Ecole Marceau would nevertheless be shelled, and they sent him and his little three year old brother to his grandmother Auduc's. He then went to school in Parigné le Pôlin, where the teacher, Madame Dreux, took care of two classes until her husband returned from a POW camp. He, too, had been released from the camp in exchange for "volunteer workers" going to Germany under the STO.

Mr. Dreux taught his students the true values of the Republic, the value of hard work and of jobs well done, in spite of the orders that came from Vichy. On a typical morning, he would check to see if the students' hands and teeth were clean, and they would then enter the building at the sound of his whistle, in line and silently. After having paid their respect with a "Good morning, Sir", the students would sit down in silence and open their workbooks. They would write down the date, and before the classes started, would read and reflect on the moral principal of the day which was written on the blackboard. Then, they were required to stand and sing "Marechal, here we are, we your children, standing before you...." in front of a picture of Marshall Petain, which was strange to the students since adults seemed to dislike Petain. There were students in three different grades in the same classroom, and, for example, while one grade was tested orally, the other two grades took written tests.

Their classroom was part of the city hall premises, and their teacher was also the main employee of the city hall. The Germans often needed information from him about requisitioned wheat, animals and what not. Each village had to take part in accommodating the needs of the occupation troops.

Mr. Dreux had figured out that Jean-Jacques was involved in the Resistance and he had strategically assigned Jean-Jacques the seat nearest the door. This door opened on the school yard and some fields. He had also given Jean-Jacques the task of making sure the wood stove was always fed properly. This way, as soon as he saw some Germans coming towards the building, he would hit the blackboard with his long stick that was also used to wake up those who were not paying attention. This was Jean-Jacques' warning signal, and he would quickly leave the classroom and hide in a small area he had hollowed out in the wood stack. When Jean-Jacques heard the German cars leave, he would go back to the classroom carrying an armful of wood. This tactic kept the other students from suspecting Jean-Jacques' involvement. Mr. Dreux never asked any questions about the days Jean-Jacques did not show up at school when Jean-Jacques was on one of his "missions". Mr. Dreux had figured this out too.

 The Vichy government had invented the notion of "free time" where citizens served their community and their nation. Students were handed an empty can and asked to remove the Colorado beetles which were destroying crops. This was one way Marshall Petain, head of the Vichy government, collaborated with the Germans, who wanted the potatoes that the beetles were ruining. These disgusting insects and their larvae would cause terrible rashes on students' hands and they would inevitably rub their faces with their contaminated hands. The students chose to call the Germans "Colorado beetles", for the students found them as disgusting as these bugs. Marshall Petain encouraged his countrymen to "return to the earth", as he believed that the highest moral ethic was learned through farming. Students were required to tend gardens at their schools, but at Jean-Jacques' they sowed stinging nettles over the vegetables before they left on summer break, so the Germans would be stung when they tried to harvest the vegetables.

When it was acorn season, the French would harvest them in the forests to make coffee substitute. First husking the acorns, they roasted them in a frying pan in the fireplace. They crushed them by hand in the pan to make them more soluble in water. No matter how the acorns were prepared, though, the resulting drink was disgusting. They had no coffee at all to mix with the acorn brew and tea was not used in France those days, so they had no alternative but to consume this wretched acorn drink.

Jean-Jacques's school was a two kilometer walk from his grandmother's house. He went there and back twice a day as he ate lunch at his grandmother's. Walking eight kilometers a day would easily wear out his wood-soled clogs. These were called "galoches" and had coarse leather uppers. The government issued ration tickets for only two pair a year, so when they were at home, they wore totally wooden clogs called "sabots". They did not have socks in those days, so they put straw in their galoches and sabots for modest comfort. During winters, some mothers would put embers in the shoes to warm them up, but, of course, she had to choose and tend the embers carefully. No matter what was done, their shoes were brutal and children could not wait to go barefoot in the summers. To make their shoes last, he and his chums would go to the blacksmith to have horse shoes nailed onto their wooden heels, then they would have to endure the remarks of some farmers, like "Here come the donkeys, they need the blacksmith's help, just like our horses".

The floors of their school were wooden. Imagine the noise that could be made by someone wearing sabots who wished to disrupt class! The students called this "sabotage" (there are several possible origins for this word, but all are derived from the wooden sabot clog).

In spite of all their distractions, the results of the 'Certificat d'Etudes' (*degree that does not exist today, that indicated that you had all the basic skills, with high academic standards*) were excellent: 90% of the students got passing grades, and those who failed had to come to school on Thursday afternoons. Boys and girls otherwise did not go to school on Thursdays at the time; instead, on Thursday mornings they went to Catechism class at the church. The priest and the teachers of the village, as opposed as they were ideologically, had respect for each other, and even managed to appreciate each other by strictly staying where they belonged in the village. Jean-Jacques and his classmates learned the names of the rivers and of the departements (French states) by heart, and all knew how to count and to write properly with ink pens.

Note 3-1. Young Frenchmen who fled to avoid conscription-enforced STO labor in Germany gathered in the elevated bush country, the "maquis", of southeastern France and Brittany. Cells of maquisards numbered from a handful to several thousands; eventually the Maquis became part of the Resistance. Using guerrilla tactics, the Maquis effectively harassed the Milice* and German occupation troops and aided the escape of downed Allied airmen, Jews and others. In March 1944, the German Army began a terror campaign throughout France. This included reprisals against civilians living in areas where the French Resistance was active. The Maquisards were later to take their revenge during the *épuration sauvage* when some 6,000 Nazi sympathizers were executed without trial prior to the complete liberation of France, along with 4,000 more executed after her liberation.

*The Milice was a paramilitary force composed of French collaborationists. I was created on January 30, 1943, by the Vichy Regime, with German support, to help fight the French Resistance. The Milice's formal leader was Vichy Prime Minister Pierre Laval. The Milice participated in summary executions and assassinations, and helped round up Jews and Resistants for deportation.

Alfred Auduc in 1930 proudly poses with his new Indian motorcycle

CHAPTER 4   Alfred Auduc's Service In The French Army

It was not until 1965 that Alfred Auduc, Jean-Jacques' father, wrote his memoirs, but he put his experiences and his feelings on paper so well that there would be a loss if the reader were not availed of Alfred's own story.

Alfred Auduc Describes His Wartime Experiences

"It was not by chance that I became a member of the Resistance; it was for an ideal. Like many, I could not accept the shame and dishonor of France's defeat. I swore that I would avenge the dead children of northern France, killed by the Germans during the attacks that began on the 10th of May 1940. I could not help this, as I had children of the same ages. At that time, I was a liaison motorcyclist of the sixth Regiment of engineers stationed near the Belgian frontier. In one week the Belgian army was crushed and then it was the turn of we French. The machine gun strafing's and the bombings were petrifying; the roads became blocked with refugees, troops, bodies and equipment in flames.

One day I asked a fleeing Belgian woman where she intended to go. She replied that she had known the Germans in the

Great War and that they were not like other men. It did not take long for me to understand what she meant. About 20 km from the Belgian frontier, a group of children aged six to ten years, and probably orphans as they were all dressed similarly, were being led along a road by a group of nuns. Suddenly, they were attacked by German airplanes using machine guns and bombs. Many children were left lying on the road dead or mortally wounded with many agonizing and screaming. Two of the nuns were also killed. The sight was horrible. I was a soldier, but that did not stop my tears and anger as the planes came back to finish the job. In the space of seconds, I was transformed. I became harder and crueler; it was then and there that I swore to avenge these children. I now agreed that Germans were certainly not like other people. Two days later, I witnessed another atrocity just as tragic. The road I was on was again attacked by airplanes. This time a group of French soldiers from Martinique was being bombed. I left my motorbike in a ditch and hid in a wooded area near the road. When the planes had finished their work, I came closer to the road with caution because I knew that the Germans often sent armored cars after an airplane attack. I was right; a few moments later a motorcycle with sidecars and three young German soldiers on board came along the road shooting towards the ground. I realized that they were finishing off the wounded soldiers from Martinique. Again, my impression was that Germans were not like other men. These must have graduated from one of Hitler's criminal schools. In a clear-minded way I decided to stop their carnage. Two of the German soldiers were side by side. I took my rifle, aimed, and shot the first one without the slightest hesitation. Then, I shot the second. The third was looking around for me and surely knew little about war as he should have reacted to my first shot. He did not, and suffered the same fate as his two companions. Such were my first shots fired at the Germans; and my last. I grabbed my motorbike and was leaving when a tall soldier from Martinique, who had been slightly wounded, ran to me. As he ran he was kissing a trinket hanging from his wrist and crying like a child. He said "My mother is a saint and she is the one who has sent you to help me". I offered to give him a ride, for we had to leave the area as quickly as possible. I dropped him off 40 km from there. He took a page from his notepad, wrote his address on one side and on the other wrote "To you, my friend, who has saved my life, my eternal gratitude". At the end of the war, I tried to find him, but he was listed as "missing in action". I also had the opportunity to save a fighter pilot in the Ardennes, by the skin of our teeth. On that day my friends and I witnessed a dog fight: a few French fighters had attacked a flight of German bombers. One of the fighters became disoriented and landed roughly in a field. A little farther, a German bomber crashed. I hurried towards the French plane. The pilot was uninjured and had managed to get out of his plane. He was covered in hot oil, but quickly jumped on my motorbike and I left as quickly as I had come. Hardly had we left the plane when a German fighter dove on the French plane and strafed it, the plane bursting into flames. I had time to head towards a bush where we hid. It was a wise decision as the German plane started firing in our direction. Fortunately, his aim was off, as ten meters from where we stood, we could see the bullets striking the ground. The young pilot told me he wished to return to Reims. His squadron had been promised American airplanes that were faster and better armed than what his squadron had and he could not wait to have his own. I then decided to check on the German bomber and found a member of the crew who survived, thrown 50 meters from his plane. His legs were broken. Some soldiers from my company were walking towards him without caution, wanting to help him. When they neared, the German pulled out his revolver and shot in their direction. The French shot back and killed him. To his last breath, he kept saying "Heil Hitler". We buried him on the side of the road, made a small wooden cross on which we hung his belt and his dog tags and at the foot of the cross we laid his papers. The next day, when I drove past the gravesite, everything was gone. A wreath of flowers had been put on the mound of his grave. A German soldier must have passed his grave. As I was looking at this grave, I felt sorry for this young man so intoxicated with Hitler that he chose to salute him with his last breath. I wondered how in the world these Germans were made to worship a madman who sacrificed them to satisfy his thirst for power.

In Normandy, I took care of an Englishman, finding him sitting in a ditch with a superficial wound. He was waving frantically at me. The German tanks were so close we could hear their cannons. He made me understand that he had walked as far as he could manage, but that he could make it on my motorbike. I asked him which way he wanted to go. He pointed in the direction and after 15 km we met an English convoy which he joined.

At the beginning of the German attacks, the French supply lines were destroyed and we could no longer hold our lines. After they broke, my regiment's duty was to destroy the bridges and roads to slow the German advance. My missions were made difficult by their attacks and the blocking of the roads by refugees escaping the onslaught. The strafing planes were constantly firing upon us. I lost two motorbikes. One was destroyed by a fragment from a bomb and the second was hit by a bullet from an attacking fighter. My gas tank was punctured and a bullet penetrated a cylinder. I was fortunate not to be hit. I was given a third bike: a superb Peugeot with a four cycle 500 cc motor, which finished my campaign before ending up in the hands of a German.

I often had to go to Normandy to pick up orders from headquarters of the 6th Engineer Group. This put me in a good situation to assess the demoralization caused to our troops by the "Fifth Column". These were Germans who had been in

France before the war, who spoke French, and who engaged in propaganda, even espionage; plus, those Germans who infiltrated the French military in order to disillusion the French. The Fifth Column also referred to those French who aligned with Germany and undermined the fighting spirit of their fellow countrymen or those influenced by Marshall Petain's plea to stop fighting. Petain understood that the French military was dogged by WWI strategies and equipment so he wished to avoid a slaughter.

Every day the Germans advanced some 20 km, making our job quite difficult in this strange war. One day as I was going to Normandy, I met a group of English machine gun cars which were camouflaged between two hedges. I asked the commanding officer what he thought of the situation. "You French soldiers and we English soldiers do not have enough tanks and planes. We are preparing to return to England, then, we will organize ourselves so that the Germans will not land on our coasts, as we await the Americans. The Germans will not win this war as they did not win the last one, but it is going to take a long time to defeat them". His words gave me a glimmer of hope and General de Gaulle's BBC address on the 18th of June, 1940, did the rest. In the meantime, the war continued. My company was taken by surprise by the speed of the German advance in Mayenne where many of our soldiers were taken prisoner. Thanks to the speed of my motorbike, I escaped.

Four days later in Normandy, the handful of us who remained was almost captured. We were resting on a large property after having walked 25 km. For foot soldiers it was not much, but for us engineers it was exhausting. We thought the Germans were 25 km from us, but since we met less and less French resistance and had fewer and fewer explosives to cut roads and destroy bridges, we should have realized the Germans were advancing faster. This is why the commander of my company, who had fought in The Great War and was a particularly brave person, ordered me to do a recon to see where the Germans were. I took the road from whence we had come the day before. It had wooded areas on either side. After 5 or 6 km, shots were fired in my direction, revealing the German's position. I managed to turn around without being hit and returned safely to report this information to my commander. He told me my story was impossible, that I had only gotten scared and returned out of fear. I felt offended because I had always carried out every mission I had been given. I suggested he take the car to see for himself and explained to him where I had been attacked. A young, kind Lieutenant asked if he could go with my commander. I followed them. 500 meters from the place I had indicated, I stopped, but the commander's car drove on. They were attacked by automatic weapons exactly at the spot where I had been attacked. The windshield was shattered into pieces and the Lieutenant was shot in the head. I don't know how, but the commander was incredibly lucky and managed to escape unscathed. He wasted no time giving his men the order to withdraw 20 km.

I then drove towards Angers, where I found no one from my regiment, so I went to the headquarters at Chatillon-sur-Sévres. A lieutenant told me that the Colonel would be pleased to hear from someone from my company. In my presence, he picked up the phone and said to a German commander "All my men have been disarmed. Your troops can advance without any danger". Then he turned to ask what had happened to my company. I answered "There are about 200 of us left". He seemed to find this surprising so I remarked that in Belgium we numbered 300. He ordered the Lieutenant to disarm me, for the Germans were arriving. I could not help saying to him that for me, being disarmed by a French soldier was a disgrace. I had no choice but to give the Lieutenant my gun, my grenades and the explosives from the bag I was carrying. Hardly had I done this when the Germans arrived from all sides.

A young German soldier came to me, pushing a motorbike in battered condition. He was shy and explained that his bike was "kaput", that he had done the campaigns in Poland, Belgium and France on this bike. Since the war was over for me, he wanted my motorbike. He made me understand in his own gentle way that I should wait a few minutes. Sure enough, he returned in minutes with a suitcase that he had taken from a truck. He opened it and I could see a blue pair of pants and a jacket, tins of food, chocolates, and English and American cigarettes. A friend of mine standing nearby said "Lucky you, what have you done to receive all of these gifts?" I answered "You don't understand. He wants my motorbike." This young German soldier made me understand that if I wore the blue pants and jacket, I would pass for a civilian and would not be made a prisoner and for me the war would be over. I answered in French "Don't be so sure; we may very well meet again one day". I did not then put on the blue pants or jacket, but took the suitcase and gave him the motorbike. He was as happy as a child on Christmas morning. In spite of his young age, he was quite a decent man, just like my friends. The Germans gathered us. It was all over. The Armistice came two days later. I was a prisoner, but not for long. After two weeks of walking towards a P.O.W. camp, we neared Vendée. It was now or perhaps never for me. We stopped to rest and I asked to visit the woods. Most of us were carrying canteens and bundles with our personal effects. No one stopped me as I headed off with my bundle. I pulled out the civilian clothes that the German soldier had exchanged for my motorcycle. Stripping off my uniform, I walked out of the woods in a different direction, looking like a civilian, unnoticed. I had escaped and began the long walk home towards Le Mans.

I went into hiding for a time, then, went to the Gendarmerie in Le Mans. There, the Gendarme proved to be understanding.

He gave me a demobilization certificate and I returned to my wife and children. A fellow escapee who had on his uniform reached home only to have his mother insist that he rejoin his regiment. She did not wish for him to become a deserter. He did as told, was arrested, and spent five years as a POW. Thanks, mom!

My trade was to be a mechanic, but I did not want to work in a factory. I found a job in Le Mans as a merchant delivering fruit and vegetables, including to the Germans, which allowed me to have a small Ford van powered by natural gas. I was thus free to drive around. I had already decided to become a Resistance fighter, but had no idea how to bring this about."

CHAPTER 5   Lost in the Flood of the Exodus

The Anglophone world knows little about the "exodus", the movement of an estimated 12 million refugees over the roads of northern France which included 2 million Belgians, a number of Dutch, Poles and others, and more than 9 million French who were fleeing Hitler's blitzkrieg. As the Germans raced through Belgium, the natives panicked, leaving their homes and fleeing to France. The French inhabitants of the northern departements joined the exodus when they learned their cities had been declared "open", meaning France would not defend them in order to spare those cities and their populations. On June 12, 1940, Paris, too, was declared an "open city". This induced most of the French all the way to the Loire River to flee.

Those first on the roads were the sumptuous and fast American cars, driven by uniformed chauffeurs, their passengers being elegant women clutching their jewelry boxes while their husbands studied maps of the region. Then came the less fancy older cars whose drivers were members of the middle classes; they were generally accompanied by their families and they often needed the assistance of the local populace. One or two days later came the most incredible vehicles imaginable; then came the cyclists, mostly young people. There were also pedestrians, sometimes entire families walking together. Last came the heavy carts belonging to the peasants of the rural north. They advanced at foot pace loaded up with the sick, the children and the elderly.

Several of these carts followed one another as they were generally a village undertaking a collective move, with the mayor, the priest, the elderly schoolmaster, and the local policeman. It was a colossal uprooting, the avalanche of one entire region onto another.

These refugees proved a major obstacle to French troop movements, but this contributed only marginally to the German victory. It shocked the peasants to see French officers among those fleeing. Once the troops mingled with the refugees, they offered the Luftwaffe an excellent target for creating further mayhem and troop disruptions. Columns of refugees and soldiers along open roads were strafed and bombed on numerous occasions.

Eventually, many of these 12 million refugees headed to the south and west of France (Italy had halfheartedly invaded the southeast) assuming that the French army would make its stand at the Loire River. Curiously, the French army made no such stand, but France south of the Loire did become a temporary safe haven. The Loire was roughly the line of German advance at the time the armistice was signed, which led to the creation of the free zone of Vichy France generally south of the river.

The exodus was a French and Belgian tragedy. Some 100,000 perished. The majority faced hunger and many faced starvation. Families were broken, often for several months. French industry and agriculture came to a halt. The French psyche went reeling, in part from the belief that their Third Republic had let the populace down, in part from the rampant rumors that spies, the dreaded "fifth column" were among them sowing havoc, and because the refugees realized theirs were defeated nations to be occupied by the Germans, if, as they believed, only temporarily.

In the aftermath of the exodus was born the French Resistance. For many there was little else to lose. Feeling betrayed by the former Republican government and in disharmony with Marshall Petain's collaborating Vichy government, the French became fiercely independent and self-reliant. First, Frenchmen began to assist the refugees with food, water and lodging wherever possible. Next, they began to assist those whose lives were at risk to escape to Spain, Switzerland, the French colonies in North Africa, wherever. When these exits later became illegal, the French began underground railroads to assist escapees. This remained the orientation of the French Resistance until Colonel Buckmaster's SOE group in London began to organize, administer and, later, arm the Resistance.

Refugees were in for a further surprise as they repatriated homeward. They had fled in part from the feared brutality of the invaders, brutality that became widely anticipated due to the intense propaganda against the Germans during The Great War, brutality that was often fictional or exaggerated. As refugees made their ways homeward, German soldiers offered them hard-to-find petrol. The courteous German soldiers assisted them also by providing food, directions and encouragement, sometimes even paying for the refugees' needs. Their motives were mixed as the German soldiers were under strict orders from Hitler to behave. Hitler's philosophy was to appear benign at first to create a less combative atmosphere, then to gradually tighten his fist until they were completely subjected. And, the German command wanted the roads cleared as quickly as possible for their own transportation. Also, at this early stage of the war, the common German soldier had empathy for the plight of the French.

As the Exodus raced through France, it reached the Normandy village of Falaise. This village became famous due to an Allied pincher movement shortly after D-Day that created the Falaise Gap. Had the pincher arms been able to close, a significant portion of the German army in Normandy would have been trapped. The war on the western front might have been ended abruptly.

Seventeen year-old Yvette Dufailly Billon, the former mother-in-law of this book's translator, was taken aback one June morning to see ragged French soldiers sleeping on the cobble stones of her village square, filling it. Yvette soon heard 'la tambour de ville', literally 'the town drummer', and in the U. S., the 'town crier', dressed in his cap and drumming for attention to alert the village to the news of the day, the 'avis à la population'. Only today, the news was different. "Make soup for the soldiers" was his cry. The village responded with much soup and more food to comfort their exhausted and defeated troops. The Exodus was creating havoc with the village's streets with many headed east and even more headed south. So, the Maire, the mayor, organized the citizens to direct the traffic through the city. During that afternoon, German bombers appeared over the village. Yvette and her grandmother were caught outside, so they began to run while holding hands. Only, in which direction does one run to escape bombs? It was to be more than a decade before Yvette could think of an airplane except in terms of death and destruction; she refused to ride on an airplane. One of her son's best friends was in the Amiens train station when it was bombed. Only a small child, he was separated from his parents and never reconnected with his family. To this day he does not know his family's name.

Two days later the Germans arrived. Yvette had heard that the German soldiers were poorly supplied, for example, having little soap and other necessities. The townspeople were shocked to see these smartly dressed, healthy and handsome soldiers with their shining boots and modern mechanized equipment entering their village. Shortly afterwards, a German officer knocked on the door of Yvette's grandmother's house. When ushered in, he asked in perfect French if he could have a room in their house. Yvette said "Absolutely not." Startled, the officer left their house and did not return.

Later, Yvette moved to Paris to enter a university there; life was more difficult in the large cities than in the countryside. For one thing, there was little food even for those who had ration tickets. Today, Yvette lives in Nice since the passing of her husband Jean. Her memory is clear and her stories are fascinating, as is everything about her.

Jean-Jacques Relates His Family's Exodus

The family of Alfred Auduc joined the exodus, as described by Jean-Jacques. "My father was drafted into the 6th Engineer group in Angers and was a liaison agent on a motorbike. On the 10th of May 1940, he was at the Belgium border. By mid-June, our French forces had been ousted from Belgium, then from northern France. An exodus of millions of refugees was flooding past us. We had heard nothing from my father, but mom wanted to wait for him at home in Le Mans.

For several days we had seen thousands of refugees trying to escape the advance of the German troops. Ignoring government posters which limited a family's luggage to 30 kilos, the refugees tried to save a few belongings using every means available: horse drawn carts, human drawn carts, wheelbarrows, baby carriages, anything with wheels. Pulling and pushing were heavy horses from the Ardennes, oxen, cattle, even dogs, but often entire families.

It wasn't long before my mother's brother arrived and tried to convince mom to take us and leave. My uncle was a newspaper delivery man for the Hachette publisher in Paris. He talked mother into leaving, so she packed my nine month old brother and me into his Citroën and we joined the exodus. As we dawdled along at the pace of those on foot, we were disturbed to encounter soldiers whose officers had deserted them. They mingled, confused, with us refugees. We were all frightened by the numerous stories, most of which we now know were false, of German brutality.

The propaganda and the newspapers had told refugees that the enemy would never go beyond the Loire River. This became our destination. Along the way we heard many diverse opinions on what was happening, how it happened and what was to happen. There was such gloom. The Germans were using their 5th column, who were German civilians that had lived in France and were thus fluent, to intermingle with us refugees to convince us that all was lost. An oft heard slogan was "the French Army was inglorious in defeat and only Petain can save the situation". Since many refugees were WWI veterans who worshipped Petain, these 5th column lies were readily accepted. Adults whispered about the "fifth column", but they never told me who they were. I was able to glean they were a malevolent group that everyone feared, but none was ever pointed out to me.

We crossed the Loire River at Saumur where the bridge was guarded by cavalry cadets from the Cadre Noir horse academy of Saumur. Safely across, we spent our first night in an Angora rabbit farm near the bridge. That night I slept with a little rabbit in my arms and told him how sad I was to have left my home, the rest of my family and my friends.

Up early the next day, we rejoined the mass of refugees. Suddenly, an airplane roared behind us and began strafing our road. Everyone raced for the ditches along the road, ducking our heads from the machine gunning that we could hear and see as bullets kicked up dirt around us. After the plane disappeared, groups formed to lament what just happened. One man remarked that the plane had Italian markings. We learned later that the Germans had instructed their Italian ally to strafe these French roads in order to clear them for German mechanized forces. The roads were crowded with defenseless refugees and the Italian aviation again and again cowardly shot them down. NOT VERY GLORIOUS!

Again and again during this never ending day we leapt for the ditches at the sound of a fighter. Late in the day, a fighter suddenly appeared. An elderly lady, a grandmother, was too exhausted to flee to a ditch and remained in her car; she was hit. After the plane left, we discovered she had been killed. She was the first dead person I had ever seen. The dreaded war had reached us even in our supposed safe haven. My grandparents had been wrong: the horrors of war were about to start anew and last for five long years. Our war would take the form of resistance, but the horrors would be just as awful as in the Great War.

The machine gunned grandmother's story is still being told today. She refused to leave her home unless her most prized possession, her grandfather clock, was taken along. The clock was tied to the top of their car and the family set off for presumed safety below the Loire. After the strafing left her dead, her family faced a dilemma over her body, as they did not wish to bury it alongside the road. Since it was June, something had to be done quickly. They took down the grandfather clock, took out its mechanism, and placed their grandmother inside, then retied the clock, now coffin, to the top of their car. Into that evening the strafing continued and a few kilometers farther everyone had to flee to the relative safety of the ditches, most leaving their keys in the ignitions and even their motors running in their haste to escape. Only, not everyone fled. Someone stole the grandmother's car, clock/coffin and grandmother. Needless to say, the culprit, upon discovering the body, did not report the find to a gendarme. Besides, the grandmother carried no ID. The family did report their grandmother's death to the gendarmes, who must have found something humorous in the story, as it spread like wildfire.

The family was soon to face a new and perplexing problem. Without a death certificate, the family could not settle their grandmother's estate. French law dictated that in such cases the estate could be settled only upon the 100th birthday of the alleged deceased. Their grandmother was in her early eighties when machine gunned. Despite repeated attempts and several testaments, the law was the law.

My mother and her brother continued south from Saumur for two or three days, making only 40 km, until our petrol ran out and we could not find any more. Refugees' other great concern was finding food. Before the arrival of any refugees, the local people had already emptied the stores. A grocer from my grandmother's village was traveling with us. His van was full of food which he was selling for four time's normal prices, but he fortunately sold to us without markups. He, like other "entrepreneurs", returned home when he was sold out.

I watch as all of the French soldiers wearily trudged past us and each time a motorcycle came upon us, I looked at the driver hoping it would be my dad. As the days passed I became more determined and tried to stop a motorcycle to ask if the driver knew my dad and where he might be. Only, the last driver barked strange, harsh words at me and I knew instantly that he was German.

While we pondered what to do, the Germans caught up with us in the Departement of Deux-Sèvres. They could not understand why all these civilians were fleeing, cluttering the roads and slowing their own rapid progression. One of their officers, who had worked in Paris, gave us a tank full of gas so we could return to Le Mans, but made us swear that we would do so. The officer then gave us a pass allowing us to eat at a German mess. Their orders were to collaborate with the French to help turn us against the English.

So it was that only a few days after we first passed the Angora rabbit farm that we passed this farm again. There was nothing left of it; it had been destroyed when the Germans bombed the nearby bridge. The bombing happened the day we left the farm. It was the first of several close calls for us. The bridge and the rabbit farm were not the only things gone. We learned that the young cadets from Saumur never gave up their positions in defense of the Saumur bridge, showing exceptional courage and heroism. Every one of them was killed in the aerial attacks on the bridge.

On the way back to Le Mans, we passed long lines of French soldiers who had been let down by their officers and were captured. They were on their way to stalags in Germany where most would stay for five terrible years. I looked everywhere hoping to see my father. Knowing him, I was convinced he would take the first opportunity to escape. This is exactly what he did."

Following his escape from the Germans, Alfred Auduc went into hiding for several months, was decommissioned and became a wholesaler of fruits and vegetables, including to the Germans. He obtained a Ford van equipped with a gazogene, a device that burned charcoal to generate gas to burn in the motor. It was grand when gasoline was in short supply, but those who rode in it were quickly covered with soot. Alfred later used his apple crates for hiding arms for delivery to other Resistants.

When Renée and her sons arrived back in Le Mans after the exodus, they knew life would be different. A most pleasant surprise was that the people who stayed in Le Mans did not loot or otherwise take advantage of the situation. Renée lost her job for several months until her office was allowed to reopen. As the Germans needed agricultural supplies, Renée's function was deemed to be valuable. Still, during these several months when Alfred and Renée had no income, food became a problem again. Shops had closed, but slowly the boulangeries and other shops began to reopen. Ration tickets helped when they began, but this too took time.

Here is a good measure of how hungry people were: residents of Paris would ride their bikes to search for food at the farms around Le Mans; automobiles now being prohibited. Not even considering their roaming around, they had to endure a 260 mile round trip on difficult roads.

Jean-Jacques was only 9 when he heard about the daily abuses of the Germans who were now controlling, censuring and plundering the Sarthe departement, as they were doing in the rest of the country. Curfew was initiated about the time the Auduc's returned, as the Germans were already in charge of Le Mans. Edicts were issued one after another: curtains had to be installed to block in all light, with offenders being arrested, checked out, but released the next day; those caught listening to a radio were sent to French prisons; while those caught writing political graffiti or printing leaflets were deported to concentration camps. The Germans even made all inhabitants walk in the same direction on one side of the street and in the opposite direction on the other. The greatest indignation was the loss of freedom; being prisoners in their own homes.

No longer was The Great War mentioned in movies or newsreels. Instead, movie theaters showed Allied bombing of French cities and later showed the powerful, destructive German V-1 and V-2 rockets which were said to be retaliating against Britain on behalf of the French. The Auduc's city of Le Mans was an example of widespread Allied destruction. Many believed the United States did more civilian damage than the British due to the higher elevations from which U. S. planes released their bombs, making their bombing runs less accurate. In spite of the destruction being wrought against their cities, French sentiment remained firmly in favor of the Allies.

Nazi propaganda against Great Britain

France would seem to have been particularly vulnerable to Nazi propaganda against Great Britain. Not only were France and England historical adversaries, but several bizarre and horrific events took place early in the war that fanned the flames of discord between the two "allies". Following France's capitulation on June 21, 1940, a consequential segment of the French favored France's joining Germany in the anticipated defeat of Great Britain. The leader among these was Pierre Laval, Petain's Prime Minister in the Vichy government, but he was far from being alone. Many saw Germany as the ultimate ruler of Europe and thus thought it in their best interest to align with the power to be.

Germany employed newsreels, films, posters and even a children's comic book, "Vica", for their propaganda. Text books were revised to show reverence for Marshall Petain and the Vichy government and to promote a bias against England, all under German supervision. Germans methodically went through libraries; tossing out all materials they found to be objectionable.

They could also draw on numerous, potent incidents such as the following:

During late May and early June of 1940, there was a massive attempt to rescue the English and French armies which had been driven into a desperate enclave around Dunkirk. Operation Dynamo sought to rescue as many of these trapped soldiers as possible. For this, the English, French and Dutch navies were to load troops from the beaches of Dunkirk and ferry them to safety across the 46.5 miles of the English Channel which separated Dunkirk from Dover, England, while German fighters and bombers made frenzied attacks against the ships and the hundreds of thousands of men on the beaches.

Unknown to the French soldiers was the decision by French Admiral François Darlan that British soldiers be rescued first. The reason for this was that England must have its soldiers safely returned if it were to have any chance against the almost certain German invasion. After two days of evacuations of British troops, Churchill decided that French and other allied troops such as the Belgians, Poles and Dutch were to be rescued alongside the British. But, by this time the omitted troops were outraged. Even after the troops were being indiscriminately rescued, there were reports that French troops had been banned at the point of bayonets and even shot to keep them from boarding certain ships; and, that French soldiers who grasped the sides of boats as they attempted to board had their fingers crushed by the butts of British rifles. When Operation Dynamo was forced to cease from the mounting losses of naval vessels, some 140,000 French soldiers had been evacuated, but 40,000 were left on the beaches and were captured. And of the 140,000 rescued, some 26,000 were saved on the last day of Dynamo.

In March of 1940, England and France signed an agreement that neither would negotiate a separate peace treaty with the Nazis. By June of that year France had fallen and Premier Paul Reynaud petitioned Churchill to be released from that pledge. Churchill responded with the caveat that France could explore an armistice only after its fleet set sail for British ports. The French response came from Admiral Darlan who gave Churchill his word that the French fleet would never fall into Nazi hands. This was insufficient for the British who had every reason to insure that the French fleet would not fall under Nazi control.

The main body of the French fleet was anchored at Mers-el-Kebir near Oran, Algeria. On July 3 a major British fleet stood off Oran while its Admiral, Sir James Sommerville, delivered four options to French Admiral Gensoul: 1) he could join the British fleet; 2) he could sail to British ports; 3) he could sail to

Martinique or the United States where his ships would be decommissioned; or, 4) he could scuttle his ships where they lay.

Thus these two allies were on the brink of an unqualified disaster that was due in no small part to vagaries and misinterpretations of correspondences which had to be translated to and from the English and French languages.

Admiral Gensoul did not reply before Britain's deadline and the British set about to destroy the main body of the French fleet. By the time it was over, most of the French fleet had been sunk and 1,297 French sailors had been killed. No British personnel were lost. This catastrophe was avoidable and both sides bore the responsibility.

It took little time for the Nazis to plaster the walls of Paris with posters which read "Remember Oran".

Although the British Royal Air Force (RAF) bombed the Rouen airfield in June of 1940, it was not until January of 1941 that consistent RAF air raids were made against German objectives in French cities. Between 1940 and 1945, the Allies bombed 1570 French cities and villages, causing some 70,000 deaths and 100,000 casualties. 432,000 houses were destroyed and another 890,000 damaged. When the U.S. Army Air Force began its high altitude, and therefore imprecise, bombing, the French Resistance begged for explosives so they could destroy the objectives without the severe civilian casualties the Allied planes were causing. Here the Nazis could use film and photographs to try to convince the French that the English were their enemies.

For the Resistance, Nazi propaganda had little impact. Germany was occupying their country and had wrested away their liberty. Germany had invaded France in 1870 during the Franco-Prussian War which followed years of tension and in 1914 during World War I, and was the more recognized enemy than was Great Britain.

The Auduc family and their fellow Resistants were not swayed in the least by Nazi propaganda. Among other reasons for this was the complete loss of credibility which the Germans earned. Most members of the Resistance did not go to movie theaters, did not have radios (they were forbidden), did not read comic books and did not purchase newspapers tainted with Nazi propaganda.

Although the British had provided the Nazis with a windfall of incidents for the Nazis to exploit, the French people remained clear as to who their real enemy was.

CHAPTER 6   Britain's Special Operations Executive (SOE) spawns the Resistance

The establishment of coordinated resistance to German occupation among French citizens who denounced the Vichy government of Marshall Petain was initiated separately but coincidently by those two giants of history: Prime Minister Winston Churchill and General Charles de Gaulle. De Gaulle's rousing call for resistance was contained in his epic, and sadly unrecorded, radio address of June 18, 1940, but his address was heard by few and rejected by some who listened:

"The high ranking officers who have been at the head of the French armies for many years have formed a government. This government, on the grounds of our defeat, has contacted the enemy, and wishes to cease fighting.

We have definitely been and still are, overwhelmed by the power of the equipment of the enemy, on the ground as well as in the air.

The tanks, planes and tactics the Germans used, more than their numbers, have compelled us to pull back. It is those tanks, planes and tactics of the Germans that have caught our commanders by surprise and led them to where they stand today.

But is this the last word? Should we have no hope? Is defeat final? The answer is no! Believe me, for I know what I am talking about, and I am telling you that nothing is lost for France. The same means that have defeated us can pave the way to victory.

Remember: France is not alone. She is not alone. She has a vast empire behind her. She can join her forces with the British Empire who rules the sea and is fighting on. She can, like England, freely use the giant industry of the United States.

This war is not limited to the unfortunate territory of our country. The battle of France is not the outcome of this war. This war is a world war. All the faults, all the delays, all the suffering do not obliterate the fact that on the scale of the universe, there is all the necessary means to crush the enemy one day. Today we are struck down by mechanical force, but in the future we can win, thanks to a greater mechanical force. This is where the destiny of the world lies.

I, General de Gaulle, presently in London, summon the French officers and soldiers who are on British land, or who would happen to be there, with or without their weapons, I summon the engineers and the workers in the weapon industries who are on British land or who would happen to be there, to contact me.

Whatever happens, the flame of the French resistance must not go out, and it will not go out.

Tomorrow, like I did today, I will speak on the radio from London."

What a contrast de Gaulle's message of hope through resistance makes with that of Marshall Petain's in October, 1940: "It is in a spirit of honor, and to maintain the unity of France, that I enter today upon the path of collaboration".

Prime Minister Winston Churchill and Minister of Economic Warfare Hugh Dalton established England's Special Operations Executive (SOE) on 22 July 1940, to empower resistance initiatives in Belgium, Holland and France "to stir the torpid Frenchman and to set Europe ablaze". The SOE, headquartered at 34 Baker Street in London, became known as "the Baker Street Irregulars" after Sherlock Holmes' fictional spy group. Dalton based the SOE's tactics in part on those used by the Irish Republican Army (IRA) during its fight for Irish independence, for hadn't a few thousand "resistants" thwarted 100,000 English regulars? The SOE's mission was to conduct espionage and sabotage behind enemy lines. According to the authoritative book <u>SOE in France</u> by Michael R. D. Foot: "In every German occupied country there were spontaneous outbursts of national fury at Nazi rule. SOE's objects included discovering where these outbursts were, encouraging them when they were feeble, arming their members as they grew, and coaxing them when they were strong into the channels of greatest common advantage to the allies." Allied and German generals alike believed that the activities of the SOE shortened the war by some six months, a considerable contribution.

Headed by Colonel Colin Gubbins, the SOE, in general terms, was organized into sections with each section responsible for a country. France had two principal sections: F Section under British control and RF Section under General de Gaulle's. Two smaller sections were "EU/P" which dealt with the Polish

Vera Atkins

community in France and "DF" which was responsible for escape routes and coordination. During the latter part of 1942 another section known as 'AMF' was established in Algiers. F Section was eventually headed by Colonel Maurice Buckmaster. His deputy was Major Nicholas Bodington. Buckmaster was thought to have been outwitted by the Gestapo on occasion. Buckmaster's personal secretary, Vera Atkins, was so effective she was thought by some to run the entire SOE.

(When Ian Fleming, then a Commander in the British Naval Intelligence Division, wrote his James Bond novels, he is thought to have modeled the character "M" on Maurice Buckmaster and "Moneypenny" on Vera Atkins, both of whom Fleming knew well).

Maurice Buckmaster was born in 1910. He was educated at Eton until his father was declared bankrupt. After leaving school he moved to France where he worked as a reporter for the newspaper *Le Matin*. Later he was a banker before becoming a senior manager with the Ford Motor Company.

At the outbreak of the Second World War, Buckmaster returned to England and joined the British Army. He served with the British Expeditionary Force in France in 1940, being rescued at Dunkirk and arriving back in England in June, 1940. He was at the point of leaving for the Middle East divisional army headquarters when a posting was received for him to join a secret organization in the War Office. He reported on March 17, 1941, to the headquarters of this branch and found to his delight that he was appointed to the newly formed French section. He was given the task of building an organization that would carry out acts of sabotage, gather information on the enemy and provide money and equipment to the French Resistance

A tall man, with a gentle, slightly self-deprecating manner, Buckmaster was thought by some to lack the aggressiveness that his job description called for. Not in doubt were his dedication and his awareness of what was owed to his agents in the field. He worked an average of 18 hours a day. He sometimes had an evening break when he would bicycle home to Chelsea for an early dinner, returning to Baker Street around 8:00 PM and usually remaining there until 4:00 AM. When considering, after the war, a complaint that the records kept by F Section were somewhat incomplete, he commented: "Those who finish work at any time between three and five in the morning feel little desire to tabulate the events of the day in order to earn the gratitude of some hypothetical historian of the future."

Buckmaster was deeply aware of the importance of mutual trust between himself and agents who were sent on missions in which they would feel lonely, would be thrown on their own resources, and would almost certainly begin to doubt whether those in offices at home understood or even greatly cared about their problems.

From Buckmaster's book <u>They Fought Alone</u>: "Often I would go down together with others from headquarters and would cross-question recruits, taking on the roles of the Gestapo men, in order to try and break their cover stories. By this means the story itself would become ingrained in their minds and they would gain some small idea of the rigors of interrogation. If they survived without cracking, their confidence would be greatly increased and they could face the thought of genuine German interrogation in the knowledge that they had already withstood a similar grilling successfully. These rehearsals were grim affairs and we spared the recruits nothing. They were stripped and made to stand for hours in the light of bright lamps and though, of course, we never used any physical violence on them, they certainly knew what it was to go through it by that time we had finished. If they cracked badly under the strain, it was tolerably sure that we would not send them, for it was clear that the man who caved in when questioned by HQ staff, in however realistic conditions, would be only too likely to wilt in the face of the Boches. A minor slip would not be held against a man, but too general a collapse most certainly would; we derived no pleasure, I need hardly say, from those occasions when our cruel gibes, our reiterated and shouted questions and our implacable persistence broke a man's spirit, but we could console ourselves with the fact that his cracking at a rehearsal might well have saved his life and others' by preventing the possibility of his doing the same thing with the enemy. We were not playing a game."

As the number of agents increased from a meager 7 in 1941 to 50 by the middle of 1942 and 120 by June of 1943, so the F Section in Baker Street was able to plan more and more ambitious and destructive raids against the German supply machine. By February of 1944, at the stage of some of their most important work, F Section had 200 agents in the field, many of them veterans of more than one tour of duty, all either in liaison with large sections of Marquisards or acting as wireless operators. On D-Day itself, there were 220 agents putting into effect plans which were relayed to them from headquarters in Baker Street. In all, 480 active agents were employed by the French section of SOE. From uncertainty even as to its purpose, the F Section grew to be a confidant and deadly fighting force.

Buckmaster continues:"By the beginning of 1943, we had managed to organize ourselves in a manner which was to set the pattern for the duration of the war. We had our headquarters in Baker Street where all operations were planned and where intelligence was collated and filed and where new reports from agents in the field were received. We held our briefing sessions at a flat in Orchard Court, not far away. Here, men who were about to be dropped into France were given the latest details about conditions, both generally and as they affected their own particular districts. It might be that a certain operator was suspected of working with the Germans. We would warn the outgoing agent and tell him in what circumstances he should take appropriate action to silence the man.

We quickly learned that the courage, endurance and tenacity of the patriots living in occupied territory were in direct proportion to the brutality of the occupying force's repressive measures. No occupying power can break the spirit and blunt the retaliatory power of a patriotic and proud people.

Conversely, no occupied country can take really effected action against an occupying power without aid from outside. Coordination of effort was essential, for uncoordinated sabotage contributes little to the destruction of the occupying power's potential. It merely invites reprisals, which in turn provokes further retaliation by the Patriots. But if the occupied people feels that it is being neglected or left in the lurch by its allies, if it begins to listen and, by the force of repetition, to accept as truth the enemy's propaganda, the reaction becomes more and more feeble, until it finally peters out."

F Section candidates for initial interview were selected on the basis of personal recommendations by SOE staff from friends and former associates whom they thought might prove an asset to the organization, while others were gleaned from the Military Services and even some came from newspaper job advertisements seeking French-speaking nationals. While most of F section's agents were not French nationals, most of RF section's agents were.

The candidate's first interview would be carried out in a bare room at the Northumberland Hotel where the only furnishings were a deal desk and two chairs; even the light bulb was bare.

The interviewer would then have a general conversation with the candidate in French. If the interviewer thought that the candidate's French was good enough for the candidate to pass off as a French national, he would close the interview and say he would be in touch. The candidate's file would then be passed to MI5 for a security check. Following security clearance the candidate would be recalled to a second interview at which the true nature of the job was outlined. No punches were pulled as the candidate was told that he or she would have only a 1 in 2 chance of surviving their missions. They were given a few days to think about it before coming to a final decision. To their eternal credit many accepted. In fact, out of 418 agents sent to France, 104 failed to return and one vanished, making the odds of surviving a more benign 3 in 4.

The candidate, now referred to as a "student", was initially sent to Wandsborough Manor for 4 weeks of training in physical fitness, the use of small arms, reading maps, etc. Next, the student underwent parachute training at Ringway Manchester for 2 weeks. At this point the student was evaluated and not all passed.

Graduates then moved on to Arisaig on the western coast of Inverness-Shire, Scotland. There, SOE had taken over a group of large houses in the deserted and beautiful countryside, declared the area prohibited and got on with the task of teaching all forms of commando and clandestine warfare. The students were awoken in the middle of the night by soldiers dressed as Nazis, who would interrogate them. At the end of their training, they were assigned a fake mission in the UK where they were spied on to assess their progress. Radio operators, the most critical position in a Resistance network, then went on to Thame Park in Oxfordshire for fourteen weeks of w/t (wireless telegraphy) and cipher training. Perhaps the greatest lesson taught was "He that has a secret should not only hide it, but hide that he has it to hide".

Between SOE agent Georges Bégué's first parachute drop in May 1941, and August 1944, more than four hundred F Section agents were sent into occupied France, about the same number as de Gaulle's RF Section sent. It was Bégué who had the idea of sending seemingly obscure personal messages via the BBC to SOE agents in France to reduce w/t radio traffic to and from SOE agents. Prior to the arrival of SOE agents, Resistance networks were asked to collect intelligence such as the effectiveness of bombing missions, to rescue and repatriate downed Allied airmen and to prepare for eventual droppings and landings of agents and munitions. The agents' responsibilities were to organize Resistance groups, to train Resistance fighters in the use of arms and sabotage equipment, to gather and deliver information, to operate radio transmitters and to liaise with London. During the war, F section lost 13 women and 91 men, far less than the 50% loss rate anticipated. For 'good luck', Colonel Buckmaster presented each F section agent with gold cuff links or a gold compact, without British markings, knowing these might be sold for needed funds if necessary. He also gave agents the insightful advice: "If you are arrested by the Gestapo, do not assume that all is lost; the Gestapo's reputation has been built up on ruthlessness and terrorism, not intelligence. They will always pretend to know more than they do and may even make a good guess, but remember that it is a guess; otherwise they would not be interrogating you."

At its peak the SOE employed some ten thousand men and thirty-two hundred women. Section F carried out about 50% of the successful munitions drops in France over four years, some 5,000 tons. 120 drops of munitions per month were made in 1943, with 570 drops per month in 1944. Dropped in 1944 were 100,000 Sten guns, 400,000 grenades and 300,000 kilos of explosives. In all, personnel drops included 1,700 men and 50 women.

While many SOE agents were parachuted into France, Belgium and Holland, others needed to be flown in. The necessity of plucking agents, escaped POW's and others from these occupied countries called for a special aircraft. In 1941, the British Westland Lysander III was chosen by a new squadron, #138 'Special Duties', for clandestine flights into France on behalf of the SOE.

This high wing two seater, nicknamed 'Lizzie', had a stall speed of only 65MPH which enabled it to land on very rough terrain and short fields. On occasion three passengers would be crammed into the passenger seat in extreme discomfort. The Lysanders were painted matte black for protection since they almost always flew within a week of a full moon. The

moon's light was essential for visibility as the pilots' only navigational aids consisting of charts, a compass and visuals. Hence, the pilots were nicknamed the "Moon Squadron".

The SOE developed an aura in the eyes of the Resistance. With all hope seemingly disappeared, the Resistance was empowered by having an SOE agent assist in the organization of their network and establishing their missions, by hearing their own messages aired on the BBC, by receiving parachute drops of arms and munitions, and by the assurance that, indeed, a massive invasion force was forming to liberate their country. So it was that many French gathered around forbidden radios to listen to the BBC's 9:00 evening news in French, followed by the airing in French of prearranged messages to various Resistance groups. They were no longer alone. They were also comforted by the coffee and tobacco they often requested and were delighted to receive in the drops.

Radio or w/t operators were the heart of SOE's activities and losing even one could prove to be disastrous, severely limiting a network's scale of operations. How grave losing a w/t operator could be was vividly demonstrated in Holland. As early as 1942, the German Abwehr captured SOE radio operator Huub Lauwers and forced him to send their messages to London. But when he did so, Lauwers omitted the security signal which should have alerted London that he had been compromised. Instead, the SOE failed to pick up even this clear signal that something was wrong and continued to send more agents to certain death. By April 1943, the Germans had captured more than 50 agents, seized control of at least 18 radio transmitters, and had begun to infiltrate Britain's Secret Intelligence Services' (SIS) operations in Holland. Most of the captured SOE agents had been greeted by the Gestapo as they parachuted into Holland. SOE only became aware of the disaster in September of 1943. Who was responsible for this the largest espionage disaster for the SOE? Was it Charles Blizard, head of SOE operations in Holland? But Maurice Buckmaster had stood by an SOE agent who had worked with the Gestapo as a double agent. The longevity of the "English Game", as the Germans called it, must be conceded to the bitter rivalry between the SIS, which had given a rib in the contested formation of the SOE, and its SOE offspring. So sensitive was this debacle among the highest reaches of the British government that as recently as 1993, five important Cabinet documents were deliberately destroyed. So secretive was the very existence of the SOE that it was years after the end of hostilities before the public became aware, as the SOE had been quietly absorbed into Britain's MI6.

On June 13, 1942, only one week shy of two years after the fall of France, the United States established the Office of Strategic Services (OSS) under Colonel William J. Donovan. Donovan was the most awarded U. S. soldier of World War I. Patterned after the British SOE and SIS (Secret Intelligence Service), this forerunner of the CIA was slow in becoming effective as its authority and scope were challenged by the FBI and the intelligence arms of both the Army and the Navy. No wonder that OSS Captain Fred Floege lamented his lack of support as he established Resistance networks in France.

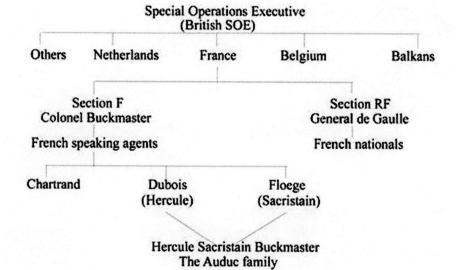

CHAPTER 7   The Hercule Sacristain Buckmaster Network

From its inception the Hercule Sacristain Buckmaster réseau or network parted from the norm. Its two organizers, under the direction of Colonel Buckmaster of the British SOE, were an American of the OSS, Captain Fred Floege, whose mission was code named 'Sacristain' and a Frenchman from Tours, André Dubois, whose field name was 'Hercule'. The network of necessity found its leadership from those living around Le Mans as Floege and Dubois were occupied with other responsibilities. The success of this network was provided by the Auduc family from its considerable financial contributions, from the nine members of the family enlisted and from the impassioned leadership of Alfred and Renée Auduc.

For security, most networks had a triangle as its formation. The organizer of the network would enlist two members, not known to each other. These two then each enlisted two others unknown to each other, and so on. All other members were known only by code names. In this way, if a réseau member were arrested and broke during interrogation, he could name only the member who enlisted him plus the two he enlisted. It was a system that worked remarkably well. But, Alfred had witnessed members of other réseau openly smoking the English cigarettes disguised with French packaging, but readily detectable from their smoke, that were included in weapon drops. He had heard the boasting of foolish ones who wished to impress by stating their membership in a réseau. No, Alfred sought more control.

He chose instead to enlist family members and friends he felt he could trust. Alfred felt he could control his family members better than he could others. But, with nine members of his family placed at risk by Alfred's solicitation, there were bound to be repercussions. After the war, certain family members held Alfred responsible for the death and incarceration of their loved ones. What a cross to bear for someone who had given so much of himself to liberate his country!

But, Alfred was not in an informed position to evaluate the risks to his network, for he had acted in late May of 1943, with the allied invasion thought to be coming that summer. Wasn't this the reason for the frequent weapons drops, weapons that the resistance did not know how to use and were therefore stockpiles for the invading allied forces? How could he know that these weapons drops had as their dual purpose the demoralization of the German soldiers who discovered them or gained knowledge of how extensive these drops and the weapons caches were? Alfred could not have known how well this tactic was working! And he could not have known the invasion was a year away.

Like most networks, Alfred's was scattered across his region. Its members were arrested throughout its lifetime with most being tortured and some revealing names of other members. After the war Colonel Buckmaster helped to put Alfred's mind at ease when he assured Alfred that the five month life of his network had been accomplished through brave and discreet operations. Buckmaster added that the average life of an active network was a short three months.

André Dubois Became One of the SOE's Most Heroic Agents

A notable SOE agent was the Auduc network's organizer: Jean Roger André Dubois. From September 1939, until June 1940, André had been a w/t (wireless telegraphy) operator in the French army. Upon demobilization, he joined a Resistance group in Saumur which he served for ten months as its radio operator. Eager for more responsibility, he was introduced to SOE agent Lt. Raymond Flower (Gaspard) who recruited André in the field to be a fellow SOE operative. He became agent number 121459 in the summer of 1942, with the field name of "Hercule" and the operational name of

"Lighterman". For another assignment, he was given the field name "Mistral".

André was born May 19, 1906, the second of three sons, to Jean Florent and Jeanne Poujet Dubois, in Saint-German-du-Puch, Gironde, France. At age nine, his family moved to Tours. André's first military service was in Niort from 1926 to 1928. During the years leading up to the war he worked in a plastics company, where in 1935, he received training in plastic casting and moulding in Berlin. Perhaps his fierce opposition to the Nazi's fomented during this period. After that, he was employed by a division of Firestone. Later, he launched his own business recycling fuel and lubricants. In 1938, he married Marcelle Angele Emelie ('Mimi') Meneau and by the end of that year welcomed his cherished daughter Francoise ('Fanfan') into his family. André next became a sales representative for pharmaceutical and veterinary products travelling the Sarthe, Indre-et-Loire, and Loire-et-Cher departements, a propitious assignment for someone who would later need a cover for his movements on behalf of the Resistance.

Dubois first became involved with the Resistance in Saumur in July of 1942, when he was also recruited for the Monkeypuzzle network by Marcel Clech to be a w/t operator. Monkeypuzzle came into existence following the demise of the short-lived Autogyro réseau. Monkeypuzzle was headed by Lt. Raymond Flower, a 30 year-old who was born in Britain, but grew up in Paris where he worked at a hotel, possibly his parents'. He became a chef in the British Army before being recruited by the SOE due to his knowledge of France and her language. Gaspard parachuted near Tours on June 27 with the mission of identifying drop zones in the neighboring Sarthe departement. Author M. R. D. Foot characterized Lt. Flowers as "brave and cheerful enough, but undistinguished for security sense or forethought". Monkeypuzzle's w/t transmissions were under constant surveillance from German goniometers which severely handicapped the network's effectiveness. Monkeypuzzle received the first female SOE agent parachuted into France, Andrée Borrel, code named 'Denise', who had earlier worked with the Pat Line to repatriate Allied military personnel. She was later captured and, at age 24, executed.

A rift over Lt. Flower's lack of security discipline developed with Marcel Clech which led to the breakup of Monkeypuzzle. Both men were later safely returned to England. André Dubois was now without a network.

During the early hours of November 18, 1942, Captain Michael Alfred, code named 'Captain Michel' or 'Sylvestre' was parachuted with several other SOE agents into an area southwest of Paris. Sylvestre's mission was to organize a Resistance network in the industrial area of northern France around Lille. His group 'W. O. Lille' became more and more important despite many obstacles. Sylvestre asked Hercule to be his w/t operator as earlier in 1942, Lt. Flower had mentioned Dubois as one who impressed with his work ethic and fearlessness. André had taken grave risks in transporting w/t sets and other wireless equipment through enemy control points. Hercule was hungry for more responsibilities after serving seven months on antiquated equipment and an association with Sylvestre provided the opportunity. To become an effective SOE w/t operator, André needed additional training in the use of more advanced w/t equipment and in clandestine radio procedures. Lt. Flower arranged Dubois' training with London then arranged his flight out through Henri Dericourt (Gilbert), the coordinator for all flights into the region. **Note 7-1.**

Two Lysanders from RAF Tangmere, Squadron 161, piloted by Flying Officer Rymills and Flying Officer Vaughn-Fowler, delivered the ill-fated agent Roland Dowlen, who was going to the Chestnut network, to a landing strip just south of Poitiers on March 17, 1943. For their return flight, André climbed into the rear seat of his Lysander along with Lt. Fowler. Occupying the second Lysander were two important Section F agents: Claude de Baissac and France Anteime, both returning from missions. Hercule was now to receive the training he wanted. His fame preceded him to London, but he added to this high regard. André was sent to STS 52 in Thame Park, Oxfordshire, for security training on the latest W/T sets and coding techniques. His trainer, Lt. Holland, reported on March 27 that he had formed a very high opinion of André's 'courage, determination and seriousness of purpose: "He is very French, very patriotic and vitriolic in his condemnation of the moneyed 'bourgeois' for their being lukewarm towards the cause, but full of praise for the 'petit people'. He has a very likable personality and is capable of single-minded devotion and self-sacrifice." Lt. Holland's observations following a brief association proved to be particularly perceptive. André was now prepared and was to return to France 'during the earliest possible moon period'.

The two Lysanders from RAF squadron 161 landed Dubois plus three other section F agents including Henri Frager, Philippe Liewer and Gabriel Chartrand together near Amboise on April 15 on an airstrip named Bronchite ('bronchitis', possibly because of its foggy clime). For Frager, who later headed the DONKEYMAN network, and Dubois, the landing was terrifying as their Lysander, piloted by Flying Officer McCairns, struck a tree;   the plane was fortunate to receive only slight damage. Landings were precarious with only moonlight for guidance. The second Lysander, again piloted by Flying Officer Vaughn-Fowler, transported Marcel Clech, who had recruited Dubois, back to England.

André's assignment was to work as a freelance w/t operator for any organization not having its own w/t, and in particular the SALESMAN network. One of the most prolific radio operators in the Resistance, from time to time he supported the Monkeypuzzle, Salesman, Donkeyman, Inventor,

Sacristan, Farrier, Farmer and Prosper networks, in addition to his own Hercule network. Doing so was an intentional breach of SOE security, as transmitting messages for several networks placed the W/T operator at exceptional risk both by making his identity and location known to many and by the great number of messages he had to send, rendering him especially vulnerable to German detection via triangulation. His first task was to find a safe house for his transmissions. He contacted Jean Meunier, aka 'Farina', and Gaston Papin, aka 'Williams', of the Castille network, who provided an introduction to a former Great War pilot named Mulot who lived near Amboise and had amassed all the weapons he could find during the German invasion. Later, on November 2, 1943, the Gestapo surrounded Mr. Mulot's house. He barely escaped, but his large cache of weapons was confiscated.

W/t operators had to move frequently to avoid detection from the German goniometers which enabled them to triangulate the position of an active transmitter and André was soon housed by Madame Rigat, a teacher in Artigny. In total Hercule transmitted 138 messages to five different London based organizations. His messages included the precise locations of 75 ramps and storage sites for V-1 rockets ('buzz bombs').

André was also to form a new network around Le Mans. Mr. Mulot's sister, Gisele Baron, who owned a boulangerie, introduced Hercule to Alfred and Renée Auduc.

The story of Hercule's Resistance activities from this point on is told in other chapters by those who knew him best.

A Courageous Section F Agent Having An Innocent Flaw

Jacques Christian Gabriel Chartrand was born on August 14, 1907, in Montreal. He became a devout Roman Catholic. After completing his commercial courses at McGill University, he started a career with Dominion Life Assurance of Canada. Gabriel enlisted in the army on September 10, 1938, finding himself in England in 1942. Now Sergeant Chartrand, he became one of the first Canadians to offer his services, on August 27, to the SOE for assignments on the continent. During his SOE training, Gabriel was found to be always in good spirits and popular with the other 'students', but with a serious appreciation for security. His three practice parachute jumps went well. However, there was a problem: Gabriel had a strong Canadian French accent. Canadian French is an older dialect than that spoken in France. Not only are the accents different, word usage may be as well. But, at this point, Gabriel was to proceed in his training. On February 11, 1943, he was promoted to Lieutenant in the Canadian army, which at this time loaned Lt. Chartrand to the SOE for six months, the normal period for loaned personnel. His responsibilities were to support the head of a network and train its members in the use of firearms and explosives.

On April 14, 1943, at 2200 hours, Lt. Chartrand, code named "Dieudonné", boarded one of the two Lysanders headed for Tours. His three companions were his leader, Major Geoffrey Staunton (Clement), André Dubois (Hercule) and a Frenchman code-named Paul. Chartrand recorded: "We landed at 0015 on the 15th and were met by a Resistance party led by a chap named Gilbert. Together we carried 12 pieces of luggage, but were met by only four men and two bicycles. We solved our predicament by hiding most of our luggage in a haystack, with Paul and Hercule taking off on the two bikes towards Tours, some 30 km away. Clement and I walked the 15 km to a train station in order to take an 0815 train to Tours. We became concerned when a plane roared back and forth over our heads around 0200, hiding in a ditch until 0400 when we proceeded to the station. Dubois met our train in Tours and took us to his mother-in-law's flat on the grounds of L'Ecole Superieure pour jeunes filles. Shortly after, the superior of the school rushed to our flat warning that German soldiers had just entered their grounds. We hurried out the back door and made our way to Dubois' mother-in-law's cottage some 5 km outside of Tours. How in heaven's name had the Germans discovered so quickly our presence? We had the answer the next day. It was merely a commission visiting school's libraries to examine books in the hands of children to make sure only the 'right kind' of history would be taught.

On April 17, Clement traveled to Paris to establish contacts and order two bicycles and radio sets that we intended to bring with us to Rouen, where we had decided to establish our headquarters. I remained in Madame Meneau's cabin getting acquainted with French habits, expressions, etc. and to stay close to Hercule, our w/t operator, who had established himself some 25 km from Tours in Saché. Around April 28, Clement came back for me and together we proceeded to Paris where I remained while Clement sought a flat or house in Rouen. I did nothing but liaise among Paris, Tours and Saché.

During this period Dubois put me in touch with a friend who had a friend, a charming woman named Micheline, who owned a store in Paris and another in Rouen. She offered to put her flat in Rouen at our disposal and to introduce us to her manager there, Jean Sueur. This was an intelligent and very patriotic man, so Clement and I moved into the Rouen flat. Jean Sueur also arranged a safe house for one of us and that was where Clement stayed. With help from others, we found what would be a good landing field for receiving goods, but London rejected the site."

With Rouen's location in Normandy, not far from the coast, German surveillance activity was especially tight and several networks had been broken with numerous arrests. Naturally, those still carrying out resistance activities were on edge. Chartrand's Canadian accent began causing alarm. But, Chartrand preferred to remain in Normandy or Brittany as he fully expected the Allied invasion would be that summer. He continues: "I met a fellow Canadian called Max, who was working with a network near Tours, and arranged to be transferred to his network due to the security risks in Rouen. I was to organize and instruct a Resistance group near the village of Château-du-Loir in the Sarthe, where I stayed at the home of Dr. Goude. His group had received two munitions drops and the material remained scattered in the field with perhaps dozens of people knowing about it. I sorted out the munitions, supervised the making of explosive charges and planned their course of action upon the invasion. They were to blow up the four railroad lines going through the village. I obtained a plan of the château headquartering the Germans and even enrolled the caretaker there in our schemes.

Hearing of plans for another munitions drop, I found this unnecessary and risky, so I traveled to Tours to discuss this with Hercule. Alas, the German police had raided his house and he was on the run. I was arrested leaving the area, but used my bicycle to entangle the policeman long enough to escape. Hurrying back towards Dr. Goude's, I realized I could not return there. I telephoned Dr. Goude and had my belongings sent to me. I then joined an American airman, David Butcher, that also had to flee his safe house and together we fled to Mr. and Mrs. Monéris' in Vouvray-sur-Loire. I remained there for almost five weeks during which Max visited to inform me of the arrest of five of our associates in Tours on August 6 (in fact, those arrested included Hercule's wife, mother-in-law and an associate). Max decided it was time to remove me back to London. In response I asked to be reassigned, to no avail. I was then taken by the underground to Rennes, where I was picked up and flown to London, arriving on December 4, 1943." Although Lt. Chartrand wished very much to return to France, it was deemed too risky to send him due to his heavy accent and the fact that the Gestapo knew about him.

In May of 1943, Alfred Auduc managed to find what he had been seeking for a long time. "Friends of mine introduced me to André Dubois, whose code name was "Hercule". He had been flown to Touraine, a region he knew well, since before the war he lived in Tours where his wife and daughter were still living. This is where he organized his networks. He immediately began to organize a group of local Resistance fighters into a section called the Hercule Buckmaster network. Its duties were to provide intelligence to the SOE and to receive and hide parachuted arms and equipment. André also helped to establish two other networks: the Lighterman in the Touraine and Sarthe areas plus the Mistral."

Alfred continues: "André first tested me before I was accepted into his group. Satisfied, he asked me to form a group of resistance fighters around Le Mans, Sarthe, where I lived. In Touraine, the Germans had discovered his presence and he had to find another place to run his operations. I took him to Cérans-Fouilletourte, about 20 km from Le Mans, where he first stayed with l'abbé Julien Lelièvre. But, the Germans had stationed an armored company near his church and Dubois asked to move to my mother Marie's more remote farm, "La Bouguelière", which was 2 km from the village and proved to be an excellent choice. It was thought that the Germans were able to locate a radio transmitter in a city within 30 minutes. Dubois lived in the attic where he set up his two w/t transmitters. His antenna ran from his window to the top of a pear tree. As moving his radios around was prudent, Hercule also stayed with my brother, Roger Auduc. During this time Hercule also sent messages from his radios in Chenu and Artigny. In all he prudently used four radios of different powers, all running on batteries.

In the meantime, Hercule introduced an American officer to me: Captain Floege, who had parachuted into the area. Floege needed help organizing his group, both staff and equipment. For this reason, I contacted members of my family, including my three brothers: Roger, André, and Edmond, as well as my brother-in-law Florent Beaury and a few of my best friends.

Soon everything was organized and I became the acting head of this network." Alfred's operations differed from what he anticipated with no confrontations with any Germans. Many of his activities were in organizing and administering his network. His was 'an army of the shadows' and oh how this tried his patience.

André heard about the wishes of certain students of the military academy in nearby La Fleche who spontaneously formed a network with Guy Garry at its head. This network called on André for guidance. One of these students was seventeen year old Marcel Veau. He and 23 others were arrested on Oct. 9, 1943, by German Feld gendarmerie (German field police) due to an informer. At the time he had been a Resistance fighter for two years. When the Gestapo arrived to arrest six members of the Bizot family, a fight erupted with one being killed and the other five being deported. Today, there is a rue de la Family Bizot in La Fleche. At age 17 Marcel remembers not being afraid of death. He had been in charge of messages and formed groups of patriots in Clermont-Créans. He also concealed weapons and with his friends began weeding out collaborators: 'those who smiled at the Germans'. He had to be wary of everyone as there were a lot of collaborators in La Fleche. Marcel recalled crying a lot for his friends who had fed him, then suffered death for their patriotism. He also went through six 'muscle interrogations' at Gestapo headquarters in Angers. At age 77, he still has marks on his neck left from blows with a slag and on his feet from the cigarette burns.

Marcel was taken to Compiègne prison on Jan.3, 1944, then to Buchenwald on Jan. 24. He keeps his memoires in a box because "one's memory may fade and I do not want to forget. There were 120 of us stacked in a cattle car; the trip lasting three days without food, and worse, without drink. When we arrived at the camp, the SS hit us and their dogs bit us. We were shaved and were made to wash in a tub of disinfectant.

In the camp, it was all about work. Those not strong enough lagged behind and the dogs would bite their calves. Some of my friends lost all the flesh on their calves." After more than a year of this inhumane treatment, he was liberated on April 29, 1945, "but it wasn't over. I caught typhus a few days later". Marcel was saved by Dr. Richard Grunberg. He returned to La Fleche on June 19, weighing 30 kilos (66 pounds).

In all, Hercule contacted some 200 persons to solicit their involvement, a number that was considerably risky and placed him in jeopardy.

After the war, Alfred Auduc defended his network: "Some people had malicious intentions and sought to give the Resistance a bad image by spreading the word that the members were given important sums of money. This was categorically false. In our network all the members volunteered and made huge sacrifices. I only knew two who asked to be paid and they were immediately dismissed. No one in our network received any money; it was quite the contrary, as each member was asked to give FF50,000 minimum (equivalent to FF500 at the time of the franc's conversion to the Euro). This amount was to be reimbursed after the war at the rate of FF300 for one pound sterling because the English were short of French currency. The guarantee was as follows: any person who could give FF50,000 or more chose a message to be broadcast from London. The donator was told when a confirmation message would be broadcast and would contribute the money after hearing this acknowledgement. One of my friends, a business man, had given a substantial amount of money. The message he chose was: "The violet is a modest flower", Violet being the first name of his wife. Hercule was pleased as he appreciated that in such dangerous times when everyone knew the risks, this man still thought about his wife."

Alfred and Renée Auduc had each contributed FF50,000 to the SOE to fund the activities of their network. When they applied for reimbursement after the war, confusion abounded. The radio message confirming Renée's contribution had been garbled and it took months for its confirmation. And, André Dubois had quoted an incorrect reimbursement rate of FF200 to the pound rather than the approved rate of FF300 to a pound. Only after a mountain of paperwork did Alfred and Renée receive their 166 pounds, 13 shillings and 4 pence each.

Alfred concludes: "One member of our network was Captain Floege's son Claude. I was able to recruit l'abbé Julien Lelièvre, Colonel Mauffrey, Dr. Richard Grunberg, and family members André Auduc, Edmond Auduc, Jean-Luc Auduc, and Roger Auduc. Our network was now formed and active.

Chanoine Lelievre   1902-1958

It was named: Hercule after the code name of our radio operator André Dubois; Sacristain after the code name of Capt. Floege's mission; and, Buckmaster after the head of F Section of the SOE. The Resistance became known as 'L'armée de l'ombre', 'the army of the shadows', as many of our activities were carried out during the night."

L'Abbé Lelièvre: Priests were among the most patriotic

Julien Lelièvre, like most other priests, opened his home to people on the run. When Hercule arrived in June of 1943, to form a network, he was hidden by l'abbé Lelièvre. Julien became totally involved with the network under the influence of Alfred Auduc, participating in most missions. Julien provided information about the presence of German vehicles in the several villages he regularly visited. He assisted young men to escape from STO service and sheltered liaison agents and downed airmen.

Note 7-1. Henri Déricourt (Gilbert): the most mysterious agent in the SOE and perhaps the deadliest

Was Déricourt a double agent? Was he a triple agent working for MI6? Or, was he simply an opportunist? André Dubois crossed paths with Déricourt on several occasions and even wired messages for him, but there is no evidence that Déricourt compromised Dubois.

Henri Déricourt was born in France in September of 1909. He was a civilian pilot before joining the French Air Force as a test pilot in 1939. When France surrendered to Nazi Germany in June 1940, Déricourt went back to civil aviation, but in August 1942 he escaped to Britain. After being checked out through the

Royal Patriotic School's vetting process, he joined Section F of the Special Operations Executive.

Déricourt was parachuted into France on 22nd January 1943. His main task was to find suitable landing fields and organize receptions for agents brought by air. He worked mainly for the Prosper Network and over the next few months arranged air transport for over 67 agents including Noor Inayat Khan, Vera Leigh, Yolande Beekman , Eliane Plewman, Diana Rowden, Jack Agazarian, Francis Suttill, Pearl Witherington and Lise de Baissac.

In the summer of 1943 the Gestapo arrested several British agents working in France. It became clear that a double-agent had infiltrated the Special Operations Executive. Several agents, including Francis Cammaerts, Jack Agazarian and Francis Suttill became convinced that Déricourt was the man responsible. These suspicions increased when it became known that Déricourt was living in Paris in a flat next to one rented by Hugo Bleicher of the German Abwehr.

Another agent, Henri Frager, told Nicholas Bodington, second in command to Buckmaster, when Bodington visited occupied France in July 1943 that Déricourt was a German spy. Bodington dismissed this theory arguing that Déricourt had arranged his own journey to France and he had not been arrested. When Bodington refused to take action some agents began to think that he also was a double agent.

Soon afterwards Georges Pichard informed Maurice Buckmaster that he had heard from a good source that a "Frenchman in charge of air operations in the Paris and Angers districts" was working for the Abwehr. Buckmaster, like Bodington before him, dismissed the charges and Déricourt was allowed to continue his work in France until February of 1944, when he was brought back to London.

After the War the interrogation of German officials provided evidence that Déricourt was guilty of providing information to the Abwehr and the Gestapo that led to the arrest and execution of several agents including Noor Inayat Khan, Vera Leigh, Yolande Beekman, Eliane Plewman, Diana Rowden, Gilbert Norman, Jack Agazarian and Francis Suttill.

In November 1946, Déricourt was arrested by the French authorities but did not appear in court until June 1948. At the trial Bodington testified that he had been in charge of all of Déricourt's work in the field. He admitted that he was aware that Déricourt was in contact with the Germans but maintained that no important information had been revealed. During the trial the defense council argued that although the prosecution could bring plenty of suspicious indirect evidence against Déricourt, they could not actually pin any definite act of treachery on him. Largely on the evidence provided by Bodington, Déricourt was acquitted.

When Jean Overton Fuller interviewed Déricourt for her book, *Double Agent*, he told her that leaders of the SOE knew the organization had been penetrated by the Gestapo. Men and women were deliberately sacrificed in order to maintain the flow of false information to shield the planned landings in Sicily and Normandy. For this reason, some also believed that Déricourt actually worked for MI6. The comparison has been made with General Haig who, during WWI, sent hundreds of thousands of British soldiers to their destruction. Was it not expedient to sacrifice a few agents to protect the plans for massive invasions of Sicily and Normandy? But, were these reprehensible decisions for the families and friends of the sacrificed agents then hidden through the destruction of classified files?

His defense grows thin when we learn that Déricourt was paid handsomely by the Abwehr. Others may conclude what they wish. The author believes Déricourt was a cowardly opportunist who played both sides.

Déricourt was reported to have been killed in an air crash while flying over Laos on Nov. 20, 1962. Was even his death faked?

CHAPTER 8   American Captain Fred Floege in Britain's Special Operations Executive

Captain Fred Floege

Contrary to the poor evaluations of him by the SOE's training staff, Fred Floege was to prove himself an especially clever agent. Here, in his memoir The Little White Boat, he writes in third person: "The man was peddling hard in the night. His bike was heavy and creaky, in bad condition. In fact, he had to work so hard to keep it moving that he felt like giving up. In addition to his fatigue, he knew he had to be cautious. Should he go all the way to Nuillé? The Gestapo probably knew about that place, too. He had realized for several weeks and even more so since this morning that the Gestapo was well informed. A moment ago, in Mée, he had almost fallen into their trap. It had been a good thing he had been particularly wary of the fact that the village was too dark, too silent, too hostile. In one of the houses next to the one he had rented, he was told the Germans had come, had arrested people, including the café owner, had loaded unidentified items into their vehicles, and perhaps not all of them had left. It was clear to him: the weapons depot had been discovered and a mouse trap had been set out for his network, for him.

They must have been aggravated and revengeful to have missed him this morning. It had been such a close call. He still had this vivid image when he went out at dawn to do a first reconnaissance in his in-law's yard in Angers. He had spent a bad night; his son Claude, whom he was to meet, had not shown up the evening before. What had happened? And then, suddenly, like in the movies: steps, moving shadows and words yelled in German had sped him back into the house as he heard the first gun shots. He jumped from the window on the second floor, landed unharmed thanks to his good training, ran across the second little yard and then as fast as he could down that narrow street. 'Major Paul', American Captain Fred Floege, was slipping away from the Gestapo!

500 yards down the street he reached the boulevard where he was harbored by some trusted friends. They had dug out what you could hardly call a bicycle. To think that he, back in 1925, had sold bicycles, and now had to ride that thing! He started off late that afternoon to find some members of his group and inform them. It was hard to believe the Gestapo had captured everyone, or had they? How could these monsters manage to learn so much in so little time? Only at the end of the war was it learned how when the survivors told their stories."

Floege had experienced a great disappointment in Mée as yet another part of his network had fallen. Was his invaluable radio operator and friend, with whom he was still traveling the day before yesterday, now a German prisoner? Floege continues his story:

"No doubt it was dangerous to go all the way to Nuillé, still five or six km down the road. The night was pretty clear, and he soon made out a big haystack, far from any building. It could be tonight's substitute for a hotel room. In the village he had just passed, he had tried to find a room, but to no avail. At the presbytery, the priest's maid had sent him away and in the only café they would not give him a room. People were suspicious of a stranger on a bike who claimed he was arriving late due to a breakdown.

To himself: "Alright, Fred! Now that you have escaped the Gestapo, you need to build yourself a shelter, or the cold might get to you!" It was a cold winter night and digging into frozen stacked hay to make a hole large enough for a man was not an easy task. When the hole was made large enough, he wiggled inside and covered his shoulders the best he could. The hard work had warmed him temporarily, but soon he could feel the bitter cold again. "I ache all over, I'm freezing, and yet I need sleep."

He did not go to sleep right away and it came back to his mind: "This is Christmas Eve, 1943; Merry Christmas, Fred!" Things were not looking so good for the head of an underground network, lost in the middle of Mayenne, who did not even know what had become of his group. So it was that Major Paul and his friend and fellow Resistance fighter, Alfred Auduc, spent Christmas Eve, 1943, apart, but together in their solitary, freezing, Gestapo fearing, outdoor habitats.

He had been reminded that it was Christmas Eve when he was pedaling towards Mée: it was dinner time and he went through a village appropriately called St. Quentin of the Angels; he could hear people singing inside several houses. Yes, it was December 24, the day before the 5th Christmas of the war. Some people were obviously trying to do some kind of celebrating.

To himself: "If all of my friends in America only knew what kind of Christmas I was having; they had tried to talk me out of going back to Europe."

U. S. Captain Ernest Frederich Floege, "Fred", with the sobriquet "Major Paul", was born in Chicago in 1898, to naturalized German parents. He was not at all conflicted:

Germany had invaded his beloved France and he was to drive them out. His family had moved to France for his father's job when he was ten. At the start of The Great War, Fred enlisted in General Pershing's U. S. army and became a colonel's driver. After The Great War, he married a young girl from Le Mans and settled there. Fred started a family when son Claude was born in 1922, but his next child, a daughter, died from meningitis. Son Claude lost the use of a hand due to a severe scalding when he was two. In 1927, his wife died. Fred ran an auto shop and developed a passion for auto sports. He wed a second time, to Julia Brossard, and they had six children. In 1933, driving his Bugatti, he participated in the 24 Hours of Le Mans Grand Prix race. Fred then sold his business and moved to Angers where he started the city's first bus line. He cleverly added an axle to used buses he had purchased and his business did well until the French army requisitioned half his buses in 1939 and the Germans took the remainder in 1940. When the U. S. entered the war after Pearl Harbor, he learned that the Germans were now seeking to arrest Americans living in France. He escaped south through the demarcation line, over the Pyrenees and into Spain. Making it to Portugal, he managed to book passage to New York.

As early as the fall of 1940, Fred was hoping to organize a group of Resistance fighters. In spite of his American friends advising him against it, and of the administrative hassles (the Pentagon was not yet familiar with the French Resistance), he impressed the newly formed Office of Strategic Services (the "OSS") enough to become an American OSS officer, asking to be assigned to France. Fred sailed to England. Upon arrival in London, he checked into the Lancaster Court Hotel, W.2., and immediately offered his services to Colonel Buckmaster's F Section of the British SOE.

With his WWI army service plus his fluency in German, English and French, Fred appeared to be an excellent candidate. The SOE wasn't so sure. His evaluator, Lt. Searle, had mixed impressions and noted several strengths and weaknesses: on March 5, 1943, Searle wrote: "He is a strong character who has himself well under control. One feels that somewhere in him are the qualities of leadership. He is, however, very much a man of his own. He does not get along with the two candidates closest to his age. …. He is very willing to learn, but at the same time gives the impression that he thinks himself rather better than the others. Is rather impatient in small things which annoy him" On March 24, Searle commented: "Still occasionally irritates people by his spirit of contradiction and anxiety to prove that he knows more than anyone else." and on March 26 Lt. Searle made his most scathing report: "He is not the type to hit back for long; not to be a leading example of courage, fortitude or resource should things persist in going wrong. ….. He is not a leader. He is rather a disappointment." The reader should note that Capt. Floege's performance in the field was diametrically opposite of Lt. Searle's evaluation. One must wonder to what extent personality, age and cultural differences colored Lt. Searle. Fred Floege showed extraordinary courage under the most difficult of circumstances. He later proved to be an exceptional organizer and leader.

Following thorough training for secret agents, he boarded a Halifax operated by RAF squadron 138 and parachuted near Tours on June 13, 1943, to organize resistance fighters around Le Mans, his mission being coded "Sacristain". Aged 45, Capt. Floege, who had the code name of "Pascal" in addition to "Major Paul", was one of F Section's oldest field agents. Capt. Floege was to prove an excellent resource for F Section and administered his networks with a flare. Not long after setting up his operations, his radio man was arrested. After that, he afforded the assistance of the SOE's André Dubois as his radio operator; André was now experienced in setting up networks so the two worked together. This is how cooperation between OSS and SOE operatives took place out of necessity. Over that summer Pascal and Hercule set up the Pascal Sacristain Resistance network that covered several departements, a network that the SOE considered to be 'powerful'. During the summer Pascal set up his headquarters in Mée and acquired the services of Michel, the code name of radio operator André Bouchardon, who proved himself invaluable to Pascal.

Fred Floege (Pascal; Major Paul) continues his story in third person: "Between the early morning run under the Mauser bullets and his evening bicycle trek, it had been a rough day and Major Paul would have had a good sleep were he in a good bed. But, at the foot of his haystack, with the cold piercing him, he could only doze and was awake most of the night. While awake, he would think about his important moments over the past six months. His thoughts were all muddled. He thought about the day when he was in front of the train station of Le Mans and was having trouble putting his heavy suitcase containing his radio transmitter on his bicycle rack; a thoughtful German soldier had offered to hold his bike while he installed his load. He thought about a nice evening at the Auduc's; rue de Tourniquet, with three American aviators who had survived the shooting down of their Flying Fortress near Sablé. They were on their way to Poitier and thence to Spain. One of the airmen had shown them how to dance the jitterbug. He also thought of another evening at the Auduc's, a strange evening with two German officers that were so relaxed that they had put their Lugers into a cabinet drawer upon entering the Auduc home. Poor Auduc's, they were among the first ones captured in early November. As they were supplying fruits and vegetables to the occupation troops, they were able to get valuable petrol tickets and driving passes that served his network well. Where were they now?

The most vivid memories he was thinking about were the parachute drops of munitions and supplies, the good ones as well as the bad ones. "What an emotion when we heard the distant roaring of the plane's engines that confirmed that the communication with London had worked well. The large plane would deadhead towards our impromptu strip; its engines singing: 'one day you will be free'!

We would send the reconnaissance signal and on the plane's second passage it would drop its containers. Sometimes there were ten, even twelve, of them and we had to hurry to collect them, load them and take them away. It was exhausting, but also exalting! Sometimes the plane dropped only one container after we had spent four nights waiting. The disappointment then was hard to get over."

All of this equipment was either piled up in a barn or buried under a heap of beets. Would it end up in the Wehrmacht's trucks? Fred Floege could not accept this. He must have these machine guns and ammunition for the big day. He was dreaming of the day when the Allies, with their material superiority, would set foot on the soil of France. He and his network were eager for the Allied invasion. He remembered that early November morning in a room at the back of the restaurant in the Hôtel de la Calandre; Madame Brault's husband, the owner, had just been arrested. She had taken Fred's hands into hers and had told him in a tearful voice "Mr. Paul, it is high time they came; when are the allies going to come?" He didn't know what to answer. He was silent and she added "Can't you see that we will all be dead?"

His haystack had become too uncomfortable and it wasn't even dawn yet, but he had to get out of there. He felt so stiff and achy that he thought he would never get out of his hole. At last, when he was standing, he had to lean on his bike to manage to take a few steps. Gradually, his blood circulation came back and he felt better. He was soon back on the road and was pedaling towards Nuillé. He arrived in Nuillé as the village was just wakening. It was time for the first mass and a lot of inhabitants were walking towards the church.

Everything looked normal. The innkeeper in front of his door was harnessing his horse.

"Here's one that hasn't been arrested yet", thought Floege as he walked towards the man. They shook hands and the man said "You know the guy that was with you when you came by the day before yesterday?" That was Michel, his radio operator. Floege dreaded what he was about to hear. "He's here, with a bullet in him." Fred forgot his fatigue and ran as fast as he could to the room where his wounded friend was lying. They were both emotional and Michel, actually André Bouchardon, told the story of his incredible escape.

When the Germans suddenly entered the café in Mée, they arrested him. Michel fought them so hard that one of the soldiers eventually took his Luger and shot him in the chest. The bullet was deflected by his sternum and thereby did limited damage. Michel then changed his tactic and decided to act badly wounded. The officer gave the order to take Michel to Angers so he could be cared for: his orders were to take radio operators alive as they possessed invaluable information.

They made two big mistakes that would cost them dearly. First of all they did not search him and therefore did not know he had a loaded revolver in his jacket pocket. He was handcuffed, but they made the second mistake of doing so with his hands in front. Once in their car, nobody paid attention to him. Very slowly Michel moved his hands and eventually managed to grip his weapon. He had nothing to lose, so he fired five shots, hitting each of his German captors. The vehicle, having lost its driver, started zigzagging and ended up in a ditch. Michel managed to get out of the car, but not before shooting his last bullet into the head of the German who still was holding him back.

It was dark and Michel was handcuffed. He knew the area well enough to find his way to a farm where he knew the owner would assist him. The farmer used his tools to break open the handcuffs. He waited for daylight and, in spite of his wounds, managed to return to Nuillé.

Major Paul (Floege) was impressed and congratulated his radio operator. He then told Michel his story. They were so happy to be together again that they were both laughing and saying "They will never get us". They also agreed on the fact they could not stay in Nuillé. The next day, they left and headed towards the Sarthe. Michel pretended that his wound was not bothering him much and refused to be separated from his friend. The village postman had changed bikes and had given his old one to the innkeeper. The two men were riding bicycles that were equally decrepit. Things were looking worse and worse: the Gestapo had swept their network from Neuvy and Montreuil-le-Chétif: their network was almost erased.

Michel did not have his radio transmitter anymore so he asked a friend to inform London of this. Upon hearing of their plight, Buckmaster was eager to get his agents back to London. Michel and Paul had to wait until mid-March to receive instructions. First, they were escorted by a young lady to Lyon, then by two guides that helped them cross the Pyrenees near Perpignan. From there they took a train to Barcelona, then to Madrid and Gibraltar. They had been given some money and forged ID's and an RAF plane flew them back to London.

Captain E. F. Floege, the American who was so attached to France, had refused the capitulation of France as early on as 1940. Eventually he did get his revenge. On May 5, 1944, he parachuted again with his inseparable Michel into France's eastern department of Doubs near Montbéliard where he organized a Maquis in the forest of Lomont. Floege formed a group of guerrillas which eventually numbered 3,000 men and inflicted heavy losses on the German troops. His mission was to sabotage rail lines and communications plus to organize guerilla activities in preparation for D-Day; it was carried out beyond expectations. In September, he joined French General Delattre de Tassigny's army group when it reached eastern France, thus serving in the same outfit as did Captain Charles d'Orgeix, the father of Claire d'Orgeix Kirk, the translator of these memoirs. Captain d'Orgeix was a tank squadron commander whose tank, numbered '29' and named 'Paris', had been one of the first to enter Paris as part of General Leclerc's liberating 2nd Armored Division. Captain d'Orgeix later became an advisor for the book and for the movie "Is Paris Burning?".

When France was at peace again, Captain Floege experienced more comfortable and happier Christmas's than that of 1943. He received the Distinguished Service Cross from the United States, the Distinguished Service Order from the United Kingdom and from France the Croix de Guerre avec Palme and the Légion d'Honneur. Fred lived to the ripe age of 98 and is buried with honors in Arlington National Cemetery, Fredericksburg, Virginia. His son, Claude, who served in the Hercule Sacristain Buckmaster réseau that his father established, remains a good friend of Jean-Jacques' who continues to see him from time to time.

Claude Floege was born in Le Mans on February 11, 1922. He attended a Catholic boarding school before going to Antibes to a horticulture school. When the Italians attacked the Nice area, Claude bicycled the long distance back to Angers, passing distraught refugees in the exodus. He reached Angers in July and found it under Nazi control. Claude found a position at a nursery while he awaited his father's return. He joined his father in Mée near a house where parachuted munitions were being hidden. He became a liaison agent and scouted the region with his dad and Pierre Gagneau and also assisted Michel with radio transmissions from Neuvy-en-Champagne, Beaumont-sur-Sarthe and Montreuil-le-Chétif where Dr. Richard Grunberg lived. In October, 1943, the Gestapo infiltrated the Hercule-Sacristain network; on November 3

Victor Brault and the Leproust's were arrested; and, five weeks later Juliette Brault and Olga Vinçon as well. On the evening of December 22, the Germans stormed Maurice and Yvonne Pitout's house in Le Mans; they were arrested and taken to rue des Fontaines where they were tortured. Oh, Christmas Eve 1943, how much misery were so many to see. They confessed that Claude, who was staying at their house, was the son of the head of the Pascal Sacristain network. At 4:00 that morning, Claude was arrested and tortured. He was taken to the Gestapo headquarters in Angers and, on January 27, 1944, sent to Buchenwald, becoming prisoner number 43709. For 15 months he suffered from hunger, lice, dysentery and hard labor. When the Allies neared, his captors sent Claude by train to Flossenburg in an open rail car and then he had to walk for days, stopping finally near the Czech border. Along the way, some kind Germans threw his group food, but the SS would club those who ate any and shoot those who stopped for it. American soldiers liberated him in late April, 1945, and he soon was on trains to Metz and then to Paris.

As he had upon entering the concentration camp, Claude again felt he was entering an unknown world when he returned to Paris. He was sent to La Baule to convalesce, but had a difficult time adjusting to 'normalcy'. Claude was awarded the high rank of Commander of the Legion of Honor. He married Solange and they spent 16 years in the Congo and Gabon where he worked as an agriculture engineer controlling the quality and the packaging of coffee and cocoa. In 1962, he returned to France to work in a school in Angers.

CHAPTER 9   Fourth of July's Fireworks Were No Celebration

The Fourth of July, 1943, broke with clear, blue skies, a beautiful early summer Sunday, in Molesworth, England, home to the 303rd Bomber Group (the "Hell's Angels") of the U. S. Eighth Air Force (**Note 9-1**). It was a day of great irony possible only in wartime. At their morning briefing, pilots learned that their mission, number 48, was to attack with 500 pound bombs the Gnome et Rhône aircraft engine plant in Le Mans, France. The plant was building BMW 801 engines used in many German planes and extensively in the advanced Focke-Wulf Fw-190 fighters. (**Note 9-2**). The strike force comprised of 166 B-17's was to be protected by the 4th and 78th Fighter Groups, yet these Spitfires and Thunderbolts were prematurely recalled due to deteriorating weather conditions in Great Britain. Sixty-six B-17's were to split off and bomb the U-boat pens at La Palice. Secondary targets for the main force of 100 B-17's were the train station and the airfield at Le Mans.

Following their morning briefing, pilots joined their crews for an 0900 takeoff. Lt. Robert S. O'Connor, a 25 year old from Milwaukee, joined his crew of nine in their B-17 named "The Mugger" for what seemed a short mission over the moderately protected city of Le Mans. Weather was good with 1/10 cloud cover and unlimited visibility. En route, three B-17's turned back due to mechanical failures. Otherwise, the mission was uneventful until the IP (Initial Point) was approached, when the accompanying 379th Bomber Group appeared to be on a collision course with the 303rd. "S" turns were executed for correction, causing the 303rd to scatter dangerously. Lacking fighter escort, tight formations were the key to a B-17's survival, especially as the chin turret machine guns had yet to be introduced.

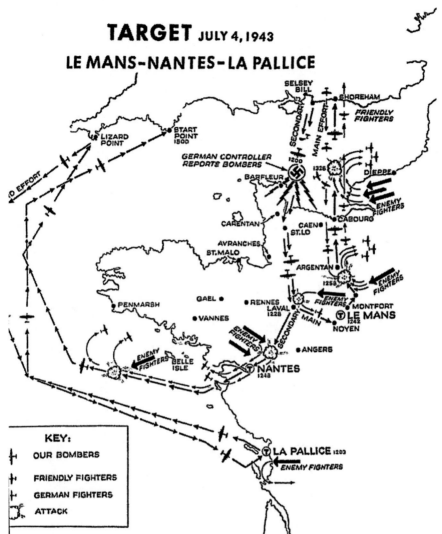

TARGET JULY 4, 1943

LE MANS-NANTES-LA PALLICE

KEY:

┼ OUR BOMBERS

╫ FRIENDLY FIGHTERS

┼ GERMAN FIGHTERS

ATTACK

That same Sunday, Alfred Auduc took his two sons, Jean-Jacques and Michel, to his mother's in Cérans-Fouilletourte, 16 miles SSW of Le Mans, for dejeuner (lunch), when they heard the roar of innumerable bombers almost overhead. Around 12:30, the four ventured outside, walked to the crest of a nearby hill and watched a giant aerial clash. The din of the exploding bombs was deafening. Immediately, they saw a bomber diving towards the ground, watching as the tail section broke off. Only one parachute was seen. Soon afterwards, they saw a bomber in flames and counted five white parachutes dropping (there were eight). 35 German fighters were attacking the now 97 B-17's; the sky seeming to turn black from the planes and their smoke.

According to The Mugger co-pilot Lt. Donovan B. Manifold: "Our RAF Spitfire escort had to leave us due to low fuel shortly after crossing the Channel. We were soon attacked by the elite Hermann Goering squadron of 'Abbeville Kids'. Their Fw-190's were distinguished by their yellow noses. One blasted our No. 2 motor and nose. Flak set a second engine on fire. Then, our No.3 propeller spun out of control and was braked automatically, causing The Mugger to fall behind its formation. The Fw-190's leapt on us. Our gunners defended us well, but Lt. O'Connor and I did not know whether we hit any Fw-190's as we were too busy in the cockpit to observe. Some of our instruments were damaged. We did not want to drop our bomb load over land, but could not make it back to the Channel; a village (Malicorne-sur-Sarthe) was ahead of us. One of our wings was on fire and there was fire in the cockpit. Lt. O'Connor sounded the alarm and through the intercom gave the order for the crew to bail out. I unbuckled my harness, opened my oxygen bottle and headed for the rear. We wore the parachute harness and gathered the parachutes near the exit. When I reached the exit, I saw Lt. Halioris there. I pushed him and he jumped. Just as I was putting on my parachute, there was an explosion. I do not think O'Connor had enough time to put his parachute on before the explosion, which knocked me out of the plane while rendering me unconscious. When I came to, I was close to the ground, but able to deploy." Lt. Manifold had attempted to maneuver his parachute away from a fire in the field below him. A group of people were fighting the fire, a disparate group consisting of Wehrmacht, gendarmes, firemen and townsfolk. Lt. Manifold continued: "I soon touched ground. I landed in a wheat field that had just been mowed. There were pieces of metal from the plane around me, but no important parts. It was impossible to hide, but I saw a wooded area 150 meters away. I quickly folded my parachute and ran towards the trees. I soon heard shots and yelling and looked behind me to see two German soldiers running towards me with their rifles in their hands. Unfortunately, I had landed near a German Army encampment. My helmet, boots, dog tags, survival kit, even my oxygen bottle had disappeared. In addition to my scalp wound, I had serious burns on my face and hands. I was taken to an officer who spoke a few words of English. He wanted to know where the rest of the crew was. I did not know, but would not have told him anyway. I was taken to a civilian doctor in a nearby town. This doctor gave me emergency care that stopped my hemorrhaging. I was then taken to a hospital in Le Mans where I was questioned by a member of the Gestapo, a most unpleasant fellow. Ten days later, I was transferred to a large hospital in Paris where I stayed for five weeks. I was treated well. Next, I was sent to Dulag Luft at Oberursel near Frankfort, the main center for questioning. After four weeks of isolation, I was transferred to Stalag Luft III near Sagan, Poland (where The Great Escape occurred). The Germans had no information on me and as I also had no dog tags I was questioned thoroughly."

Here is the account of top turret gunner Sgt. Buddy Koenig of Spencer, Nebraska: "I was shooting at planes almost overhead when half a dozen others smashed into us from the rear. They blew the turret cover right off me. I was showered with glass and metal, but by some kind of luck I wasn't hit and could keep on firing my guns. I then heard Bob O'Connor on the intercom 'Pull out those fire extinguishers', his last message, but Bob kept the plane level so we could bail out. As I descended, an FW-190 circled me; I thought I was a goner, but the pilot waved a salute to me and was gone. I landed in some woods where French Resistants helped me to cover. I was to walk some 400 miles to the channel where a boat took me back to England. I weighed 170 pounds when shot down and only 130 when I got back to England. I returned to my unit amid war whoops and the biggest celebration our squadron had had."

Co-pilot Lt. Manifold and seven other crewmen hit the silk, with Lt. O'Connor and Lt. Richard W. Peterson, the bombardier and the only son of Dr. and Mrs. Peterson from Denver, Colorado, staying on the plane to keep it level while the crew bailed out. Local villagers were sure the two airmen stayed with The Mugger to steer it away from their village, Malicorne-sur-Sarthe.

Navigator A. N. Halioris, badly burned, landed on the Leloup farm where the Leloup's rescued him. Only, a collaborator informed the Gestapo. The three were arrested with First Officer Halioris being sent to a stalag and the Leloup's to a concentration camp from which they never returned.

Upon the erection in 1948 of a monument to Lts. O'Connor and Peterson at the crash site of The Mugger, the Leloup's daughter, Colette, began placing fresh flowers in memory of her brave parents and she has continued her memorials ever since.

In addition to Lt. Manifold, machine gunner Harry Thompson-Brundige and radio operator Earl Hogue became POW's. Tail gunner John Zioance was captured, but managed to escape. Turret gunner Albert Carroll, waist gunner Edward Chonskie from Shenandoah, Pennsylvania, and Zioance were rescued and later taken into the home of Alfred Auduc in Le Mans. These three airmen travelled the underground through France and across the Pyrenees to Spain, from where they returned to England.

This sympathetic letter of August 20, 1943, was written by Lt. Robert O'Connor's mother to the parents of a previously lost B-17 pilot, Joe Hass:

"Dear Mr. and Mrs. Hass,

For months I have tried to bring myself to write you to express my sympathy in the loss of your fine son, Joe, but each time I thought of doing it, I felt at a loss of expressing just how I felt about it all. I am the mother of Robert O'Connor, who was Joe's co-pilot on the Hunga Dunga when they went to England.

Joe had allowed Bob to "buzz" our neighborhood on one occasion when they flew over Milwaukee, and it gave the boys and us a chance for joking when, in Oct., we met the boys in Battlecreek, Mich., the day the boys left for England. Bob phoned us to come, as they were soon leaving, and we had a very hard drive on roads under construction etc., arriving in Battlecreek near midnight on Sat. eve – Bob had Joe, and "Scoop" Anderson (the navigator), Earl Steele (the bombardier) and another lad, not of the Hunga Dunga's crew, at the hotel to meet us. Hard as the trip was for us, we have said a million times that it was well worth while. The boys were so fine, so grand, so wonderful! Joe seemed such a fine balance for Bob, who was younger than Joe and much more impetuous. We were so happy to think Bob would have such a steady pilot from which to learn his lessons.

Early in Jan., I sent Joe a 3 lb. round tin of assorted candies, but it came back to me with the dreaded words stamped across the label-Bob, of course could not write us much. The first intimation that something was wrong came in Bob's Jan.

27th letter, written in the evening, and in small writing down in one corner of the paper was the word "Joe!!" We feared then he was trying to tell us something was wrong. We did not know then that on that day Bob was in the hospital with pneumonia. A Jan. 28th letter followed in which he referred to a raid a week earlier, in which he wrote "Scoop and a G.I. on "Hunga Dunga" received the air medal and Joe would have gotten it, too." That worried us.

On Mar. 8, Bob wrote that, "ever since Joe went down, I've been lost in the shuffle and with no extra planes, there's just not a place for me at present. My one wish is to get my own plane and the old crew and carry on for Joe. Boy! How I miss Joe!! He was more than just my pilot; he was a real friend. He just didn't have a ghost of a chance when he got it. Perhaps it was a blessing in disguise that I was in the hospital that day. You may be darn sure that when (and if) I get my own plane that I'll be a flying fool and show those boys over there a thing or two."

Then in April in answer to his young brother's questions, Bob wrote "We got definite news from Geneva about him-he never had a chance, but he got most of his crew out, which is so typical of Joe."

Now, I hope, my writing this will not re-open an old wound and that it will not cause you more heartache, but I thought you might like these little bits of Bob's letters, for it is all to the credit of Joe's character. I wanted to write this before, but not knowing whether it would help or hurt I hesitated. I had asked Bob for your address, if he could get it for me, but as he did not do so, I wrote to the postmaster in your city for your street address. It came at about the same time as we received a blow in a telegram from the War Dept. stating Bob is missing in action over Laral, France (in fact, Laval). The raid was on July 4th and we got the word on July 12th. So you can know that we are a heart broken family, too. –Enclosed is a copy of the information we received. Since then there is no other news obtainable—I have written to the parents of all the boys on the crew, in hopes that some of them may get news about the ones who parachuted to safety, but it may take months.

One reason for writing to you, too, is to ask you if you ever received a photograph taken in Battlecreek, Mich. a few days before the boys left there, of the Hunga-Dunga and its crew—I had a film made of it and so can have more prints made, and will be glad to do so for you if you wish more of them—

I hope this letter hasn't caused more anguish. I crave any news at all of Bob, and I thought you might, too. I wanted you to know that we thought very highly of your son, even though we had only a couple of hours with him. Again let me express my sympathy in your great loss. Should I get any good news (but I am fearful) of Bob, I will let you know.

Sincerely, Helen O'Connor"

The Mugger crashed on Count Armand's property just three miles from the village of Malicorne, killing the two lieutenants. Born in Paris on April 1, 1900, Jean-Francois Armand was the 4th of the 5 children of Abel Armand and Francoise de Brantes. His parents had a house in Paris and one in Fribourg, Switzerland. His father fought in WWI and was at the head of a squadron in Verdun, being killed in action in 1918. The young Count was educated at the Agriculture School in Grangeneuve near Fribourg. Owning to his frail health, he did not serve in the military. He married Renée de Moustier on January 10, 1928. In 1935, they purchased Château de Montabon in Noyen-sur-Sarthe (next to Malicorne-sur-Sarthe) and settled there with their 4 children.

In Sept. 1939, Count Armand was drafted into an Engineering Group at the train depot in Le Mans. Now a soldier, for several months he was assigned to repairing roads, mainly in the Vosges. Demobilized in early 1940, he returned to Château de Montabon. After the German invasion, he hosted members of his family from conquered Belgium. Shortly after that, his father-in-law, Count Leonel de Moustier, the governor of the Doubs departement, became part of the "Eighty", the governors who, on June 10, 1940, refused to vote full power to the government of Marshall Petain.

At the time, Jean-Francois Armand, a devoted Catholic and patriot, discretely sympathized with Resistance fighters of the l'Organisation Civile et Militaire. He harbored Colonel Rémy (the code name of Gilbert Renault, one of the Resistance's most important organizers; **Note 9-3**) during one of his missions between England and Portugal. In 1943, he hid three young boys who refused the STO (Service Travail Obligatoire) at his brother's apartment in Rue de l'Universite, Paris. Their names were Maurice Chailleux, Albert Joly, and Claude Sireau. After a few weeks, he took them to different farms near La Fleche, some 20 kms from Château de Montabon

On the 4th of July, 1943, John Zioance, a Mugger crewman, parachuted onto his property. Jean-Francois took part in his rescue as a member of the "Manipule" network. Later, he met Resistance leaders Jean Moral in Château d'Amenon and Victor Daum from the Armée Secrète several times at Captain Morin's bookstore, rue Auvray in Le Mans. At the time of the allied invasion, his network's task was to act at the rear of the enemy lines when the time arrived. In his network were Mssrs. Calendreau and Ratier, who were teachers in Sablé and Malicorne, and Mr. Legendre from Courcelles-la-Forêt. About this time, his friend, the abbey Joseph Pannetier from Sablé, warned him that he had a family to take care of and cautioned him about informers.

On Sunday, March 26, 1944, Count Armand was arrested by the Gestapo as he was biking home from mass. On May 30, after two months, at the Archive in Le Mans, he was transferred to the Compiègne prison. He briefly sighted his father-in-law, who had been arrested near Rougemont in the Doubs. Between the 4th and the 7th of June, he was deported towards Neuengamme and met Dr. Jean Papin. On arrival, he was branded with #33791. He heard about the D-Day landings, but soon became disappointed with his unabated incarceration. He was taken to Bremensarge where his father-in-law was and assigned to carrying metal bars in this submarine base in the estuary of the Weser River. This is where, on Dec. 14, 1944, he died from exhaustion without having ever seen his youngest daughter Inès who was born during his captivity. His father-in-law died in March, 1945. The citizens of Noyen-sur-Sarthe, who had not heard about Jean-Francois's death, elected him mayor in 1945. They then named a square in the town after him, thus honoring the man who had held high the banner of liberty at a time when most of his contemporaries were content to wait for better days. A large memorial cross was erected to Count Armand at the edge of his property near Malicorne.

Countess Renée Armand, showing a lot of courage, became the advisor for the Malicorne district between Sept. 1945 and October 1967. She became the President of the War Widows Assn. in the Sarthe and took care of families of the widows with the utmost of devotion. On Nov. 1, 1947, her eldest son, Philippe, who was 18, received on his father's behalf the Medal of the Resistance and the insignia of Chevalier of the Legion of Honor. The family was again devastated in 1959 when Etienne, the youngest son, died fighting for France in Algeria.

How could this wealthy aristocrat with his lovely family of four children risk everything? One cannot answer unless their own freedom has been taken away.

Second Lieut. Thomas Brzoznowski, son of Mrs. Thomas Brzoznowski, Gibbs City, has been missing in action over Hoyen, France since July 4 according to word received on July 12 by his wife, the former Miss Gertrude Zyskowski Nash district. He was a bombardier in the army air corps.

Lt. Brzoznowski Missing Since July 4 In France

Second Lieut. Thomas H. Brzoznowski, commissioned a bombardier in the army air corps from the Victorville air base, Victorville, Calif., last January 2, has been missing in action over Hoyen, France, since July 4, a telegram received Tuesday by his wife, the former Miss Gertrude Zyskowski, Nash distrist, stated.

Another bomber group, the 384th, also took part on the July 4th mission against Le Man's Gnome et Rhône factory. Based at Grafton Underwood, England, the 384th was on only its sixth mission. The 384th was paying the price for its inexperience, having lost 2 aircraft on their first mission, 3 on their second and 5 on their third, while their fourth and fifth were turn backs due to poor weather. In the 545th Squadron, the B-17F captained by Lt. Lawrence Wayne Myer was named Lakanuki; you know what that means don't you? The Lakanuki, a Douglas Long Beach B-17F, was one of the 20 B-17's of the 384th that took part, with 2 returning to base due to mechanical problems. Near the IP, their Flying Fortress was hit by D.C.A. (defensive counter air or flak), belching smoke as it plummeted, its tail section breaking off. A sole crewman appeared from the severed tail section.

Tail gunner S/Sgt David L. Butcher, age 25 and on his first mission, had been knocked unconscious and thrown providentially out of the tail section. He descended unconscious to 2000 meters, when he awoke to pull his ripcord. His B-17 plunged into the ground at Poillé-sur-Vègre. Local residents, exiting from Sunday mass, reached the downed bomber within minutes, about the same time as did German soldiers. One crewman was still alive and was seen injecting himself. Local villagers assumed it was a lethal injection for he soon succumbed, but it must have been morphine. Alfred Auduc soon appeared, but because of the German soldiers, could not even access the crewmen's papers. Butcher's nine crewmates were lost. Two days later, the village priest conducted rites for the nine downed airmen with all of the citizens of Poillé-sur-Vègre in attendance, in blatant disregard of the strict prohibitions against such tributes.

Affidavit of Alfred Auduc

I, the undersigned Monsieur Alfred Auduc, residing at 2 rue de Tourniquet, Le Mans, belonging to the Hercule Buckmaster réseau, certify that the American B-17 bomber #42-3235 crashed on July 4, 1943, between noon and 1300 hours at Poille-sur-Vègre in the Sarthe Departement. The plane was hit and the tail section broke off. Only the rear gunner, David Butcher, was able to bail out. When the plane hit the ground two bodies were thrown from the aircraft. These were Myer and Davidson. The seven other crew members had been carbonized.

The following day I noticed from a distance of 200 meters what I believed to be the bodies of nine airmen. Later on I was told by the Germans that there were 11 corpses, among whom two came from another plane having crashed near Malicorne-sur-Sarthe. The 11 bodies were placed into five coffins and buried in the Le Mans civil cemetery. I attended to their burial, at which time it was confirmed to me that nine airmen from the Poille crash and two from the Malicorne crash were being interred. The five graves were marked with five wooden crosses and were Plot 21, row 1, graves 17 through 21. The two bodies from the Malicorne crash belonged to the same crew as E. Chonskie, John Zioance and Albert Carroll who we sheltered and assisted their return to England. The serial number of the Malicorne plane is not known to me.

Signed: Alfred Auduc   May 21, 1947

Affidavit of Charles Liard

I, the undersigned, Charles Liard, caretaker of the Cimetiere de l'Ouest at Le Mans, certify as follows: on July 7, 1943, five coffins containing the remains of 11 airmen have been buried by the Germans in this cemetery, Plot 21, Row 1, to the left, grave 17, 18, 19, 20, 21. Nine corpses came from Poille and two from Noyen-sur-Sarthe. Peterson, R. W. has been interred in grave 17; and, O'Connor, R. S. #0661542 T 42A, who fell at Malicorne is in grave 18, both of them coming from a plane having crashed at Malicorne on July 4, 1943, around 1300 hours.

Graves 19, 20 and 21 were unidentified at the time of interment. On July 17, 1945, Americans came and took the remains in graves 17 through 21 to St. Andre de l'Eure. When the Americans removed the bodies they told me grave 19 contained Jack Davidson, #35327696 T42; grave 20 contained Lawrence Meyer 0733702 T43B, and grave 21's name was unknown, but was #0671093 T42A.

Since the disinterment of American bodies from graves 17 to 21, these have been used by the British. There are no American soldiers or unknowns remaining in this cemetery. Signed: Charles Liard

From the Le Mans cemetery, the bodies were first moved to Saint André du l'Eure, before their final resting places in the U. S. Normandy cemetery at Colleville. Seven of the airmen from the B-17 the Lakanuki are interred there: the pilot, 2nd Lt. Lawrence W. Myer from California at plot A, row 9, grave 13; the co-pilot 2nd Lt. Norman A. Gauntt from Texas at plot J, row 27, grave 10; the navigator 2nd Lt. James C. Crouch from Indiana at plot J, row 27, grave 16; the bombardier 2nd Lt. Thomas H. Brzoznowski from Michigan at plot J, row 18, grave 28; the radio operator T/Sgt Jack NMI Davidson from Indiana at plot I, row 25, grave 32; the right waist gunner S/Sgt Floyd NMI Hubble, Jr. from Michigan at plot J, row 27, grave 26; and, the left waist gunner Kenneth E. Christensen from Oklahoma at plot J, row 27, grave 14. The remains of the engineer/top turret gunner T/Sgt James L. LaRue and the ball turret gunner Sgt James T. Carter were interred in the United States.

The Odyssey of a Downed Airman

David Butcher, the sole survivor of the Lakanuki, was quickly hidden by Mr. and Mrs. Gouin from Fontenay-sur-Vègre. Any delay enabled the Germans to reach downed airmen first. It was the first day of David's eight months behind enemy lines. His story:

The soil of France was getting closer...bend your knees, David, bend your knees and keep your legs together...the landing was a little rough but without any damage. David Butcher, the tail gunner in a B-17 that had just been hit, did not have to jump; he was thrown out of the tail section. His bomber named Lakanuki had suddenly been broken in two and the front part had exploded. David had been ejected some 20,000 feet up and knocked unconscious. He remembered: "The tail busted off and I must have gone out a hole. When I came to, I was outside the plane lying upside down in the air. I didn't know where I was at first because my face was all bloody. First thing I knew I thought I had better pull that cord outta there so the parachute opens. So I pulled the cord and I must have thrown it back to London."

His 'chute unfurled only at the last minute. He was on the ground now and was beginning to gather in his parachute when he saw a man pedaling towards him. They did not say much, for neither could speak the other's language. The Frenchman helped him hide his parachute in the bushes nearby and motioned for him to sit on the handlebar of the bike .... and off they went.

That Sunday, the 4th of July, 1943, their mission's objective was the destruction of a factory south of Le Mans in Arnage. It was too far for the fighter escort to protect the B-17 flight, making it a great opportunity for a group of FW-190's who soon came to attack the bombers. These Germans were clever and knew where the weak point of the B-17's was: its nose. It was lucky for David Butcher, for he was the tail gunner. He was also lucky to happen to fall near the right farm. Madame Gouin, the owner of the Grand Breuil farm in Fontenay-sur-Vègre, was a patriot who made it her duty to harbor those fleeing the mandatory STO labor. She had even harbored an escaped prisoner, Paul Thion, the same man who now biked to rescue the American airman.

At the farm, the first thing was to help David get rid of his flying equipment. His padded jacket was certainly useful at 7,000 meters, but a little warm for a summer Sunday in the Sarthe. It was also too conspicuous. He was given civilian clothes that were tight on his American frame. He was shown upstairs to a small bedroom and the only person he saw in the house was the farmer's wife, who brought him food. She made him understand that he had to be very cautious. The Germans would soon find the parachute and would be going from one farm to another threatening to shoot those who would not turn the airman in.

On the evening of the fifth day, the door of the small bedroom opened and two men walked in. One of them spoke a little English and explained that, for security reasons, he had to change locations. The three men set out towards Le Mans.

"Monsieur Butcher, welcome to the Hercule resistance network of the SOE. From now on, I, Alfred Auduc, am going to take care of you."

During his long hours on his own, the aviator had had the time to realize he was the only survivor of his crew; the other nine crewmembers were mangled and burnt in the plane's wreckage. "So long, my friends, we shared good moments together drinking beer at our Grafton base between missions."

Butcher soon learned that another plane had been downed the same day and three airmen were harbored somewhere else. Alfred Auduc wanted to organize repatriation of these cumbersome men, cumbersome by their build but also by their ignorance of the French language. Moreover, the airmen were getting claustrophobic with the four now in one small room of his house, rarely able to go outside for fear of being noticed. One of the airmen, Edward Chonskie, was dressed as a maid and 'her' outings soon caught the eyes of some German soldiers who were not indifferent to 'her' charm.

Alfred had been asked to shelter the airmen for one week, until arrangements could be made for their repatriation to England via the French underground. As time passed, it became apparent that something had gone wrong. Much later they learned that the members of the underground who were to assist with their airmen had been captured on the French side of the Pyrenees.

The two people in charge who could do something about the airmen's situation were Dubois, the radio operator of his own Hercule network, and Floege, the head of the Sacristain network, but the two did not seem to be in a hurry. Auduc had had to speak his mind and at last their messages to London received a response: the airmen they harbored were not German imposters. By this time in the war German soldiers were being dressed as allied airmen to infiltrate the underground escape networks and Resistance members had to be even more careful.

As Sergeant Butcher was going from one hiding place to another, he discovered how a Resistance group functioned, how important the radio transmitter was and how secretive it was; he also saw how weapons and explosives were being used for sabotage. Noticing how inexperienced these patriots were, he volunteered to become their instructor. Sometimes he was treated to short walks in Le Mans, escorted by the Auduc's son, the twelve year old. He understood he had to pass for a deaf and dumb person and he was given a new ID card. He was now Louis David, a mechanic who was staying at a hotel in Le Mans.

After he had resided in the Sarthe for a month between Le Mans and the family farm of the Auduc's in Cérans-Foulletourte, Hercule explained to him that he would have to move again. They set out for the Touraine region where Dubois knew several safe houses. One of these was at Madame Rigat's house; she was a primary school teacher in Artigny, a little village near Amboise.

The Germans were now on the trail of Hercule and on the 13th of August, 1943, David was going to experience another extraordinary day. On that morning Hercule was in Tours at Madame Meneau's house; she was an early Resistance fighter and his mother-in-law. About noon, another SOE agent, Canadian Gabriel Chartrand, showed up unexpectedly. Chartrand had been advised against going to Tours, but the heart of the Quebecois was beating for a young nurse in the clinic where Dubois' wife was working. Madame Meneau's house was one of the mail drops of the SOE and that is why Chartrand had gone there.

The older lady was concerned because she was being watched. She asked Chartrand to take charge of Monsieur Butcher. The two men biked towards the outskirts of Tours. Suddenly Chartrand said "wait for me here; there is something I need to do". Chartrand returned to Madame Meneau's house. She was not alone as her house was now full of Germans. Chartrand, who was quick on his feet, threw his bike at the two Germans trying to detain him and ran away so fast in the little streets of Tours that the Germans lost track of him. He reunited with Butcher, but they now had only one bike and forty kilometers to travel. Never mind, they managed to reach Chateau-du-Loir in spite of German patrols which caused them to jump into the ditches on the sides of the roads several times.

Sergeant Butcher eventually, after having lost count of the number of houses where he was in hiding, found himself back in the Sarthe. It was now the responsibility of Dr. Goude of the local Buckmaster réseau to find him new safe houses. Among other places he stayed was with Monsieur and Madame Oscar Monéris who lived in Vouvray and whose garden concealed as many machine guns as leek plants.

To Alfred Auduc who had come to Chateau-du-Loir to make a fruit delivery in early September, it was quite a shock for him to see David again. So, the American had not escaped to Spain! To celebrate their reunion, Alfred Auduc took David, again in the Ford named 'Marlène', for dinner to his home in Le Mans. The next day, as planned, Alfred escorted David back. On the way, they met Madame Monéris who was waiting for them on the side of the road, obviously upset: "The Germans have arrested Dr. Goude and his crew last night and it will soon be our turn". Auduc took his passenger to a safe place for the day; he had to urgently move all the weapons hidden at the Monéris' before going back to Le Mans. Sergeant Butcher had been lucky yet again.

These arrests in Chateau-du-Loir happened right after those in Tours and gave reason for Alfred Auduc to become pessimistic. He knew people from other networks and asked Alain and Nicot from the Chinchilla group to take care of David. This is how David found himself in yet another farm in the Sarthe, at Mr. Champion's farm in Bazoge.

Unfortunately, "Chinchilla" was also under the watch of the German SD and Nicot hardly had time to direct David towards Paris before being arrested on the 23rd of October, about ten days before the Auduc's arrest.

Thurs., May 11, 1944

Oak Park Airman Escapes from Enemy-Held France

What happened to Technical Sgt. David L. Butcher between Independence Day of last year, when the Flying Fortress on which he was a tail gunner went down dur-

Sgt. D. L. Butcher

ing a mission over France, and Easter Sunday, when he wired his family from New York that he was safe and well, cannot be told until after the war.

But Sgt. Butcher somehow got out of occupied France almost without a scratch, turned up in England, and then came home to spend three weeks with his family. He left Sunday to report at the readjustment center of the Eighth Air Force at Miami Beach, Fla.

Sgt. Butcher is the son of Mrs. Mary A. Butcher, of 739 South Taylor. He enlisted in the air corps in August, 1940, attended gunnery school at Las Vegas, Nev., and armorer's school at Salt Lake City, where he was an honor student.

News of his safe return from enemy territory was received with special rejoicing by the former Gertrude Langhart of St. Louis, who became his bride shortly before he went overseas.

It was only in February, 1944, after having spent Christmas in Paris at a Mrs. Heissat's, that David Butcher was able to utilize the French underground. His small party stayed in a little town about 100 km from Toulouse and then in Toulouse. It was a risky trip because the train was always full of Germans. Next they were directed to Carcassonne by bus. They then stayed in a smuggler's hut at the foot of the Pyrenees. They stayed in the hut about two weeks and then crossed the Pyrenees towards Barcelona. It was very difficult due to the winter weather. The Spanish guide and one of the English men got frostbite on their feet. David survived although he experience minor frostbite.

In Spain, those caught by the police were sometimes exchanged in Gibraltar for sacks of flour from America, but without incident the party crossed Spain all the way to Gibraltar. An English colonel tried to convince David to provide the names of those who had assisted his escape, but he refused. They detained him, but for some unknown reason released him shortly thereafter.

Upon reaching London, on Easter Sunday, David cabled his family that he had safely returned to England, but security restricted his sharing of any details. The war was over for this admirable survivor, but his wartime experiences were to leave indelible impressions and even determine his final resting place.

Aerial bombardments at this juncture were so inaccurate and civilian casualties so great that the Resistance pleaded with the Allies for more explosives so they might conduct greater sabotage which caused fewer civilian casualties. The July 4, 1943, bombing of Le Mans sites was from 22,300 feet and resulted in many more French casualties than the combined Allied and Axis ones.

Note 9-1. The 303rd Bombardment Group (H) "Hell's Angels" of the Eighth Air Force was stationed at Molesworth, England from 1942 until 1945. Their motto was "Might in Flight", which was earned on their record 364 combat missions. The Mugger was a B-17F, #42-5792.

Note 9-2. The Gnome et Rhone factory under German control became famous for slow production, building only 8,500 engines by 1944, when the Germans had been estimating 25,000. French resistance took many forms.

Note 9-3. Colonel Rémy was the field name of Gilbert Renault from Vannes, France, the oldest of nine children of a Catholic family. With armistice declared on June 22, 1940, he refused to accept Marshal Philippe Petain and went to London with one of his brothers on board a trawler. He was one of the first men to respond to the call of General de Gaulle, and was entrusted by 'Colonel Passy' (Major André Dewavrin), then captain and chief of the BCRA (France's Central Bureau of Intelligence and Operations) to create an information network in France. In August, 1940, he met with Louis de la Bardonnie, and together they created the Notre Dame Brotherhood, which would become NDT-Castille in 1944. Initially centered on the Atlantic coast, it ended up covering much of occupied France and Belgium. This network was one of the most important in the occupied zone and its information allowed many military successes, such as the attacks on Bruneval and Saint-Nazaire.

Convinced that it was necessary to mobilize all forces against the occupation, he put the French Communist Party in touch with the exiled government of Free France in January 1943. Renault later admitted it was Pierre Brossolette who got him in touch with political groups and trade unions.

He wrote an article that appeared in *Carrefour*, April 11, 1950, entitled 'La justice et l'opprobre' (Justice and the Opprobrium), in which he preached the rehabilitation of Marshall Pétain. A short time afterwards, he adhered to the Association of defense of the memory of Marshall Pétain (ADMP). Repudiated by de Gaulle, he resigned from the RPF.

Renault wrote many works on his activities in the Resistance. Using his code name of Rémy he published his *"Mémoires d'un agent secret de la France libre et La Ligne de demarcation"* (adapted for cinema by Claude Chabrol in 1966), which are regarded as important testimonies on the French Resistance.

CHAPTER 10   Downed Airmen's Tortuous Road Home

One of the Resistance's most important contributions to the war effort was rescuing and repatriating downed allied airmen. Trained pilots were a critical resource to both sides, but especially to the ravaged RAF following the Battle of Britain, which was exclusively an air battle. Not only were capable pilots in short supply, but the cost of training them was dear. It was imperative for the Resistance to reach downed airmen before the Germans. Once located, the rescued airmen were swiftly secreted into "safe houses". Now known as "parcels", these airmen were provided with civilian clothes, forged identity papers, food, and, often, medical assistance. Preparations for their repatriation could take weeks. Arrangements had to be made for these airmen to be taken from one safe house to another along a route that eventually would land them in Gibraltar or Portugal, from where transportation back to England was virtually assured. This long and treacherous escape route required a coordinated network of Resistance members and their safe houses.

Two different Belgian groups formed separate but similar underground escape routes (other less significant routes through France were also formed). Allied bombers taking off from England were often intercepted as they crossed into continental Europe, especially over Belgium in their routes to Germany. The largest network, known as the Comet line, was established in August of 1941, by a courageous twenty-four year old lady from Brussels, Andrée de Jongh, code named "Dédée". Her organizational skills were applied to the many complex issues facing the formation of an underground network and her first move was brilliant. She, along with two Belgian accomplices, escorted a British soldier by train from Brussels to Bayonne, near the Spanish border. Enlisting a Basque guide, the group hiked over the Pyrenees, reaching Dédée's destination of the British Consulate in Bilboa, Spain. Once there, she requested assistance from MI9 (British

Military Intelligence, Section 9). The consular staff was cautious, fearing she was a Gestapo operative, until Dédée produced her three companions who corroborated her story. Dédée now had the financial and personnel support of MI9 along with the experience of transporting downed airmen over this great distance.

But the challenges facing the Comet line operations were severe and often fatal. Curfews not only stifled movement at night, they raised the possibility of certain death as German soldiers had been ordered to "shoot on sight" anyone breaking curfew. Language was a great hindrance as few downed airmen could speak French, thus requiring that a

Andrée de Jongh "Dédée"

member of the Comet line accompany airmen along the underground network. Food was rationed and in short supply, yet the airmen had to eat to retain their strength, necessitating that network members sacrifice their own meager rations.

In spite of every opposition the Gestapo could mount, the Comet line successfully repatriated some 800 airmen. Dédée alone escorted 118 airmen over the Pyrenees. The cost was great, too, as Dédée's father was captured and executed. Dédée was also arrested, on January 15, 1943, and deported to a concentration camp, but although she was tortured for information, the Germans never understood who she was. After all, how could this petite, attractive young woman be the head of a large, complex network? Dédée survived and lived until age 90. The Comet line first staggered after Dédée's arrest, but quickly resurrected to become as effective as before.

The second most effective underground network was the Pat line, derived from the code name of its founder: Pat O'Leary (in reality Medical Captain Albert M. Guerisse who was a Belgian communist). As the war progressed, anti-Fascists and Communists from other countries joined the British SOE as secret agents. It was not a giant leap to initially be anti-fascist and then become communist. The Pat line ferried some 600 airmen and escaped POW's to safety. Guerisse faced a too similar fate as he was captured, in March of 1943, and subsequently deported to Dachau concentration camp where, under terrible torture, he revealed nothing of the Pat line. Captain Guerisse survived to receive Britain's George Cross, among his 35 decorations.

For their part in the French resistance eleven female SOE agents were executed, four at Dachau and four at Natzweiler, a Category III, meaning the harshest, concentration camp. The three remaining female SOE agents were shot at Ravensbrück. But for some strange reason, Guérisse and de Jongh were not executed despite the important part they had played in rescuing fliers so that these airmen could live to bomb German cities again in what the Nazis termed "terror bombings". Nor was the captured Marie-Madeleine Fourcade, who headed France's largest Resistance network, the Alliance réseau, executed by the Gestapo. Instead, they tried to convince Fourcade to become a double agent, but she refused. (Madame Fourcade's best-selling memoirs, L'Arche de Noé, have been published in English under the title "Noah's Ark").

Don Lawson, author of the book "The French Resistance," wrote the following with regard to the downed fliers who were saved by the resistance fighters:

"How many Allied military escapees and evaders were actually smuggled out of France into Spain will never really be known. Records during the war were poorly kept and reconstruction of them has been unsatisfactory. Combined official American and British sources indicate there were roughly 3,000 evading American fliers and several hundred escaping POWs who were processed through Spain. These same sources indicate that on the British side there were roughly 2,500 evading fliers and about 1,000 escaping POWs. (American and British escapees and evaders in all of the theaters of war totaled some 35,000, which amounts to several military divisions.)

Operating these escape and evasion lines was not, of course, without cost in human lives. Here, too, records are incomplete and unsatisfactory, since many of the Resistants simply disappeared without a trace. Estimates of losses vary from the official five hundred to as many as several thousand. Historians Foot and Langley estimate that for every escapee who was safely returned to England a line operator lost his or her life."

All told, 14,000 Belgians and French were involved in ferrying some 5,500 airmen to safety. Even as it became known that informers and collaborators were sending Resistance members to concentration camps and to their deaths, volunteers stepped up to insure that the underground escape routes fulfilled their missions.

With André Dubois, Alfred Auduc organized the Lighterman Resistance network which took on the responsibility of rescuing downed Allied airmen. He and friend Louis Fournier, who spoke some English, set out on July 5, 1943, the day after the crashes of the B-17's The Mugger and Lakanuki, to search for downed airmen. Learning that one might have landed on the Gouin farm near Fontenay-sur-Vègre, they called on the Gouin's, whom they knew, but only after a long, convincing conversation were they led to David Butcher's hiding place. Convincing the airman to leave with them, they set out in Alfred's old Ford, which Butcher named "Marlène", its name ever after, for Alfred's home at 2 rue de Tourniquet in Le Mans. Now needing papers,

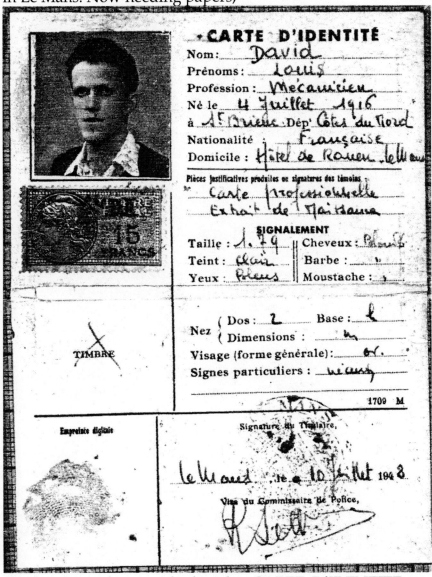

Butcher was photographed and a CARTE D'IDENTITE was forged. He became Louis David, a deaf mute who worked as a gardener, and was dressed in Alfred's clothes, which were sadly too short. On July 8, the Auduc's learned that an informer had turned in the Gouin's. Madame Gouin was

captured and deported to Ravensbrück concentration camp, from which she eventually returned, extremely weak but alive, at war's end. Monsieur Gouin escaped capture.

Alfred contacted Hercule who thought it best for David Butcher to be sent to a villa deep in the woods of Touraine, in spite of the airman's wish to remain at the Auduc's home in Le Mans.

Staying at the villa was diminutive, moustached French-Canadian Captain Gabriel Chartrand of the SOE, who had recently been flown in to assist the Resistance to prepare for the Normandy landings. In the first of several close calls, the two heard the Gestapo was nearby and escaped to Tours on bicycles, but Chartrand was briefly arrested there. Somehow giving their captors the slip, the two headed for Vouvray near Château-du-Loir, to the home of Mr. and Mrs. Oscar Monéris, he a retired schoolteacher, where they stayed for two months. The Monéris' were members of the Buckmaster network who were storing arms parachuted in to Doctor Goude's group.

On the night of Sept. 9, 1943, the Germans were informed of the Hercule network from a collaborator, possibly the wife of a local pharmacist, but in Vouvray this had been anticipated; Butcher and Capt. Chartrand were moved earlier that day to another location.

Butcher was to stay in France for eight months, assisting in distributing arms which had been dropped in to Resistance members and instructing them in their use, for example, showing how to load clips into Browning automatic rifles (BAR's). After the war, the Auduc family received a letter from David Butcher describing his escape. He hiked to Spain where Basques assisted his traverse of the Pyrenees Mountains, then made it safely to Barcelona. From there, he booked passage on a ship back to London. The war was over for him and he was shipped back to the United States. One of the toughest tasks to confront him was not responding fully to his crewmate's families' requests for information, as he could not respond due to security restrictions. David married and had two children, settling down in Ferguson, Missouri, and becoming a carpenter. He tried not to think about his wartime experiences, even throwing out his uniform, as nightmares sometimes disrupted his rest. When he returned to France in 1984, he became more open to talking about his wartime experiences. He was deeply touched by his visit to the crash site of the Lakanuki and made his pledge to have his ashes strewn there with his crewmates'.

CHAPTER 11   The Short life of the Hercule Sacristain Buckmaster Network

The average life of a network was less than six months, as collaborators were paid handsomely to be informers and as captured network members were not always able to withstand Gestapo torture, coerced to reveal critical information. So many networks were compromised that the ones which were not, such as the Darius network around Amboise, were notable.

Albert Auduc knew his network was especially active. He was aware that even less active networks were being compromised, but this knowledge did not deter his activities. He explained:

"Resistance networks had the primary mission of preparing for the Allied invasion, which we were informed would occur in 1943. This is what we thought the parachute drops of arms and munitions were all about. We were willing to continue our activities under the mistaken understanding that the Allied invasion was imminent and its launching would so disrupt Gestapo surveillance that our network would remain undiscovered."

So it was that the Auduc's arranged for an especially dangerous drop to fall on Marie Auduc's farm. Alfred explains: "In our network our tasks were to receive equipment drops by parachute, to communicate information and to organize repatriation of downed allied airmen. As far as the drops were concerned everybody had their own dramatic stories to tell. It would be too long to present all of them, but let me tell you about one. A drop was made in September of 1943 on my mother's farm in Cérans-Fouilletourte. Close by was Château St. Michel de Perrais (now a business school) where a German armored unit was headquartered. A parachute drop was confirmed by London with the BBC message 'Hitler is going to commit suicide', as we had arranged. This message was to cost me dearly later on. Most of the time, there were ten to twelve canisters in each drop, representing about three tons of weapons and equipment. The drop I am relating had been received by my three brothers, my brother-in-law, my wife, Hercule and me.

We had been told that the drop would take place between midnight and 2:00AM. At half past midnight, a plane flew over the drop site. As we were sending signals to the plane, we suddenly realized by the sound of its motors that it was Luftwaffe. Hercule became very worried because this crew could have alerted Luftwaffe fighters. We were lucky that it did not happen. About 1:00AM, we heard a second plane. This time it was the four-engine plane we were expecting. It was flying low. We sent this second plane the signal and it answered. It continued for several kilometers before turning back and aligning with our lamps. They dropped twelve containers over a distance of only 200 meters, a great job! In addition to the usual equipment, we had been sent a box of supplies and instructions. We knew what was in each container as the colors of the parachutes designated the contents of the canisters. In other drops, the containers had been dropped over long distances and were not always retrieved. In certain cases these containers were reported to the Germans by people who hoped they would receive a reward. A few minutes after our plane had disappeared, it came back at a low altitude above the drop zone and Hercule was able to contact it using the "S" phone connected to his radio transmitter. Taking advantage of a very bright moon, the plane had come back to check if all was OK. After turning above the drop zone, it left, but not without receiving our "OK, OK" signals. The Germans had on occasion intercepted a drop, receiving needed arms and ammunition. Without an OK signal from the Resistance, the drop plane was to bomb the drop zone to insure that none of the munitions served the wrong purpose. Later we learned it was not a total catastrophe when these arms fell into German hands as it deflated German morale to think that the Resistance was being so well armed.

The noise of the plane had wakened everyone in the area. This drop had gone well, but had given us a few concerns. In addition to the several neighbors who heard the drop, we worried about our errant signal to the German plane. There had been two lights we noticed at the end of the drop zone while the containers were being dropped. I later learned that these two lights were from two young men's bicycles, students from Brest. They were in hiding at the Château Perrais in Parigné le Poilin and were riding their bikes when they became so scared that they hid in a ditch, forgetting to turn off their bicycle lights.

For a drop like this one, six men were barely enough. Four were needed to mark the drop zone while two more were to guard the area with Sten guns to protect the group. The Sten machine guns were cheaply made and produced as much noise as protection. This is why with Hercule we managed to get some German submachine guns, the best ones at the time. We felt strongly about acquiring these submachine guns because we needed good protection and these were good defensive weapons.

By 6:00AM, everything that had been dropped was in a safe place, an uninhabited house. For the first time, we had been sent recent equipment, for example, booby traps that looked harmless but were very dangerous, even for those installing them. These booby traps were connected with a very fine metal thread that could be attached either on a door that would set them off when opened or an object that would set it off when moved.

During these nights, my mother, Marie Auduc, who was the best cook in the world, prepared us wonderful meals. This particular night, while we were eating, we heard our neighbors, Mr. and Mrs. Gaulupeau, arrive outside and call to my mother. They told her that they heard airplanes and had seen 12 parachutes dropping onto our farm. My mother told them that they must have been suffering from hallucinations, but they insisted and Hercule told us that the two of them would either have to be included in our plans or be eliminated. I undertook to involve the neighbors and took them to see the material we received that night. They accepted our terms and from then on became part of our group. We returned inside the farmhouse and made a good pot of coffee, real coffee, which had been dropped from the sky that very night! This was the first drop witnessed by my son Jean-Jacques who was 12 years old at the time.

For the security of the radio operator it was very important that our agents did not know where he was. An arrested operator was a very big prize for the Germans, who could always use him to send false messages. After receiving such, the English were usually able to recognize these contrived messages due to small prearranged irregularities which the operator always transmitted, and thus London was even able to send false messages back to the Germans.

All our agents utilized the Hôtel de la Calandre as a message drop point. The hotel was run by Mr. and Mrs. Brault, at rue Gambetta, Le Mans. In one of the rooms, a radiator had been modified. One simply unscrewed a plug and put in or took out messages. Messages for our group were taken from the hotel to our radio operator at our farm, La Bouguelière, by me or, in my absence, by my 11 year old son who carried them inside the handlebars of his bicycle. My wife had become a real artist in the manufacture of false documents. From her position with the Société des Agriculteurs" (*Farmers' Association*), she had access to helpful items. Every city had a duty to provide food to the occupation troops. Renée's responsibilities necessitated that she worked in different mayor's offices, which gave her access to the city's stamps. She was able to copy stamps of the prefecture of Sarthe, the Town Halls of Le Mans, Caen, Versailles and Nantes, and even created the well-known German stamp that represented the eagle holding the swastika in its claws. This last stamp was critical to forging the documents. The cars that needed to go beyond the departement also had to have forged titles and forged passes.

We had a good team in that period, which included l'Abbé Lelièvre, whose prayers seemed to protect us, and Colonel Mauffrey, the former captain of the airfield in Chartres, who was an excellent organizer and a good advisor. We had a lot to do, so Renée also learned to decode messages. She learned how to use the grid which enabled an agent to translate the code. On each hour the grid was rotated. A message received between 9:00 and 10:00 would translate an "a" to an "r", while at 10:30, the grid would have been rotated and the "a" would now be translated as an "m", and so forth. The grid itself was changed daily. Eventually, Hercule relied on Renée exclusively for decoding.

One day Captain Floege told me he urgently needed to go to La Guerche de Bretagne and asked me to go with him. During these missions there was a constant risk of being caught. We had to be very cautious so we carried no true ID papers, everything was forged: driver's licenses, passes, car titles, even our wallets contained nothing but forged documents and pictures. We carried envelopes whose stamps were changed to show false post offices. This way, if we were captured, the Germans could not know where we were from. On this occasion, Capt. Floege took the identity of a Mr. Letessier who supposedly ran a lumber yard and I was his employee. We concealed weapons and radio transmitters in the car. We wanted to look like two friends going fishing and installed fishing gear and nets that stuck out of the car windows. Apparently it worked as we went through the German checkpoints without any problem, but the French police did not look pleased when we two fishermen showed them our passes that were valid any time of day or night, weekday or

Sunday. Often they took us for collaborators and on several occasions fined us for any reason they chose, but we never heard about these charges later.

As far as handling intelligence was concerned, it was more complicated. One courier, Jacques Frager, who was as courageous as Jean Moulin, (**Note 11-1**) came from Paris. Captain Malfait came from the north of France and Madame Rigat was in charge of the intelligence for Touraine. To insure the safety of the radio operators, the couriers never knew where one was, indeed, the Germans were always after radio operators.

As for me, I had my safe entries to the Hôtel de Paris in Le Mans which was the German's headquarters for our region. Since I often had to deliver fruits and vegetables to their headquarters, it was easy for me to gather information there, some of which was quite valuable. I managed to get in touch with two interpreters. One of them was Charles Vasseur, an Alsatian who worked at the Renault factory. I also became acquainted with his German superior, Captain Baumeister, and his assistant, Fausson, who had been a conductor in Cologne, as well as two German officers of the Kommandatur, Dr. Kunter and Captain Siebers, who managed the Hôtel de Paris. They turned out to be very valuable acquaintances. I managed to get a pass for days, nights and holidays as well as a blank pass and 60 to 80 liters, and even more, petrol per week.

 I was able to obtain three Simca 5 automobiles, two of which my wife equipped with false papers and all three had the same license plate. The forged papers were so perfect that later we couldn't even tell which

one was the original. However, it was obviously dangerous to have the cars in the same region at the same time. This happened once when all three were in a garage in the village of Château-du-Loir where the owner, Mr. Gacher, very politely asked me to remove them because his clients were beginning to remark on the license plates! My cars were available to other resistance fighters for their missions. The cars always came back except for one occasion when the car and the driver disappeared. I almost lost a second car one day when Hercule asked me to provide a vehicle to one of his friends. It was urgent. I was to fill up the tank and add five liters in a container. Hercule also told my wife he needed several passes. For security reasons, I was never told where the cars were going. Hercule told me he needed my best car with tires in good condition. Then, I did not hear about the car for three weeks. I received a letter from a car shop in Bordeaux telling me that someone had left a Simca 5, with no car plate, in his shop and this person had asked the shop keeper to send the car to my address in Le Mans. The letter also indicated that the vehicle would be put on a train and that I had to pay for the trip plus the days in his shop. I paid for everything; my car came back without any damage and I noticed that it had been driven over 600 km. I never knew where it had been or who had driven it. My little cars were of great value to the cause of the Resistance.

A lot of sabotage was carried out, unfortunately taking a heavy toll on civilians as well. I would like to tell about one such incident. At the end of the summer in 1943, on a Saturday morning, Hercule asked me to go to Tours with my wife, giving me the name of a café where I was to meet him between 11:00 and noon. At about 11:30, there was a violent explosion and the front window of the café was shattered into pieces. A factory making gunpowder and ammunition for the Germans had been blown up. In this factory the change of shift was taking place at the time of the explosion. One stockpile of ammunition had blown up, igniting the entire factory. In many cases sabotage was chosen over a bomb drop in order to save civilian lives. Hercule did not show that day; he came back two days later in a car I had lent him. We had been very worried about him. He never said where he had been and we knew better than to ask, but his actions had been witnessed.

Another kind of sabotage was carried out at night. For example, the telephone line between Paris and Bordeaux was severed by Hercule's Mistral Resistance group in Touraine. I had the pleasure of joining in this escapade. This was not an easy undertaking. It was not enough to simply cut the line; at least 50 meters of the line had to be removed in order for the sabotage to be effective. I still have a piece of that line as a memento.

Hercule on occasion escorted me when I delivered a load of apples to the Germans. One day my load happened to come close to a train full of German equipment such as cannons, munitions, trucks, etc. German sentinels were keeping watch. When they saw our apples, the soldiers asked if they could have one. We suddenly became generous and gave them three boxes. They quickly filled their pockets. As this was happening, Hercule opened the door closest to the German train and intentionally spilled a box of apples. This was the opportunity we had hoped and planned for when we hid a bomb with a magnet in the box of apples. These were time bombs for which we inserted fuse sticks depending on when we wanted the bomb to detonate: in one, two or three hours. As Hercule was busy picking up the apples that had rolled under the train, the sentinels looked on and found this quite normal. He put the bomb under the train; the train left; and, later on, it blew up as planned.

In September of 1943, I carried out a careless sabotage that infuriated Hercule. My Simca had been requisitioned by the Germans, but I was allowed to use it when they were not. I was ordered to drive it to the Hôtel de Paris and hand it over to a German civilian. One look at him and I was convinced he was a member of the Gestapo. This convinced me to place a time bomb in the steering box for an explosion to take place three hours later. I handed the key to the civilian and wished him a "safe trip". But, two and a half hours later, he had not left. I was worried because this meant it would blow up very close to Le Mans. Sure enough I later learned that Charles Vasseur wanted to see me. He told me my car had an accident and he had been asked by the Germans to inquire because they thought the car had been sabotaged. We went to the scene of the accident near Bouloire with Captain Baumeister. I looked under the car and reported that the steering rod had snapped. Vasseur leaned over and confirmed "Yes, the steering rod is broken". Actually, he had not seen anything. Baumeister, who was at the head of transportation service for the Kommandatur, also leaned over to take a quick look. He echoed what Vasseur had said and commented "Serves him right to have had an accident; it is against the rules to drive a car yourself". He ordered me to take the car to the shop, have it repaired, and send him the bill! The next day I confessed to Hercule what had happened. He was furious and told me that next time I wanted to get rid of someone I should place the bomb under the intended's feet.

Yet another example of sabotage occurred when Hercule asked my wife and me to go to Chartres and meet with agents and Colonel Mauffray in order to obtain information about aircraft landings. Colonel Mauffray was the former commandant of the airfield and his house was only 1500 meters from the landing strip, a great location for getting information from those who worked at the airfield and for documenting activity there. Colonel Mauffray was also able to obtain information from his former employees who were still working at the airfield. In the evenings, groups of German bombers would take off on missions towards England. That night Madame Mauffray had cooked a delicious dinner and we were in no hurry to go to bed. Later, we heard the German planes returning from their mission and landing. Suddenly the house shook owing to bombs being dropped on the airfield. As the German bombers returned, and unknown to them, English planes, probably flown by French pilots, tailed them. The English took the Germans completely by surprise and destroyed all of the German planes, their hangers and also the officer's mess. Nothing was left. Their DCA gunners did not even come into action, probably fearing some German planes were still airborne.

As far as we were concerned, this called for a celebration. Colonel Mauffray opened a bottle of his best champagne and we drank to those who had so well planned and carried out their mission and were now on their way home. The next day I reported the evening's event to Hercule; he laughed because he already knew. Hercule said "In England, they call this a surprise party". I later learned of his participation in planning this raid and that through his "S" Phone he was able to talk with the Allied pilots from his radio transmitter. The S-Phone was an ultra-high frequency duplex radio telephone system developed for SOE agents working behind enemy lines to communicate with friendly aircraft and coordinate landings and the dropping of agents and supplies. The "Ground" set, used by agents on the ground, weighed about 15 pounds including batteries and was typically worn attached to its operator with two canvas straps. It was a highly directional unit which required the operator to face the path of the aircraft. It had the useful trait that transmitted signals could not be picked up by ground monitoring stations more than 1,600 meters distant; however, its signal was only good to an altitude of 3,000 meters which brought the aircraft within range of flak. It permitted direct two-way voice communication with an aircraft up to a range of 50 kilometres. While the S-Phone provided directional information to the pilot it gave no range information, although a pilot could tell when he was directly over the "Ground" operator because at that point no communication was possible. I was in awe."

Albert.CARROL.   Mr. GORGET.   John ZOUANCE.
VION. Sarthe.

On July 4, 1943, the mission of a group of Flying Fortresses was to drop bombs on factories in Le Mans that produced armaments for the Germans. These Allied planes were constantly attacked by German fighters and several of them were downed including two in the Sarthe: one near Poillé and the other near Malicorne. In the Poillé crash there was only one survivor, the tail gunner who was thrown out of his plane as it exploded. In the Malicorne crash, eight of the crew managed to bail out, four of whom were harbored and helped by farmers, as was the one from the Poillé crash. They were later taken care of by Mr. Georget who spoke English. I had actually seen these airmen bail out. Therefore, it was not difficult to find them. They were taken to Le Mans by a farmer. They wanted to stay in Le Mans as they expected the Allied invasion to take place soon. I reported them to Captain Floege who agreed to meet them.

He questioned them and told them they were of no special value for the Resistance and that he had better things to do than take care of them. Floege added that we should never have taken them to Le Mans to see him. My wife and I could not believe what we were hearing and we decided to ask Hercule to take care of them. But, we had no more luck with him. Hercule eventually accepted to report their presence to London when we threatened to leave his Resistance group. The answer from London was no more encouraging. They told us to be very cautious because there were a lot of Germans impersonating downed airmen. London wanted to know their names, their serial numbers and the names of the captains of their planes. We waited for their decision for more than a month. At last we were told to take them to Poitiers to a clinic managed by Madame Blanc. Our password was: "I have come on behalf of Dauphin". When we got the message from London informing us that we were to take the aviators to Poitiers, my wife and I drove two of them. On the way to Tours there was a German checkpoint. The Germans were easy to spot from a distance because they were wearing a shiny plate on their chests and looked like prize cattle wearing their grand medals. I was too close to turn the car around. I told my wife "We are going to roll the dice and try to go through". The Germans made me stop the car and one of them, holding a submachine gun, opened the door demanding: "Controle papirs". The two Americans were shaking with fear. I produced my documents slowly in order to give my passengers time to gather themselves and produce their own documents, which, of course, my wife had forged. The Americans were petrified and couldn't move. My wife quickly figured out what was going on and reached into their pockets to take their documents. All of this happened without the Germans noticing and after looking at our papers, they gave them back to us. The Americans were still petrified and my wife had to take the documents being returned to them.

The German policeman closed the door and waved us through. A few miles down the road we stopped to check on our passengers. They told us they felt a lot more comfortable up in the air than down on the ground. From Poitiers the airmen were escorted to Spain by the underground and managed to return to England in spite of numerous difficulties.

The crew member who survived the crash in Poillé remained in France for eight months. His name was David Butcher, a very intelligent man who became our instructor for automatic weapons. Shortly before we were arrested, we managed to start him along the underground to Spain with the help of Alain Nicot, who was our specialist for difficult missions.

I would also like to tell the story of an unarmed little airplane, a Lysander. This airplane was made to carry out missions in enemy territory and often carried secret agents. In the early days of summer, 1943, a Lysander landed in Touraine on an improvised landing strip. It was carrying out a mission for our Hercule network. For some reason, the plane could not stop at the end of the landing strip, went over a ditch and eventually stopped on a road. It was quite a problem because it could not take off from where it stopped and had to be put back onto the field. Valuable time was going by and we did not know what to do until we saw two young men riding their bicycles towards us. We stopped them and when they saw our submachine guns, they got scared and said "We didn't do anything wrong". We explained to them what the situation was and they were very proud to be able to help us. Together we had no trouble getting the plane back onto the field. The pilot tried to start the engine, but it did not turn over. The rule in this case was to set fire to the plane, but before doing this, the pilot decided to try one last time. To our surprise the engine started, but did not run for very long. The plane rolled over a hundred meters and stopped. We had to work on the engine more and eventually it started again. It took off and disappeared into the darkness of the night. Hercule was concerned about the fate of this plane, but the next day he was informed that the plane had successfully made it back to England after going through German flak on the French coast. Hercule was fond of this story.

Like a lot of people, we sometimes were not cautious enough. Captain Floege and Hercule wished to meet the Germans I was in contact with. I thought it would be so easy to stage a dinner and so invited everyone. Hercule arrived first with two automatic pistols. He put one of them into the drawer of the credenza in the dining room. When we sat at the table, he chose to be close to the credenza for obvious reasons.

The German officers came with their interpreter. The officer who provided me with petrol took his revolver out of his pocket and told Renée "I'm putting this despicable piece of junk in the drawer". Did he see Hercule's revolver? It was hard to say, but in any case he didn't show it. As we waited for dinner, we went outside to have a drink and enjoy the pleasant weather. There is no need to say the American officer had not been introduced as such, but as an uncle of mine, while Hercule was passed off as a cousin from Le Mans. Everyone was enjoying a pleasant evening until one of the German officers offered cigarettes to everyone. The American officer said "Thank you, but I don't smoke". The German looked at him eye to eye and asked "Are you French?" On hearing this, everyone except the Germans put their hands in their pockets. The American answered "Yes sir, I am French". "Where are you from?" "From Mayet." "Oh, I know Mayet, I have a friend there, Mr. R......, and he sells mushrooms." "Yes, I know him very well. Remind me your name and I will tell him I had the pleasure of having a drink with you." "Doctor Kunter, teacher of foreign languages." The American officer soon after excused himself saying he needed to return home. As I walked him to his bicycle he told me "This is too much of a challenge for me". Colonel Mauffray was also there that evening. At the time, I served good meals and excellent wines. Everybody drank a little too much and at the end of the meal was very lively and in certain cases very funny. The French were saying to the Germans that they would not win the war since the United States was helping France and the Germans agreed. Everything turned out well, but it could have been different and I was very pleased when everyone went home.

Without realizing it, the Germans had revealed a good deal of useful information on this occasion as well as on others. After the war, I traveled to Koln to visit Captain Baumeister, who ran a service station. We had an interesting discussion about those earlier days. When these German officers learned of our arrest, they became concerned about their association with revealed Resistance members. When I described the information he and his associates had unwittingly dropped into our plates, he was clearly shaken. But, I assured him that even under torturous interrogation neither I nor anyone in our network had revealed anything about himself or any German officer we had come into contact with. After all, he was not Gestapo; he was a good man. Before my arrest, Baumeister had given me a picture of the Koln cathedral. The Gestapo found it when they ransacked my home and the picture puzzled them. The Alsatian interpreter for Captain Baumeister, Charles Vasseur, was arrested after the war, but I was able to secure his release by attesting that he was a good man, not guilty of any crime against France.

Here is another example of a funny situation. The city of Sillé-sur-Sarthe in July of 1943, organized a fund-raising event for POW's who unfortunately were quite numerous. It attracted a lot of people including my wife and me. When we arrived, I was surprised to see the German officer who provided me with petrol tickets. He had come with a few friends and his inseparable interpreter Charles Vasseur. They were in plain clothes and were thoroughly enjoying themselves. It wasn't long before someone noticed they were not speaking French. Some people suggested they were the American aviators who had parachuted from imperiled planes. Others were adamant they were Americans. People started to gather around them. Some of the Germans understood French, knew about American aviators parachuting into the area, and were amused by the situation. Then, some people wanted to shake hands with them. I was observing the scene and wondered whether the Germans would play along and pass for Americans. They did not, but if they had, they could have seen how enthusiastic people would have been to have met allied pilots.

The next day I went to the Kommandatur to get my weekly allowance of petrol. The officers there told me the story about being taken for American aviators. I asked them "Have you heard about these American aviators?" And the officer answered "As far as I am concerned, I couldn't care less".

While I was still in this office, a man walked in and saluted the commandant with "Heil Hitler". He was French, a Mr. de .... ("de" denotes of the aristocracy). He started talking to the German officer in German as if he was reciting something he had just learned. The officer asked his interpreter to tell this man to get out. The man did not appear to understand, so the German officer told him "Speak French or I cannot understand you". The man wanted some petrol, but did not have a pass for his car. The officer told him "Sir, when you don't have a pipe, you don't need tobacco". The man insisted so much that eventually he was given a voucher for 5 liters. He was not pleased and left without saluting this time. The German officer turned to me and said "This is sad. We see S.O.B.'s like him every day."

On the evening of July 8, I had invited two German officers and their interpreter, Charles Vasseur, for dinner at the Hôtel de la Calandre. While we were having dinner, a young, beautiful lady came in and chose a table close to ours.

Suddenly, the German Captain Baumeister's face changed and he whispered: "Beware, she works for the Gestapo." I looked at her carefully and remembered having seen her before, but couldn't remember where. She was Italian and lived in Le Mans. The next day, as I often did, I went to Château-du-Loir on business. Once this was cared for, Hercule and I decided to have a drink near the station. Just as we were about to walk into the café, I noticed that the pretty Italian was on the terrace, smoking a cigarette. I immediately told Hercule: "Careful, let's walk on". This is when I remembered I had often seen her in the cafés of Chateau-du-Loir which must have been where she carried out her surveillance. We headed towards the city hall while I told Hercule about this female Gestapo agent. His reaction was to tell me "I am going to play one of my old tricks on her", but I never knew whether he did. We walked into a distant café and ordered a beer. All of a sudden Hercule indicated that an agent of the British Intelligence Service was there. Across from where we sat an elegant man was also drinking a beer. I asked Hercule "How did you spot him?" "His tie pen. It is the way these agents recognize one another." "He doesn't appear to be interested in us". "You're wrong; watch when he drinks his beer as this is when he observes us". And that is exactly what he did. I asked: "Should we buy him a drink?" "Certainly not. He could be a real agent, but he might just be an imposter. And, don't forget there is a bitch on the watch."

That same evening we returned to Le Mans through the back roads and were careful not to be followed. Château-du-Loir was becoming a dangerous town, but the next day, as usual, I went back. My friend Albert Jamin was the owner of the hotel where I stayed. He informed me that a man wished to see me. After asking him to describe the man, I decided to introduce myself. When I met him, he asked: "Are you Mr. Fred?" I replied: "You can call me that, it doesn't matter." He explained that someone staying with him was desperate to see me. The house was about 600 meters away and before going in I observed the outside while my hand clutched the revolver in my pocket. I felt very nervous when I walked in, but what a surprise when I saw the American aviator that I had delivered to Hercule a month before and who I thought had left some time ago. He had stayed several months with me; his name was David Butcher. David had ended up there at the Monéris' house, together with a Canadian (Gabriel Chartrand). They told me their story. They had been concealed in a house owned by a friend of Hercule's in Touraine. The Germans found out about it and surrounded the house, but by an extraordinary stroke of luck they managed to escape. They fled to Tours where they were arrested, but again managed to escape by throwing a bicycle into the legs of those who had arrested them. They then fled to Chateau-du-Loir.

I called my wife and told her that I had a surprise for her and she should prepare dinner for an extra person. I had decided to take David to Le Mans and give him the opportunity to spend a nice evening and see a few people he knew. It was agreed that I would take him back the next morning. As we were driving off, about 300 meters from the house Madame Monéris came to us, trembling, and said "Dr. Goude has just been arrested, together with the entire team from Chateau-du-Loir." She added: "We expect to be arrested at any moment because we have weapons hidden in our house." I told her: "Let me take the American to a safe place and I will come back to move the weapons if it isn't too late. There was no time to waste and I went to see someone from Chateau-du-Loir who I hoped was a good patriot. "Can you do me a favor", I asked. "Depends; what kind of favor?" "I would like for you to conceal an American until tonight." "Out of the question. You have the wrong address." "So I see, but it is in your best interest that you forget this conversation." Instead, I went to my friend Albert Jamin who provided the American with a bedroom. My plan was to pick him up that evening and take him to some friend's house where I knew he would be safe. After all these events, we eventually managed to organize David's trip to Spain through the underground and from Spain he was able to return to England.

The most dangerous part of this long day was yet to come. I had to return to Madame Monéris' to move the weapons. Two of my associates went with me. We were armed with submachine guns and courage. When we arrived we found empty barrels that we filled with the weapons and loaded the barrels in my little van. During this time the Gestapo was arresting one person after another in the village of Chateau-du-Loir. We were very lucky as everything went well and I could take the weapons to a secure location a few kilometers from there. I then met the head of the La Chartre-sur-le-Loir network and informed him of the weapons cache available to him.

During the final month of our activities, life had become extremely complicated for everyone due to real or false secret agents, German espionage, the Gestapo, the Abwehr (the German Military Intelligence Service) and the German goniometers that were trying to locate our transmitters and were after us. One night in Cérans-Foulletourte they had established their surveillance less than one km from La Bougueliere where our transmitters were. They saw no electric lines and concluded that the transmissions could not come from our farm. Actually, our equipment got all the electricity it needed from batteries under the responsibility of my brother, Roger.

Part of our mission was to watch for "rats". Thanks to a man from Alsace, whose name I cannot remember, I could get access to anonymous letters that were sent to the German police every day. Generally, these letters fell into three categories: personal vendetta accusations; ladies wishing to get rid of their husbands (more often than not two letters would accuse the same person, one by the wife and the second by her mother); and, letters from landowners: in these letters some unscrupulous landlords tried to get rid of their neighbors so they could take their land and farm. All these letters had one point in common: they were written in a coarse and stupid way. Even under the occupation these cowardly missives backfired on their authors. The Germans despised these letter writers and did not take them into account, except in certain cases. There was the case of a railroad worker who had been accused in a letter that described him as being dangerous and capable of criminal acts. The letter indicated his address; he lived at a railroad crossing. The Germans left for his house and on the way they stopped at a café in a nearby village in order to have a cognac. As they were enjoying their drink, they asked a few questions to the waiter "Do you know Monsieur ….. who is a railroad worker?" "Oh yes, he's a very nice man: honest and wouldn't hurt a fly. On the other hand, his wife is a real bitch." So they decided to go to the local Gendarmerie where they received the same information. Then they went to the RR worker's house where they found his wife and this is what they said to her: "We have come to rid you of your husband." "Take him; I'll be glad because he is a horrible person." She then gave them a list of all the bad things about him. It was exactly what was in the letter that the Germans had with them. "Oh, so it was your letter we received?" "Yes, I'm the one who sent it to you." She thought she had at last gotten rid of her husband. The Germans explained to her that they had decided the following: "Since it is forbidden to send anonymous letters, the husband is the one who is going to get rid of you. You are going with us." She was taken to jail.

The rats also had to be taught lessons. Here is what happened to one of them who lived on a farm between Le Mans and La Suze. Wishing to take revenge against his neighbor, he took his gun from his attic and concealed it in his neighbor's hedge.

At the time, the Germans would not hesitate to shoot those who concealed weapons. The next day he went to Le Mans to the Kommandantur to report that his neighbor was hiding a gun. But, his maid, who was not very intelligent and did not get on well with her boss, went to the neighbor's house and told him what her boss had done. The neighbor decided to get the gun and put it back in its original place. Then, an anonymous letter was sent to the Kommandantur that same day accusing the farmer and showing a sketch of where the gun now was. When the Germans arrived they were confused. They didn't find the gun in the hedge, so followed the sketch and went to the rat's house and asked him "Wouldn't you be the one who is hiding a gun in his attic?" The farmer was shocked and led them to his attic where, naturally, the Germans found the weapon. The man didn't know what to think. He was taken by the Germans. Many people in the area were pleased because he had reported clandestine animal slaughters to the Gendarme in La Suze. Two days later he was back home which did not seem right to us. We were pretty sure that in order to be released he had promised the Germans he would work for them. So, I decided to take care of him. My brother-in-law at that time was a strong man weighing 130 kilos. The day after the rat returned home, we knocked at his door at 5:00AM. The door was not locked, so we stormed into his room. He panicked and dove between the bed and the wall. My brother-in-law lifted him from his position, handily. I asked him a few questions and he begged us not to hurt him and promised it would not happen again. We enjoyed seeing the look of fear on his face. My brother-in-law slapped him, then pulled his nightshirt up and spanked him. He had probably never been spanked before. Then he held him above the floor and said "If you ever do this again, this is how I will drop you into the Sarthe River, dropping him on the floor. We didn't want to be meaner than this because he was a veteran of The Great War. This story quickly spread through the area and no one talked to him anymore. He died shortly afterwards.

Hercule had also taught a lesson to another person of the same ilk: he put a plastic bomb on his door, but did not rig it to explode. It was an effective warning. Most of the time, these lessons were enough to stop those people from doing their dirty jobs.

The last time I saw Hercule was in October of 1943. When we said good-bye, we had the feeling we would never see each other again. We knew that a lot of people from our network had already been captured. When I was captured, there was one car left in my garage and it was probably taken by the Gestapo. When I returned in 1945, I learned that one of my vehicles had been bought by someone from Le Mans. I went to the Prefecture to explain my case. The governor asked that one of the cars taken back from the Germans should be repaired and given to me. It was a Citroën.

Note 11-1 Jean Moulin, the son of a professor of history, was born in Beziers, France, on 20th June 1899. He was conscripted into the French army in 1918 but the First World War came to an end before he had the opportunity to see action.

After the war Moulin joined the civil service and rose rapidly to become the country's youngest prefect. Influenced by his friend, Pierre Cot, a radical pacifist, Moulin developed left-wing views and gave assistance to the Republican Army in their fight against the Royalists in the Spanish Civil War.

Moulin refused to cooperate with the German Army when they occupied France in June 1940. He was arrested and tortured by the Gestapo and while in his cell he attempted to commit suicide by cutting his throat with a piece of broken glass. After recovering he was released from prison.

In November 1940, the Vichy government ordered all prefects to dismiss left-wing mayors of towns and villages that had been elected to office. When Moulin refused to do this he was himself removed from office.

Over the next few months, Moulin began to make contact with other French resistants who wanted to overthrow the Vichy government and to drive the German Army out of France. This included Henry Frenay, who had established Combat, the most important of all the early French Resistance groups. He also had discussions with Pierre Villon who was attempting to organize the communist resistance group in France. Later, Moulin was accused of being a communist but there is no evidence that he ever joined the party.

Moulin visited London in September, 1941, where he met General de Gaulle, André Dewavrin of the BCRA and other French leaders in exile. In October 1941, Moulin produced a report entitled *The Activities, Plans and Requirements of the Groups formed in France*. De Gaulle was impressed with Moulin's knowledge of the situation and decided he should become the leader of the Resistance in France. Moulin was parachuted back into France on January 1, 1942, bringing with him a large sum of money to help set up the underground press. This included working with figures such as Georges Bidault and Albert Camus who had both been involved in establishing the Combat newspaper.

Moulin's main task was to unite all the different resistance groups working in France. Over the following weeks he arranged meetings with these network leaders: Henry Frenay of Combat, Emmanuel d'Astier of Liberation, Jean-Pierre Lévy of Francs-Tireur, Pierre Villon of Front National, Pierre Brossolette of Comité d'Action Socialiste and Charles Delestraint of Armée Secrete. After much discussion Moulin persuaded the eight major resistance groups to form the Conseil National de la Resistance (CNR) and the first joint meeting under Moulin's chairmanship took place in Paris on May 27, 1943.

On 7th June 1943, René Hardy, an important member of the resistance in France, was arrested and tortured by Klaus Barbie and the Gestapo. They eventually obtained enough information to arrest Moulin at Caluire on June 21. Jean Moulin died while being tortured on July 8, 1943, never revealing any information.

When his family first became active with the Hercule-Buckmaster section, Jean-Jacques was not aware how dangerous their activities were: "After my parents cautioned me, I made it a game to be clever enough not to be detected. I officially became a Resistance member on June 1, 1943, five weeks before my twelfth birthday. After the war, I was given the designation "P1" for a Resistance fighter who had not been captured and sent to a concentration camp. Those who had been were designated "P2".

In May of 1943, my father and mother had joined the Hercule Sacristain Buckmaster network of Resistance fighters. Under the code name "Francine", Renée Auduc became a leader of the network and became a P2 agent. Upon her partial recovery from deportation and after de Gaulle assumed control, she joined the "Forces Françaises Libres" (*the Free French Forces or FFC*) and was the first woman in France to receive the rank of Captain, with the responsibility to decommission their network, including recording its history. She also wrote dossiers on each member of our network in order for them to receive recognition and compensation after the war. Her position was quite rare for a lady resistant fighter. She had shown admirable bravery during a time when everything was under the control of the enemy. She skillfully forged documents: ID's, passes and car titles, among others. She was able to translate the code of the messages from the British Intelligence Service almost as if she had been trained to do this. For her dossiers on the members of the Resistance, it was necessary to obtain written support from other known Resistance members as there were many imposters and doubters. Even I found it advisable to obtain confirming letters certifying my involvements, from Messrs.' Butcher and Floege.

In late May, my father was introduced to André Dubois a.k.a. "Hercule", from Tours. André went into hiding with his two radio transmitters in Cérans-Foulletourte, in a farm called "La Bouguelière", owned by my grandmother, Marie-Augustine Auduc. It was an inconspicuous farm with no electricity. As it was prudent for a radio operator to change locations from time to time to minimize their being located, Hercule was also sheltered by my uncle Roger Auduc, by one of André's Dubois' brothers for a few days, and by the priest of the village, father Julien Lelièvre. It was necessary for Roger to daily recharge the batteries used by Hercule. Alfred Auduc's job was to forward Hercule's messages that had come from Paris or the Touraine area, to the Hôtel de la Calandre on rue Gambetta in Le Mans. It also became my assignment to carry out the dangerous missions of delivering and retrieving these messages. After hearing the BBC's message "Hitler is going to commit suicide" on the radio, our group received a drop of 12 containers holding a total of 3 tons of weapons. We were at the receiving end of 14 drops during the summer of 1943. 'Captain Fred', as dad was called, also provided vehicles that were needed for certain missions, sometimes even driving them himself. He was involved in the sabotage of telephone lines and even a train.

Once, as the team was busy sorting out and putting away the last weapons from a munitions drop, a neighbor arrived at my grandmother's. He excitedly told her he had been woken by the very loud noise of an airplane, and when he got up and looked out the window, he saw nine paratroopers stiffly making their way out of the plane that had flown low over his back yard. Everybody told him he must have had a nightmare, but he said his wife had seen the same thing. Our head of network, Hercule, gave my father the order to kill both of them. My father refused, for these people were his neighbors and childhood friends, and they had four young children. He asked them to come in, and showed them the "stiff paratroopers". When the neighbor realized he was looking at containers holding three tons of weapons and equipment, he was petrified with fright. Hercule picked up a colt pistol, handed it to him, and said **"you have just become a resistant fighter".** He was so proud to become part of the fight for **FREEDOM** that he went home to ask his wife to also be involved, then harnessed his horse to his cart in order to carry the equipment to my grandmother's quarry.

The Germans later found the weapons cache. They were both astounded and worried, for they thought that weapon depots like this one were everywhere. They could not access the place with their trucks because it was at the end of a narrow dirt road. They requisitioned our neighbor and his horse cart to pick up the weapons and take them to their trucks. The Germans never suspected our brave neighbor's connection with the weapons, and they did not question him. My father, even when he was tortured, never revealed his name or his contributions to our network.

WHAT USE CAN A BOY AGE TWELVE BE IN THE RESISTANCE?

He can go unnoticed where an adult would immediately be spotted and arrested.

One of my main missions was to be a liaison agent. I would collect the paper messages brought in from agents that came from Paris and the North of France. These messages were concealed inside a central heating radiator in the Hôtel de la Calandre in Le Mans. At the time, hotels built courtyards containing stables so that customers could leave their animals when shopping in the markets or staying overnight. I always left my bicycle in this courtyard because bicycles became very valuable when cars became useless.

I would first pull out any messages to see if there was one for Hercule, taking the ones for him and then placing all other messages, including any I had brought, back into the radiator. After collecting messages, at first I placed them into my bicycle pump. One day, unknown to me, the pump must have fallen off my bike. I returned home in a panic: what horrible thing had I done? As time went by, there were no repercussions from the lost pump with its clandestine messages. But, afterwards the messages were carefully placed into the handlebar of my little bicycle and I would deliver them to Hercule. He and his radio transmitter were hosted by my grandmother on her farm, "La Bouguelière" in Cérans-Foulletourte, Sarthe. My round trip from Le Mans to my grandmother's was 35 miles. Occasionally I did the round trip twice in the same day and made several trips each week. My trips were made more difficult from the hazards to my tires and chains. The road was unpaved and was full of silex (knife-edged flint), hobnails and other nails. I often had to repair a tube, using my repair patch and I carried an extra patch in my kit. To be extra safe, I wore a spare inner tube around my neck. Speed was important, so not being stopped by a flat tire was critical. A bigger problem occurred if my chain broke, which it occasionally did, so I carried extra links plus extra chains. Only the Germans' and a few authorized French cars were on the roads. I was never stopped on my bike, but I was more concerned about the French police than the German as the French police were often more thorough and more brutal.

Networks were arranged so that an agent knew only the code names of others in their network, and further, they knew the code names of only those with whom they dealt directly. If any agent were arrested, they could not reveal anything, even under torture: they did not know the identity of their leader or fellow network members, nor where they were. All they could reveal was the name of the place where they were heading. No need to say that Liaison Agents, such as I, were at the top of the wanted list of the Gestapo and the S.S. since I knew names and locations; at age twelve, I would have broken easily under tortuous interrogation.

Another of my missions was to gather intelligence. The English air force had noticed an unusual concentration of enemy planes on the airfield of Le Mans, so Hercule was asked to check out where these planes came from. The airfield was adjacent to the circuit where the 24 Hours of Le Mans Grand Prix races had been staged, but the racing oval and the stands were quiet now. On September 21, 1943, I was sent on location where I got very close to the airfield by innocently flying my kite. The sentries, men too old to fight at the front, started playing with me, unaware of what I was doing, and this allowed me to get close to the planes. I sat down, pretending to work on my kite, and was able to see the bottom of the planes' wings. They were wooden; the Germans had not painted the underside of the wings! The planes were fake wooden planes, meant to overstate their numbers to the Allies. We radioed the information to London, and the English, showing their sense of humor, dropped **WOODEN BOMBS** on the airfield shortly afterwards. Their message for the Germans was that the Resistance was aware of every move they made. The fake airplanes were removed and only the squadron that was usually stationed there remained.

For my action undertaking this mission alone, recognizing and reporting that the planes were wooden, I was awarded the Croix de Guerre with silver gilt star for my bravery and good work.

After the war, Sylvain Grassin, a cousin and a resident of Le Mans told me his story. The Germans had used camouflage to turn Le Mans into a rural landscape by building fake roads, rivers and buildings to fool the hunters in the sky, the Allied Air Forces. Sylvain related: "During the war I lived on the road to Laval and often saw German convoys coming from the west into Le Mans. One day we noticed two big trucks, one with a cumbersome "cigar" concealed under a tarp, the other appeared to be empty because, unknown to the driver, its load had slipped off and lay on the side of the road in a ditch close to our house. As soon as the convoy was safely away, we ran to the ditch to see what this cigar was. It was a fake airplane made of wood, probably on the way to a fake airstrip to confuse the Allies. We were impressed by this discovery and we thought it could be an important military secret. We returned home and kept watch at the window to see if the owners of the cigar would return for it. The Germans did return, very slowly, searching the ditches on each side of the road, until they found their lost cigar. They picked it up in a hurry and left. This was an important event for us because even if we weren't sure how strong the Luftwaffe was at the time, we understood that it was the beginning of the end for them. We even thought they might have wooden tanks somewhere."

Here is how I became a saboteur at age twelve. We received boxes of two pound explosives in parachute drops. They had a strong magnet attached and could be placed on any metal surface. A timer ignition stick was then placed into the explosives box: red for a one hour delay, blue for two hours, etc. (these were 'pencil fuses', of which some 12 million were produced by the Allies, showing how much sabotage was hoped for).

We learned of the pending arrest of Resistance members and even who would be making the arrests. The only way we had to stop the arrests was to sabotage the vehicle to be used. This was a very dangerous task and only one solution was deemed workable. We would use Hercule's tactic of planting an explosive while appearing to pick up dropped apples. Only, the Germans no doubt had heard of this tactic, forcing us to revise our strategy. I was to ride my bicycle and approach the unattended German vehicle. When alongside, I was to 'spill' my marbles, making sure some rolled under the vehicle. I was to lay down my bike and gather the marbles into my school bag. While reaching for those under the vehicle, I was to take out the explosive from my school bag, place the pencil fuse into it, and attach it to the chassis, then, make my getaway. The first attempt went off without a hitch. During the second attempt, after I had spilled my marbles, a German soldier quickly strode towards me. I stopped breathing. Was my tactic already known to the Germans? Was I to be shot then and there? When the soldier reached me he bent down and picked up a few marbles, carefully handing them back to me. He just as quickly walked away. As I planted the explosive and attached the red fuse for an hour's delay, my heart pounded like I had never known.

I was home before the vehicle exploded, excited to inform my parents of my success. Only, they considered it too risky for a third such attempt as I had been seen. Had these vehicles been occupied by Germans when the bomb I planted exploded? I never gave that much thought, I suppose it was because I never saw them and my only thoughts were for my fellow Resistance members who I had been proud to save.

One of my favorite assignments was serving as a lookout during parachute drops. When the head of the network,

Hercule, asked London for a weapon and equipment drop, he would send a message like "Hitler is going to commit suicide" (for which my father was later beaten beyond recognition by the Gestapo as they were questioning him), or "Edmond will become a brave man", or "The violet is a modest flower". When the same message was repeated during the BBC's French broadcast, we knew that the drop would take place the next evening. To handle these drops - about three tons of equipment – many hands were needed. I begged Hercule to allow me to participate in a drop; he agreed and the experience was marvelous! The landing strip had to be marked with "one red light, six white lights". The dropped munitions had to be gathered and put in a safe place as quickly as possible. I was the lookout boy and was to give the alarm should Germans approach. During the night, I heard a strange noise and gave the alarm. It turned out to be a herd of cows which were attracted to the lights and headed our way. Everybody got a big scare, but I was congratulated by the head of our group for my watchfulness.

An assignment that I liked very much, but that was risky, was escorting for walks the airmen staying with us. My parents were asked by Captain Floege, from the O.S.S. of the USA, to assist the allied aviators whose planes had crashed in the Sarthe area, and take them to the underground network that would enable them to return to England. The airmen would sometimes spend several weeks with us before it was safe for them to leave. Four or five of them at a time would stay all day in a small room in our house. There were curfews at night. The cramped conditions were a real problem, and something had to be done. They desperately needed exercise to retain their strength and composure. It was decided that I would walk outside with them from time to time, in the streets of Le Mans, one by one. My mother forged some ID documents for them, and it was established that they would all be deaf and dumb, since they could not speak French.

One day as I was walking with David Butcher, the Feldgendarmes stopped us. I squeezed my protégé's hand (he had never before seen a German), hoping he would understand that he should not try to do anything. I did not know what his reaction would be. All I knew was that if he tried to run away or attack them, in either case we would be killed. I reached for his papers in his jacket, and handed them to the Germans who looked at my "deaf and dumb uncle" and said: "Uncle, very sad, nix talk, nix hear, Raoust".

It was a very frightening experience for both of us, and after this mishap, this "uncle" never went out again before he left. Instead, David Butcher asked if he could move to my grandmother's farm near Cérans-Fouilletourte, where Hercule was. It was agreed and David spent a couple of months there. He was frightened by the thought of trying to escape on the underground line, but also saw that he could contribute to the war effort through our Resistance network."

After the war, David said of Jean-Jacques: "I have never seen a boy his age have such courage. He always did his very best to help us downed airmen".

CHAPTER 13   A Collaborator Destroys Their Network, Their Lives

When Marshall Philippe Pétain, the hero of Verdun during The Great War, reached an armistice with the conquering Nazi's in June of 1940, the Vichy government of Free France was established. Free France was the area south of the German penetration at the time the armistice was signed and was comprised of all of France approximately south of the Loire River, excluding the strategic coastline all the way to Spain. Free France became known as Vichy France, after the spa town of Vichy where the fleeing French government was reestablished. Pétain invoked the term "collaboration" to describe his government's buckling under to the Nazi's and urged all Frenchmen to collaborate. His top lieutenant, Pierre Laval, went further, advocating that France join Germany to defeat England. This is difficult to comprehend from today's illuminated perspective, but France in 1940 was a quagmire of political extremes. The fear of communism had pushed many to embrace National Socialism. Others simply expected Germany to rule a new Europe and wished for France to have a prominent role in this anticipated new order.

But the Vichy government was not alone in collaborating with the enemy. Depending on how the term is defined, one could support that the majority of the French collaborated. For example: were French workers in armament factories collaborators? Were those who sold information to feed their starving children collaborators? This issue so troubled postwar France that Charles de Gaulle fabricated the "great lie" that almost all Frenchmen resisted the occupation.

The Hercule-Sacristain-Buckmaster network became quite active and successful, thus becoming well known, making it inevitable that some informer would reveal their network. It was known that the Germans were searching for the network's radio transmitter. German trucks had been seen riding around grandmother Auduc's village, attempting to triangulate the position of Hercule's radio transmitter using goniometers. Only, Marie Auduc's house had no electricity, so the Germans ignored it. Hercule's radio transmitter was operated from car batteries that were regularly recharged by Roger Auduc who was an electrician. When the Gestapo finally raided Marie's house, she and André Dubois, 'Hercule', the radio operator, had been alerted and escaped into the woods.

André Dubois, like Alfred Auduc, involved his family in his network. In early August, 1943, his wife Mimi, employed at the Clinic Besson in Tours, his stepmother and two associates were arrested. André responded with a failed attempt to rescue those arrested, but the attempt, described in Chapter 15 by Alfred Auduc, failed. The four were eventually sent to Ravensbrück. Only Mimi and one associate survived.

Hercule was now on the run from the Gestapo who now knew everything about him. Finally, in October of 1943, he wired London that he feared his capture and wished to be taken out. Arrangements were made and Hercule travelled to Paris to await instructions, staying at the house of his friend, Mr. Raymond Laudet.

On November 19, an SD team, led by SS Sturmführer Scherrer and accompanied by his interpreter, Ernst Vogt, Untersturmführer Kinast and a driver, Storck, was sent from the Paris Gestrapo headquarters at 84 Avenue Foch by its head, Hans Kieffer, and were clearly furnished with the exact address of where to find Dubois. In a post-war interrogation of Abwehr agent Hugo Bleicher by the French, Bleicher claimed that Marcel Clech, arrested earlier the same day, had revealed the whereabouts of Dubois, but it is difficult to imagine the Breton revealing such crucial information, unless under the greatest pressure of torture. Ernst Vogt, the SD's interpreter at 84 Avenue Foch, in an interrogation in 1949, also stated that the details of Dubois' whereabouts were revealed by an SOE radio operator, who had been arrested by the SD, after successful interrogation. Vogt, however, described this captured operator as working for Dubois, which would not have been the role of Clech. SOE records suggest that a courier, transporting a radio set (and therefore perhaps assumed by the Germans to have been a W/T operator) had spoken injudiciously, was arrested by the enemy and revealed the location of Dubois. Dubois himself, in a letter that he managed to smuggle out of Fresnes prison in March 1944, suggested that the Germans "already knew everything from the people they arrested before me" and that they had found the Laudet's address among the documents of the W/T operator arrested before Dubois, who was due to inform London that Dubois was ready to return to England. This may well have been Clech, but at least counters the charge that he told the Germans where to find Dubois.

Whatever the source of the Germans' information, it was accurate enough to seal the fate not only of Dubois, but also of Mr. R. Laudet who was sheltering him. When the Germans arrived, they used the password and masqueraded as allied agents to gain access to the third floor apartment where they were told they would find Dubois. Entering Laudet's apartment, Vogt announced that they had come with orders from Captain Morel in London to drive him to the Spanish border so that he could escape to England. But Dubois, although indeed waiting to leave for London, knew that he could expect a Lysander flight. He therefore challenged Scherrer and, concluding that his visitors were bogus, drew two pistols and opened fire. The two Germans drew their own weapons and likewise opened fire on Dubois. A melee ensued. Hearing the shots, Kinast and Storck ran into the building and on the stairs passed the wounded Vogt who told them Scherrer was dead and Dubois was wounded. Carrying on past Vogt,

Jean-Claude Faribault, Jean-Jacques Auduc and a few of their associates had the following plaque installed at what was 80 Ave. Petain in Montrouge, but is now 80 Avenue Henri Ginoux. Jean-Jacques relates: "For the dedication ceremony, we ordered a most beautiful flower arrangement. It was delivered, and stolen, before the ceremony."

A la mémoire
des héros de la Résistance Française:
M. LAUDET
abattu ici par la gestapo nazi le 9.11.1943
A DUBOIS
chef du réseau Hercule BUCKMASTER
grièvement blessé, déporté,
fusillé au camp de Gross-Rosen le 30.7.1944
Ils ont sacrifié leur vie
pour notre Liberté.

Kinast and Storck first came upon Raymond Laudet whom they shot and killed, believing him to be Dubois. They realized their error when, as they inspected Scherrer's body, Dubois rushed out past them and, although already wounded, ran down the stairs. He passed Vogt on the way, but was pursued down the stairs and out into the street by Kinast and Storck who continued to fire at him. Dubois managed only 50 meters down the street before he was brought down, having been hit seven times and very badly wounded, including in the left and right groin, the stomach, neck and right shoulder. Vogt, having reached the street only with great difficulty, was also seriously wounded. He and Dubois were both bundled into the back of a Feldgendarmie car and rushed to the Hôpital de la Pitié-Salpêtrière in Paris. Dubois was cared for by a capable German doctor who put a silver tube into his throat. He received good care. It was not until January that Vogt was able to visit Dubois who was held in a high-security cell in the hospital's basement throughout January and February.

After he had recovered sufficiently from his wounds, Dubois was moved to Fresnes prison where he was questioned four times. He was able to smuggle messages out. Fellow inmates were later to report on his fortitude and their admiration of his courage. Dubois continued to maintain another false identity, that of Antoine Desgranges, in order to protect his family. While imprisoned at Fresnes, a hell-hole of a prison just south of Paris, Dubois penned this letter:

"Dear Friends,   March 20, 1944
The person to give you this note is to be released on April 24 and proposed to deliver this message to you. The Gestapo arrested me on November 19, 1943, at 11:00PM at some friends' house where I was waiting to leave for London. My arrest was a bloody drama: my friend was killed (Mr. Laudet of 80 Ave. Petain in Montrouge) from whom I had bought a bracelet for Fanfan (his daughter) and a gold necklace for my poor dear Mimi. I heard that there was a massive crowd at this poor man's funeral. I would ask that you go to see his widow to get the jewelry and to tell her that she will later be rewarded by means of a posthumous title for her husband.

I killed one kraut and badly wounded another. I myself was badly wounded by seven bullets. I am better now. I was interrogated 4 times, but they already knew everything from my people who were arrested before me. They took my papers, among which there were letters from my poor Mimi, a letter from Jeanne, who must have been arrested due to it, and pictures of friends.

I will no doubt be judged as this friend brings you this letter. I think it will be the death penalty. I am in Fresnes using my alias of Antoine Desgrange, despite the fact they know my real name. I am in cell 498, 3rd division. I would be happy if I could die with news from my dear Mimi and my Fanfan and my whole family.

Please give a note to this friend who will make sure that I get it. This friend will probably need money. I ask that you give him 8,000 francs (not a large amount) which will allow him to get back on his feet and will reimburse him for the packages that he will send me.

Dear friends I keep the most wonderful memories of you; you are the only ones that know of my unfortunate destiny and ask you to be the messengers of all the love that I have for my Mimi and my Fanfan for whom I wish a happy future with all my heart.

I give you a big kiss with all my heart.   André D. of Tours"

The entrance gate at Gross-Rosen concentration camp

In late March, André, only 38, was among a group of 19 SOE officers deported to Ravitsch concentration camp in Poland, then to Gross-Rosen in southern Poland. Dubois was later seen by Marcel Rousset and others after his transfer to Ravitsch and is believed to have been executed at Gross-Rosen concentration camp in late July or early August of 1944.

A German political prisoner there, Harry Wolfram, gave evidence to a British Army War Crimes investigation team in 1948 that he had seen Dubois among those executed.

The group of 19 was put into a separate barrack surrounded by barbed wire outside the camp. This barrack was nicknamed "the weather station". The group was tortured while the commandant of the camp, Johannes Hassebroek, questioned them on their roles in the Resistance. Hassebroek also demanded that they examine and name parts of Allied airplanes downed by the Germans. On July 30 at about 5:00AM, they were taken near a wall, executed and cremated in a mobile crematorium. All the evidence of this event was destroyed by the doctor of the camp. In 1948, there was a trial in Hamburg under English authority. Witnesses identified the 19 officers from pictures. A former prisoner who worked as a secretary in the political office (where political orders were received) certified that on a day late in July, 1944, the figures for the mobile crematorium appeared to be deflated. The members of the firing squad were identified and stood trial. Commandant Hassebroek first was condemned to be hanged. In 1949, this sentence was commuted to life in prison, then to 15 years without parole. He was released from prison in 1954 (ref: Archives of Gross-Rosen, Poland). In 2002, a plaque was erected at Gross-Rosen to the memory of the 19 officers assassinated in 1944.

Germany had been a signee on July 27, 1929, of the International Geneva Convention concerning the treatment of prisoners of war. The Geneva Convention stipulates that 1) prisoners of war should be treated in a humane way: they are to be protected from violent aggression, insults or public curiosity, 2) the prisoners are to be treated in keeping with their rank and age, and, 3) no information about the prisoner's army or country may be obtained by force. In spite of their signature, the Germans constantly broke the Convention. The soldiers who Germany held captive were deprived of their rights and their status as Prisoners of War. They were made to work; they were abused and often deported to concentration camps. Germany ruthlessly broke the Convention when it captured paratroopers and aviators. They employed a method they called "special treatment". The captured paratrooper/agents who wore civilian clothes were assassinated without trial. Soon, those who were wearing uniforms received the same treatment. The executions were carried out by members of the Wehrmacht.

Until July 4, 1942, the Wehrmacht had orders to apprehend only the paratroopers who were carrying out military missions. On that date, their new orders were: captured paratroopers, whether they were wearing military or civilian clothes, were to be taken to the SD (Security Service) or to the Gestapo, for questioning. The aim was to obtain information on training locations, means of communication, place and time of the parachute drop, meeting places, names of Resistance agents, etc. They used torture during these questionings and afterwards the captives were either assassinated in prison or sent to concentration camps. On October 18, 1942, Hitler sent personal orders about commandos. The 12 copies of this document were classified and instructed that commandos be executed without hearing or trial.

In 1944, two English ladies and two French ladies were captured. They were on an intelligence mission when captured and sent to Dachau where they were executed. On July 6, 1944, three paratroopers from the SOE whose mission was to liaise between the French headquarters and London were assassinated. In 1945, the members of an English military mission who were the liaison between the English and the Czech partisans were executed in Mauthausen. Also in 1945, paratroopers captured in France were executed in Ravensbrück.

In striking contrast with their own policies, Germany consistently and firmly demanded that their captured soldiers be protected by the Geneva Convention.

André Dubois' name is one of the 91 men's and 13 women's on the SOE Memorial in Valençay in France's Indre departement. This memorial was dedicated on May 6, 1991, the fiftieth anniversary of Section F agent George Bégué's first parachute drop into occupied France at Valençay, to those Section F agents who perished fighting to liberate France. Many Resistance members accepted the willingness of their family and friends to assist their cause, often with disastrous results. These ladies who André loved dearly were arrested and sent to Ravensbrück: Angele Meneau, his mother-in-law and manager of the girl's school "La Petite Bourdaisiere" in Tours who hid SOE agents and fallen airmen, died there in captivity; Mimi Dubois, his wife, who worked at the "Clinique Besson" in Tours, survived; Jeanne Stefani, a nurse at "Clinique Besson" survived; and, Jeanne Dubois, his mother, died in captivity.

André Dubois was awarded the Legion d'Honneur, the Croix de Guerre avec Palme and the Croix de la Resistance with Silver Laurel Leaf. Although he was recommended to receive the Member of the British Empire (MBE), he was not awarded. Colonel Buckmaster's summary of Dubois was: 'A most gallant and devoted Frenchman, who sacrificed everything for his country. Nothing could surpass his sense of duty and his cheerful self-sacrifice. He went all out all the time.' Dubois had transmitted for seven months, the average survival period for a radio operator in the Resistance.

Unfortunately, Alfred and Renée's house was searched by the Gestapo on November 2, 1943, and they were arrested. Perhaps the wife of the local pharmacist informed on them.

Theirs were part of a series of arrests that included Victor and Juliette Brault, the owners of the Hôtel de la Calandre.

Victor Brault was born on the 24th of September, 1895, near Château-du-Loir in Saint Pierre du Cheville. His parents, Louis and Clementine, had a farm there. When he returned from serving in World War I, Victor married Juliette Cochet in 1919. Juliette already had a daughter, Suzanne, from her first marriage, and she had a son, Gerrard, with Victor. They run a little café/restaurant situated at 132 Avenue Jean Jaures in Le Mans. After a few years, they moved to and managed the Hôtel de la Calandre, located at 94 rue Gambetta. They did good business and people enjoyed meeting there, particularly on Fridays when there was an animal market nearby. The Brault's were modest people and yet very friendly.

During the time of the Occupation, Victor had to conceal his patriotic feelings. From time to time, a number of German officers requisitioned rooms in their hotel. The Germans were courteous, but this veteran of The Great War did not like the noise of German boots on the sidewalk in front of his hotel. His wife Juliette was the cashier. She had a perfect view to the outside and made a point of discreetly writing down the car plate numbers of the German vehicles as they drove by. She knew who she would give this information to. Very quietly in 1943, la Calandre became a mailbox for several groups of Resistance fighters in the Sarthe and neighboring departments. For instance, the OCM group in the north of Sarthe, with members Camille Deletang and Victor Gaubusseau, were used to coming to the hotel. It was also the meeting point of the agents of the Donkeyman, Hercule and Sacristain networks. A few of the couriers were: Olga Vinçon, Emile Chabanne, Arsene Leproust, Andre Morand and Alfred Auduc, who lived nearby. These networks' members harbored aviators and retrieved messages for André Dubois to transmit to London. In an old hotel radiator that was not working, they would unscrew a valve to leave and pickup messages. Captain

Ernest Frederick Floege, as well as his son Claude, and Pierre Gagneau, came regularly to leave their coded messages to be sent to London. One of the hotel's bedrooms was fitted with an antenna that allowed these Resistance groups to transmit directly such information as the location of landing strips and alert messages for parachute droppings. Until October, 1943, this quiet place was one of the critical centers of the Resistance in the Sarthe. Sometimes 7 or 8 resistants stayed at the hotel, making it difficult to maintain anonymity, yet secrecy was critical for everyone's security.

The Gestapo crackdown occurred from November 2, 1943. The Gestapo quickly curtailed all the activities of these Buckmaster agents. Very few managed to escape. Victor Brault was captured the next day. On November 4, Captain Floege was about to reach the hotel when Captain Mauffray warned him of a trap set up by the Gestapo. Juliette Brault was left at the hotel for five weeks so that she could be the bait for the Gestapo to arrest more people. She was arrested on December 10, questioned at the Gestapo headquarters in Le Mans, and then imprisoned in Angers along with her husband before being sent to Compiègne.

Juliette Brault arrived in Ravensbrück on February 3, 1944, after a three day train trip. She was tattooed number 27610 and died in the concentration camp on April 1, 1945. Victor Brault was deported on January 27, 1944, to Buchenwald, tattooed number 43970. In March, he was transferred to Dora, then to Ellrich, where he died January 20, 1945. On June 16, 1946, a plaque honoring the Brault's was mounted on the wall of their Hôtel de la Calandre. This plaque may still be seen at 92 rue Gambetta on the wall of the apartment complex that replaced the hotel. Near Cérans-Foulletourte on the side of the road RN-23, now named the "Voie de la Liberté", was erected the largest memorial dedicated to the Resistance in the Sarthe. The names of the 64 victims of the networks Hercule and Pascal Sacristain are etched in the grey marble. Victor Brault and his wife Juliette who ran the Hôtel de la Calandre are among those listed.

On November 11, Alfred's brother Roger, his brother in law and Father Lelièvre were also arrested. They were taken to rue des Fontaines in Le Mans, where they were questioned. Alfred Auduc had been taken to Angers, where he was tortured for 2 months, in cell # 13. He spent Christmas night of 1943 attached by a chain to a dog house, and had to bark every time a German walked by. Early in 1944, he and his brother were taken to Compiègne prison, then to Buckenwald. Compiègne became the staging area in France for those headed to concentration camps. This city in the east of France was the site of the signing of the Armistice ending The Great War and was chosen by Hitler who forced the French representatives to sign the 1940 Armistice in the same railroad car that had been the scene of Germany's humiliation in 1918. Afterwards Hitler had the railroad car and other World War I memorials destroyed.

Alfred learned that his commander, Hercule, had been arrested and was missing. In March 1944, Alfred was assigned to the Laura Kommando in the mountains of Thuringe. Numbered 43954, he worked at the underground plant that manufactured and tested V-2 rockets. For one year he worked in the worst possible conditions, constantly beaten by the "Greens" - the kapos that the Germans had picked out among fellow inmates.

Alfred's brother André escaped arrest when he saw the Gestapo's car coming to his house and he was able to flee. His wife was arrested, but later released. Renée Auduc was sent to Angers where she was tortured for information before being sent to Ravensbrück, along with Geneviève de Gaulle, General de Gaulle's niece, on February 3, 1944. Renée was tattooed with the number 27578.

Geneviève joined the Resistance just after the occupation of France in June 1940. She expanded the existing information networks, in particular the group "Défense de la France". Arrested by P. Bonny, of the 93rd Band of Rue Lauriston, on July 20, 1943, she was imprisoned in Fresnes prison and was later deported to the concentration camp of Ravensbrück. In October of that year, she was placed in isolation in the camp bunker. This decision was taken by Heinrich Himmler in order to keep her alive and use her as a possible exchange prisoner. Geneviève was released in April 1945 and the following year married Bernard Anthonioz, a fellow resistance member and art editor, with whom she had four children.

Geneviève de Gaulle-Anthonioz wrote a book, fifty years after her release from Ravensbrück, speaking of her life in the concentration camp and the mutual help among the women. This book was called 'La Traversée de la Nuit' (literally, "The Crossing of the Night", translated into English as "The Dawn of Hope: A Memoir of Ravensbrück" [ISBN 1 55970 498 5] published by Arcade Publishing). An active member and later president of the ADIR (Association of Deportées and Internées of the Résistance), Geneviève filed lawsuits against Nazi war criminals, then took part in the rise of the political movement launched by her uncle Charles, the Rally of the French People.

In 1958, she worked with the cabinet of Minister André Malraux when she met Father Joseph Wresinski, then chaplain of the town of Noisy-le-Grand. The sufferings of the families she met there revived memories of those which she and other deportees had experienced. In 1987, she testified in the case of the Nazi: Klaus Barbie. She served with the movement ATD Quart Monde to ease poverty in the 'Fourth World', becoming a permanent volunteer and then served as the president of the movement from 1964 to September 2001.

CHAPTER 14   On The Run From The Gestapo

Jean-Jacques had to flee from the Gestapo, alone, and remained on the run for three months. He shares his story: "While my parents were being arrested on November 2, 1943, I was returning from delivering a message to the drop in Le Mans. Neighbors who had been waiting for me appeared suddenly to relay the terrible news that my parents had been arrested. I was twelve years old, had no ID, no money, no ration tickets, and I was now to be hunted by these brutes. I did not know if I would ever see my parents again. My parents had prepared me for this situation, and on that day, following their instructions, I took the train for Chartres and went to the house of a member of our network: Colonel Mauffrey. It was the start of the most difficult experience I had in the Resistance. A few days later, anticipating that he could be arrested, Col. Mauffrey called another member of the network in Paris, my uncle Marcel Brion, and asked him to take care of me.

I took the train to Paris, arriving in Montparnasse station. Everyone, including a large number of German soldiers, got off the train, and I was soon the only one left on the platform. On the station walls were posters which read 'Aid a terrorist and you will be arrested and shot' while others offered considerable sums for turning in a terrorist. My uncle Brion was nowhere in sight. I felt very scared.

A man came up to me, wearing a cap with the word 'porter', and asked if he could help. I had no idea if I could trust him, but what else could I do? He heard my story, then, told me to follow him. I followed him to his small apartment and stayed there a couple of days. It was an exceptionally cold winter and their room had only a stove in its middle; I was seldom warm. His new bride slept on the cool floor while I was awarded the warmth of sharing his bed. I had not known such wonderful people existed. My wonderful porter could not ask his bride to sacrifice for me forever, so he called my uncle Brion who picked me up and took me to a cousin's outside of Paris. Uncle Brion was terribly sorry that he had not met me at the train, but he had realized that the Gestapo sometimes trailed him and he could not even return to his home.

The web was closing in on me and the English members of the network were doing everything they could to keep me from falling into the hands of the Gestapo, knowing that a boy my age would not have been able to endure the tortures of these beasts and would have confessed to everything he knew. It remains a mystery to me, but the English found me first and managed to give me different addresses of safe houses where I could go. In order to inform those who knew me that I had safely arrived at my new address, the BBC would broadcast messages like "Tiny Tom has safely arrived at his friends' the paint dealers", where Tiny Tom was my code name because I was small for my age.

As I was doing all these moves, one of my biggest problems was that I obviously had no ration tickets while people in Paris did not have enough food even for themselves. Another mouth to feed was a big sacrifice for those who sheltered me, in addition to the great risk they were taking in harboring a "terrorist". They could easily have been arrested for aiding me.

This is why at age twelve I had to fend for myself by finding employment. I was introduced to the owners of the Hôtel de la Gare in Persan-Beaumont, a village to the north of Paris and a safer place for me at my cousin's. The owners were very nice and gave me a job washing dishes. The job was not too exhausting, but with some 150 glasses to wash and dry each morning, it was very boring. An old German soldier who came every day for a glass of red wine, except on days when serving alcohol was prohibited, took a liking for me. He had a boy my age and he would bring me some bread, bits of chocolate and very stale soldiers' cookies. I had told him my parents had been killed by the English during an air raid. On

Christmas day, 1943, he invited me to his barracks to celebrate the event with his friends: hot chocolate, cake, and an orange... a real treat, so I accompanied him to his barracks. Suddenly, somebody yelled in the hallway that an officer was inspecting the soldiers' rooms. Before I had a chance to realize what was happening, I was pushed into a stinky closet full of uniforms and had to stay locked in there until the evening. <u>I really thought my time had come!</u> That Christmas night was the worst one in my whole life. As soon as he could, the German soldier set me free and gave me a big loaf of bread. At last, free again, I was able to go home and climbed up to the attic to go to bed, but there, another ordeal awaited me. My only protection from the cold was a small duvet that my boss's mean Siamese cat was determined to sleep under at my feet, as the duvet was not tucked in. Every time I would stretch my legs, she would bite me and cause an excruciating pain. What horrible nights I spent!

I would think of the happy Christmas days I had had with my family. I felt so alone, surrounded by strangers, and I would quietly cry, thinking about my unfortunate parents. What had happened to them? Would I ever see them again? I would think about my dear grandmother, about my little brother. What had become of them? When would this nightmare end? Who would I be with tomorrow? Would I be with yet other strangers who might even turn me in to the Nazis?

When I went to bed, I fervently prayed to God that I would not wake up the next day. Fortunately, I did not know about the fate of Jewish children my age, about concentration camps and crematoriums.

I could not stay in one location for long as the Gestapo was particularly interested in anyone new in a village. I went back into Paris and found work with a broom merchant. The owners were friendly, elderly people. One day, my boss was ill, and he asked me to use the horse cart to do a delivery of birch brooms to the zoo in Vincennes, a western suburb. I had to ride across Paris through areas I did not know and I did not know how to do this. I climbed on the front seat, put down the bridle next to me and tried: "gee up". I was lucky: the horse knew the route so well that we traveled without a problem. The horse was in no hurry, and we would hold up the traffic of German cars whose drivers would yell at us, to my utmost pleasure. The horse also knew his way back to the barn where he knew he would find fresh hay. I was also glad to go back to the barn, too, knowing that the hay would provide me with a warm and dry bed.

My boss had come across a barrel of kippers that became a much appreciated breakfast, lunch and dinner for me every day. To give my meals more variety, I had learned to set up traps and catch sparrows that were feeding on the horse manure. I roasted them on a fire: delicious! It was soon time to move again and I was happy to do so this time.

My next safe house was with a lonely elderly lady. I only saw her when she came back from work. My chore was to walk her dog. Other dog owners began asking me to walk theirs. I was also asked to wait in line for hours to get food using these people's ration tickets. Very often, after waiting for hours in the cold, when at last it was my turn, there was nothing left in the stall. I had to return home empty handed, and not only did I not get my "tip", I also got tongue lashed.

The city employees in Paris were after stray dogs and cats, and the animals were impounded. For a little reward, I "helped" them by selling them the dogs of the people who had been mean and not very generous with me. I am not proud of this, but I had to find some way to buy food to survive. I would return the collars and leashes of the "lost" dogs, describing their bold getaways. I imagined that the dogs were put into the city's pound where some loving couple would adopt them. Later on I asked the dog catcher what happened to them and was shocked by his answer. These poor creatures were being fed to the sole remaining lion in the Paris zoo!

I would often spend my afternoons at the Court House as it was heated and I enjoyed listening to some entertaining trials. It was an impressive building and was to be the courtroom for the trial of Marshall Petain. I remember a murder trial in which the husband threw his wife from their lofty apartment. His only defense was: "She deserved it". To fight the cold, I also often spent time with many others in the subway system, the "Metro", where it was warmer than outside.

My happiest stay in Paris was with the "ladies of the night". I was in a nice, warm place, and was well fed. They could get everything they wanted from their German officer "clients". They pampered me as if they were my big sisters. They were wonderful ladies who had big hearts and I owe them a lot. Many of them worked for the Resistance, gathering valuable information from their German clients. After the liberation, I was very sad to learn that the "resistant fighters" who had joined the ranks at the last minute just for the glory, had attacked them and shaved their heads.

The Gestapo was still after me, and amazingly they always arrived a day late to arrest me. My instinct of survival, or my lucky star, told me it was time to move each time, even when I liked my hosts and felt safe. To intimidate me, the Gestapo would leave notes summoning me to turn myself in, or else they would pull out my mother's eyes or mutilate my father. It was tough not to give in to their blackmail, but my parents had prepared me for this situation, and I knew I should not respond. I stood up to the situation!

During my three months on the run, our Network was unfortunately broken and my parents were deported to a concentration camp. It was now safe for me to go back home to the Sarthe and attempt to rejoin my family, what little was left of it. The Gestapo was not interested in me anymore. I went back to the area where my grandmother lived. After spending a week at some cousins' in nearby Evaille, thanks to the intelligence they could get on the Nazis' surveillance, I decided it was safe to go home. My joy was immense when I took sight of my little brother and my dear grandmother again! I learned my parents were prisoners in work camps in Germany, but even this sad news was a relief for I had thought they were dead. Through the Red Cross, we were allowed to send one package a month. We could also send one letter a month, but it had to be written in German so the Germans could screen it. We found an Alsatian who could translate for us, but had to pay him dearly. They never received our packages and our letters had all been opened. Of course, we did not receive mail from them and we had no idea how horrible these so called "Work Camps" were!

Following the liberation of France, I received an invitation from Colonel Buckmaster to visit him in London. Naturally, he was like a god to us, so I scrapped together what money I could and purchased passage on a ferry from Calais to Dover.

Colonel Buckmaster made himself available to me for a whole day in London, saying he was so glad to meet his "British Army Staff's" youngest member. I was emotional when I visited his offices, and most of all the BBC offices and the room from which General de Gaulle had talked to the French people on June 18, 1940, and many times thereafter. His call to his people revived their hope in victory so much. From the same room were sent the personal messages and messages to the Resistance that we all had listened so eagerly for.

During my time in England I went to Surbiton, Surrey, and stayed with the family of an officer with the Special Operation Executive: Capt. Xavier Pierre Eduard (Peter) de Belgeonne. He had four children, and his family taught me some English "Good Manners" and a few words of the language. For the next 30 plus years, Captain Belgeonne's son Rudy sent me a hat from each country he was assigned to. He included no note but I understood well who was sending them and was fascinated by the postmarks. These 31 distinctive hats were such a joy for me to receive. I still have every one of these, storing them with great care."

CHAPTER 15   Were Concentration Camps To Be Their Reward?

Now imprisoned in the harshest concentration camps through relentlessly cold winters, Alfred Auduc never ceased his defiance which was so open that it sometimes endangered himself, his brother and his close associates. More amazingly, he never ceased to sabotage German machinery whenever he had a reasonable opportunity. But, his combative spirit explains how he survived while so many others perished. To sabotage is one thing; to do so and not be detected required a high degree of cleverness. Alfred's story continues with his network being compromised:

"In late summer of 1943, we learned that the Gestapo was becoming increasingly active in Le Mans, in Tours, and at their regional headquarters city of Angers. Hercule's wife Mimi and his stepmother were captured in Tours with other resistance fighters of the same network. Hercule was determined to liberate his wife and his friends. With the help of Colonel Mauffray and the information we got from one of the prison wardens, we organized an attack against the prison. Four members of our group were to dress as German soldiers to simulate escorting a group of six or seven men into the prison at 2:00AM. Once inside, they were to neutralize the sentinels, cut the telephone lines, open the cells and free the prisoners. A few bombs were to be exploded outside as a distraction. My three cars were to be parked nearby and serve as our getaway. Unfortunately we were delayed because we could find only two German soldier's uniforms. By the time we were at last ready, we learned that Hercule's wife and our friends were on their way to the Compiègne prison. Hercule was devastated.

From then on, we learned about other people being captured almost daily. Dr. Goude's network was dismantled, as well as the network in Sablé. Renée and I decided to put our children in a safe place, then, leave our house. After two weeks, I came back home cautiously. Everything looked quiet. We needed to take things from the house and on November 2, 1943, we spent the night there. At 5:00AM, after we had listened to the radio messages from London, somebody knocked at the door and the windows. Our house was surrounded by German police. I asked them to give us a minute to get dressed, which gave me time to put my submachine gun, my pistol and a grenade in a hole I had dug under the floor of the dining room. During that same time, my wife swallowed a message and concealed two microfilms in an aspirin tube. I opened the door and asked if I could use the outhouse at the end of the garden. They accepted after checking whether I was carrying a weapon. This allowed me to throw into the WC all of the important papers I had at my house. Renée made the same request and she was able to throw away the forged German stamps and the code grid she had in her bag. Our house was thoroughly searched and some members of the Gestapo stayed overnight hoping someone else would come. They pulled up some of the floor's wooden planks, but did not find the hole containing my weapons. My brother Roger and my brother-in-law were also arrested. My other two brothers managed to escape as the Gestapo came for them.

Renée and I were taken to rue des Fontaines, the Gestapo headquarters in Le Mans, before being transferred to Angers, where we waited several days before being questioned. One night about 10:00PM, they came for me, handcuffed me with my hands behind my back, and took me into a large room where I was violently pushed into a corner, my face against the wall. I noticed there were about 15 members of the Gestapo there drinking coffee and alcohol. There was also a representative of the Vichy government, who had come to pay his respects to the Gestapo agents that had been killed by "French terrorists". He even provided the "terrorists" names.

The Gestapo was hardly listening to this man; they were more focused on the meaning of the message "Hitler is going to commit suicide". I understood that this message was considered as the ultimate insult to their Fuhrer. We really had hit a sensitive spot with this message and I thought this was going to seal my fate. For the Gestapo, my name was associated with the English Intelligence Service. To make sure they really had Mr. Auduc, they asked the Vichy representative to confirm my identity and then asked him if he knew of anyone else they could capture. I recognized the voice of this S.O.B. He was telling the bastards "Yes, in Le Lude you can still capture two people" and he gave them details to make it easier for them. Eventually they put me in front of this rat and asked "Do you know him?" My answer was "No". The same question was put to the rat. There was a sinister smile on his face when he said "Of course, it is Auduc, Hercule's friend." And he was shown out of the room. One of the Gestapo spoke French and said "You will have to answer a lot of questions because we have captured Hercule". "No you haven't", I replied sharply. (Hercule was supposed to be in London). This is when they showed me his watch and a few personal documents. I was confused because the last time we saw each other, Hercule told me he was on his way to Paris to meet a friend, another radio operator, and then going back to London. I learned later that, unfortunately, this radio operator was a double agent. While Hercule was staying with his friend Mr. Laudet in Montrouge, the house was surrounded by the Gestapo and two of their agents knocked on the door and gave the password Hercule had given to the double agent. Hercule fired his pistol and the Gestapo returned fire, killing Mr. Laudet. Hercule shot as many Germans as he could, but he was against too many and soon was shot eight times (actually 7). The Gestapo took him away and we did not hear about him after that.

The Gestapo read me the report they had on our group and this is what I heard: assistance in landings of planes, at least twelve parachute drops, important information sent to

London, sabotages, eight Gestapo agents killed with five by Hercule and three by Captain Floege's radio operator. The Gestapo had me listed as a lieutenant in the British Intelligence Service, which I wasn't. Only now did the Germans understand that "Fred" in the Hercule network, "Fred Lemarchand" in the Sacristain and "Maurice" in the Max réseau were the same person: Alfred Auduc.

I later learned the Germans had arrested Floege's radio operator in a café following a fight where he was shot in the shoulder. Without searching him, they handcuffed him, but with his hands in front. Before getting into their car, they put his jacket on his shoulders and drove towards Angers. In spite of his wound, the radio operator managed to take his gun out of his jacket pocket. He shot the three passengers point blank. The car crashed and the radio operator managed to escape from the wreck, and then ran to a farm where he was freed of his handcuffs. He later was able to return to England.

I was aware of how serious my situation was. I was asked to give details on the parachute drops in Cérans-Fouilletourte and to tell them what the message announcing the drop was. I told them I couldn't remember. "We are going to help you remember" they said and two of these brutes went to a bag and pulled out a nerf du boeuf (a short, thick lash made from ox sinews), repeating their question "What was the message?" I answered "Hitler is going to commit suicide". They started hitting me while yelling. I could not protect my face as my hands were tied behind my back. The blows were so violent that they shredded my jacket like blades. I soon collapsed, falling to the floor. They then kicked me, broke my teeth and kept hitting me. I was in a sad state when they took me back to my cell.

My wife was also questioned and she tried to take the responsibility for the infamous message in an attempt to protect our friends.

The following day, a doctor examined me and I understood him to say I was resilient and they could question me further, as they still needed to. This was not good news as it meant that I was in for another round of questioning and torture.

On November 11, 1943, I was questioned about a weapons depot belonging to our Hercule network. They told me that they knew that the house where the weapons were was booby-trapped. I told them I did not know this house, as this depot had been established after my capture and I could not have known about it. They told me I was to go there with them because they feared a trap. Two trucks from Le Mans full of armed soldiers were to accompany us. There were also some 15 Gestapo agents with us, two of which spoke French fairly well. They inspected the hedges around the house and the soldiers stayed at a distance of about 15 meters. Everyone was instructed to lie down. One of the two men who spoke French told me "You are going to open the door and see if there is a booby trap". By this time, I had no hope of survival and did not hesitate to open the door. It was not booby trapped. The room was full of beets, which the soldiers cleared and underneath the beets were weapons and a box of booby-traps. The German who seemed to be in charge had all of the weapons carried to the courtyard and it sounded like he was explaining the weapons to his troops but I doubted he knew the weapons at all. He grabbed an incendiary grenade and threw it against an apple tree, which produced huge fireworks. One of the booby traps was new to him and he asked me about it. I said "It is a wonderful device", and bent over to take it. Before I could, I was struck with the butt of a rifle. They knew that, had I managed to pick it up, I would have used it. I could understand a few words they were saying and could make out more or less the following: "He has a remarkable wife who told us that there was a weapons cache like this in every city. What is to become of us with so many weapons around?"

On this same day of November 11, my brother Roger and L'abbé Lelièvre were captured, as well as my brother-in-law, Florent Beaury.

I was inflicted with awful tortures and questioned every day about parachute drops and sabotage. What seemed to be most important to them was to know the names of the Germans I had been in contact with. Each session they insisted more and more, becoming more determined to break me. One evening about 9:00PM, I was taken to a room where four Gestapo agents and the soldiers who beat me were waiting for me. The one who spoke French said "We want to get this over with and we will use all the necessary means for it". As I had done before, I kept denying everything and claimed I did not know any German officer. He replied "We are going to start and I am sure you will talk before the end of the first session". He took my right hand and placed it on the table, then the brute hit my hand so violently that the tips of four of my fingers were completely smashed. They then dipped my hand in ice cold water and held it there for 30 minutes, then dipped it in disinfectant. In order to endure all this torture, I used a method I had read in a book Hercule had given me. The book explained how to resist such questioning and torture. It recommended that prisoners control themselves by relaxing their nerves and emptying their minds. At the end of this session, they gave me 30 minutes to talk. My answer did not change and, thinking my situation was hopeless, I asked them to kill me. The German who spoke French then said "We are going to commence a second session and you will confess".

The same beast took a piece of cloth, unbuttoned my pants, and wrapped the cloth around my genitals. He then started twisting and crushing them. It was excruciating. I could not help yelling from the pain. They questioned me for one hour and became more and more agitated. I could not even answer their questions anymore. "Well, since you don't wish to answer our questions, we have something else for you." They put me in a car and drove to the hospital of Le Mans and took me to the surgery ward. One of the Gestapo took a box with glass ampoules from his pocket. I understood they wanted to give me injections, but the doctor present refused to do it as he did not know what the ampoules contained. The Gestapo agents became aggravated and decided to inject me themselves. They injected me in my spine. This paralyzed me and I became black from head to toe. They probably missed their aim as they had made me unable to speak. They ordered the doctor to give me a second injection. In spite of my pain I realized that the doctor had pretended to inject me because I could feel the fluid running down my back. I was then taken back to my cell in Angers; it was 4:00AM and I really thought that, as resilient as I was, I was going to die. I remained paralyzed for one week. A doctor checked on me every day. They had used an experimental "truth serum" that backfired!

My wife plus Mr. and Mrs. Brault, were the only other people who knew the names of the Germans we had been in contact with. None of them talked during their interrogations and the names of the German officers were never revealed.

It may seem strange that French people would prefer to die under torture rather than reveal to the Gestapo the names of German officers who would normally be seen as our enemies. The reason was that we did not want to be cowards. These officers had not betrayed their country; they were men who had had no choice but to serve under the Nazi regime and its terror. If we had revealed their names, there would have been no forgiveness for them. They would have been shot or they would have had a similar fate to General Rommel, who was forced to commit suicide in order to conceal his crime. Afterwards, Hitler gave Rommel a national tribute. Another general who was a friend of Rommel's was forced to read a speech dictated by Hitler: it was a string of lies and hypocrisy and the general was not able to finish. Everyone in the audience knew the truth. This story was told to me by a

German who attended General Rommel's funeral. He also told me that the Allies had shown a lot of respect for this great soldier who had always been a respectful adversary.

They put me in the same room as Renée only once. It was horrible to see her sad state. She could not open one of her eyes and her face had been badly beaten. She cried: "See what those brutes have done to me."

The Germans had a method during the interrogations of starting gently, saying they had a proposition and adding "You know what awaits: you are going to be shot unless you accept our proposition. This is what we want: the American you know (Captain Floege) has escaped us and you know how important it is for us to find him. We think that if we put you under surveillance, he will hear about it and will try to contact you. If we manage to capture him, you will be set free." I replied "Have you ever found any French people who have accepted such an offer?" They answered: "Of course, if it can save their life, there is no choice." My answer was "No, ask my wife." He turned to her and said "You have children of your own, if you love them, you will accept." Hardly had he finished his sentence when my wife yelled at him "If you have children of your own, it is high time you thought about them because you will have to answer to them; we know your names, we know the landing is near since we have been in contact with London every day." He responded "If you know our names, go ahead and give just one of them." "Yes, I can name Wolfe, he lives in Le Mans" and she even gave the name of the street and the person who was hosting him. The Gestapo men looked at each other in astonishment and ordered our wardens to take us back to our cells.

I was taken to Le Mans twice for interrogations, then to Tours and, the day before Christmas, I was taken to Poitiers where I arrived at 10:00PM. They tied me to a kennel outside. It was cold and snowing that night. A bright spotlight was on me and I had to stay outside. After all the beatings, I had a fever and I imagined I was hearing Christmas bells and Christmas songs. The only respite for me that night was to see a few birds that came into the light to find a bit of heat. That night, I thought of my wife and children. I knew the firing squad was next for me. I was so exhausted that I wished it would happen quickly. The next day, Christmas Day, at 10:00AM, I was put in a heated cell where a lady was brought for me to see. It was Madame Blanc, the manager of the clinic in Poitiers. I told her not to endure torture because the Gestapo knew all about our network. One who had gone to the clinic had been captured and had told the entire story. Madame Blanc was sent to a concentration camp where she perished. When Hercule had learned that someone besides my wife had been taken with me to Poitiers and thereby the Gestapo knew the address of the clinic, he was furious.

Two days later I was back in Angers, back into cell number 13, the one for death row. For twelve days my hands were tied behind my back without any relief, not even to eat. On the thirteenth day an old German of the Wehrmacht took my handcuffs off and whispered in my ear "you not kaput; you go with friends to Germany. The Allies have taken care of you." I learned later that Captain Floege and the SOE in London had both sent letters personally addressed to individuals in the Gestapo in Angers informing them that, if Renée and I were executed, there would be retaliation and London was prepared to carry it out. For a long while I could not believe I was going to be spared, possibly because for over an hour all I could think of was how much my hands hurt. Then I saw a cross carved into the wall with the words "I am a communist, but before I die I want to believe in God and ask Him to spare my life." I started hoping again.

A few days later, in early January, I was taken to the Compiègne prison with my brother, and then to Buchenwald. When I arrived, holding my red form, I told my story to a Canadian major who had been there for a while and this is what he told me about the organization of the camp. "Those who arrive here with a red form were condemned to death in their country. In the evening when the roll is called, they are asked to come forward and are executed in different ways depending on the wish of the Gestapo. Your only chance to survive is to volunteer for a commando work unit to get out of the camp." In spite of the cold, the earth of Buchenwald burned my feet (a French saying that meant he could not wait to leave the place, whatever the work).

That day my brother was chosen to be a member of a commando and I was determined to stay with him. I went to the kapo and explained that I did not want to be separated from my brother; at first he did not want to hear it, then, as I was insisting, he asked if someone wanted to stay and take my place. There were a lot of volunteers to take my place because a lot of people did not wish to be separated from their friends. One was chosen to take my place and it bothered my conscience: would he be killed instead of me? I never knew

the answer. We climbed into a truck, about a hundred of us, enough to make sure those who might die would be immediately replaced. We were driven to a mountain in Thuringer Wald near the border with Czechoslovakia.

The Germans were building a secret underground factory there to produce liquid air and to carry out tests of the V-2 rocket. This commando I was now a part of was named "LAURA". There were about 1,000 prisoners working in the factory. On our arrival we met a few survivors from a large French commando: they had started the works on tunnels and large chambers for the installation of machinery. These tunnels were dug into the mountain and were 50 to 80 meters long. Digging a tunnel cost the lives of many prisoners. Water would ooze everywhere, especially from the top, and after about half an hour anyone working there was soaked. The SS whose job was to take the prisoners back to their barracks took pleasure in leaving them outside 30 minutes or more in temperatures that were between -20 and -30 C; these poor men had to keep moving their arms and legs in order not to freeze to death. The prisoners in this commando never survived more than eight or ten days and those who were still alive replaced the dead ones. Among the French survivors I saw a few good friends such as André Gatignon, who had belonged to the Buckmaster network in Loir et Cher, l'abbé Labaume and Doctor Piquet who were among the first French prisoners sent to concentration camps in 1943. I also had the shock of seeing "Bouboule", the executioner at Buckenwald.

The first week my brother and I were assigned to a commando that had to work outside. The veterans had told us that it was one of the worst assignments and that each evening they would bring back the dead. It wasn't long before we realized how truly we had been informed. Four ferocious SS were in charge of this group and were helped by their two German shepherds. Our job consisted in repairing the ratchets of a steep three kilometer railroad line. This ratchet rail would enable a specially made locomotive to haul the V-2 rockets up the mountain. This locomotive could pull only one car at a time, so steep was the climb. In one curve the ratchet rail had been broken and had fallen down a ravine with a car. It was impossible to pull these out of the ravine, so the Germans cut them into pieces with an acetylene torch and the prisoners had to carry the pieces back up one by one. Oftentimes the pieces were so heavy that we could not even lift them and the Germans would beat us for it. At 11:00AM our friends would bring us bottles containing rutabaga soup. One day after we had received our ration of soup, the SS made us sit in a circle. We were quite concerned and everyone wondered what they were up to this time.

A professor from Luxembourg who had refused to give the SS the tobacco he had received was put into the middle of our circle. The SS let their dogs loose and sicced them onto the professor. What happened next was awful. The dogs attacked the man and bit him deeply in the neck. When he collapsed the dogs started eating his arms and legs. They were so strong that they would drag the poor man as if he were a puppet. He lost consciousness and we thought he was dead. The SS rejoiced in this carnage and, unfortunately, the day was not over. That afternoon we had to witness another fight that was equally horrible. A poor, exhausted man who wanted to relieve his bladder asked the SS for permission. Perhaps he was hoping that it would give him a few minutes to recover enough strength to finish his day. He walked four or five meters from his work station. The SS decided he was taking too long and again let their dogs loose. He was brutally attacked by the dogs and did not even have time to pull up his pants. The dogs attacked all the parts of his body that were not protected by cloths. No need to give any more details. It was so horrible and the poor man died. That evening we had one more body to carry. As for the professor from Luxembourg, he was still alive the next day. His friends helped him go back to work because as long as you were alive you had to work. The SS made him lie down at the edge of a precipice so that if he moved only an inch, he would fall off; he probably found the strength to realize this for he turned his back to the precipice. When the SS saw that their sinister plan was not working, they took out their guns and took target practice on him. This is how the professor from Luxembourg died. That night when my brother and I were back in our barrack, we could not even talk any more as we were ashamed to be part of the human race. I could not sleep that night as I had horrible nightmares where the world had become insane. The fact was, the Germans were not the only criminals we encountered, as we met criminals of many nationalities. My mind felt empty, but I was still trying to think about our 20th century civilization. Maybe there was no more civilization. Men who thought they had the right to decide who was to live and who to die quickly became so ferocious they were worse than wild beasts.

My brother and I managed to leave this infamous commando group; we were assigned a different job in the tunnels. We would do day work one week, night work the next. Night work was not worse than day work, but it had a major drawback: when we worked at night, we were not allowed to rest during day time. This was a major problem because sleep was the only way for us to recover our strength.

One day my brother and I were asked to carry the bottles of soup to the commando we had just left. It was a difficult task that took more than three hours off our sleep time. On the second day I refused to do this. The kapo of the barrack grabbed me by the arm, pulled me out of what was called my bed and dropped me onto the concrete floor. I got up and without saying a word I punched him in the face and stomach, but he quickly pulled himself together and I collapsed under his blows. My brother was shaking with the fear that the kapo was going to kill me. They would beat to death someone for a lesser reason, but surprisingly he did not kill me. Something out of the ordinary happened the next day. As a reward for having had the courage to stand up to the kapo, my brother and I got a double ration of soup. It was the first time our fellow inmates had seen a prisoner stand up to a kapo.

More often than not, I felt privileged when I received packages from the International Red Cross. One time within the same day I received twelve packages: from the French, the British, Canadian, Australian, American and other Red Cross's. The SS who gave me these packages looked at me in a mean way. I imagine this is why it didn't happen again. After that day my packages were plundered and sometimes I received only the wrapping. I was made to sign the International Red Cross book proving that the packages had been given to me. Whatever was left for me I shared as I was proud to be able to make some of my friends happy. Actually, we had to eat everything quickly because all of the cans had been opened before we got them. We decided to save some of the unopened food to celebrate Christmas of 1944. That night all the prisoners of all nationalities joined together. We French had decorated a table. It was beautiful. I could not believe what we managed to do with only paper. There must have been artists amongst us. Everybody had taken part in decorating the barrack, and, using our supplies we prepared a very special meal. The French had decided to invite at our table a representative of each nationality in the camp. Among these guests was a young Russian about sixteen who was so happy it is impossible to put his joy into words. Everybody appreciated our idea and at midnight Christmas songs could be heard in all the languages. The voices were weak and the songs sounded sad. They expressed the feelings of these men who were exhausted and ill, who seemed to be praying to live long enough to die in their homelands. Other men like me were thinking about their wives: where were they, were they alive? Our questions remained unanswered. This Christmas felt wonderful compared to the one the year before when I was chained to the kennel.

The Russians were not as lucky as we were, for their country had not acknowledged the International Red Cross. They had to be content with a few potatoes. They knew only one song, the International (which is the Communist anthem) and they sang so loudly that the SS heard, went to their barrack and hit them as they took them outside. The SS major then took a hose and watered them down for 15 minutes. They were soaking wet and had to stay outside for half an hour in temperatures of about minus 25 degrees centigrade. They must've gotten some divine protection on that Christmas night, for none of them became ill.

My brother and I always managed to stay together by working in the same commando group. First, we worked at the construction of tunnels where sizable areas were being prepared to receive large liquid air compressors. We were told they were the most powerful ones in Europe. There were four of them. Then, we were assigned the task of loading carts with the V-2 rockets that were going to be tested. At first, I did a good job of it in spite of the sick feelings these devices gave me. But, soon I did my best to slow things down. For instance, I often did not screw the bolts straight, in order to strip them. I was not able to do this for very long: the Germans found out about the 'problem'. From then on they kept a close watch on me without my knowing it and eventually a kapo saw I was the one who was responsible. He got into a terrible fit, insulting and threatening me. I remarked to him that I was asked to do something that was not my trade and, like my brother, I was an electrician.

The following scene took place early in 1944. The kapo was so angry, he probably wanted to get rid of us, so he took us to the engineer's office, and explained that we two Frenchmen claimed we were electricians. It was decided to test our skills all morning to see if they would keep us. One of the engineers turned to me and asked me in bad French: "What are your skills?" I answered "my brother is our electrician in lighting installations, and I am a mechanical electrician." "Why are you here?" "An American airplane crashed near where we live, and we helped the crew." "In this case, you are not criminals." The foreman took my brother to a room where he was asked to do electrical installations. Since it really was his trade, he did a perfect job. As for me, I was asked to build a tripping device. I barely finished before the end of the morning. The Germans were impressed with our jobs and it was like a little miracle in the sense that they then put us in with a group of civilian workers. Every day an SS officer would escort us to the workshop. We earned the trust of the engineers there who treated us like other civilians. This is the time when my brother and I started doing things our way without even talking to each other about it. Electric bulbs would often need replacing and my brother was only too eager to put in new ones. There were shorts here and there and the machines often broke down. We had learned from our time as Resistance fighters in France that any personal initiative to sabotage should strictly be kept to oneself. It may seem to be a simple rule, but it was so hard to never share our ideas and our successes with each other. We were now entitled to a daily ration of bread and crude sandwiches. It was such a treat compared to what we had experienced before.

In the workshop, I was curious about everything, but mostly about old radio sets put away in boxes, and the variety of other electrical equipment. This soon triggered my saboteur instinct. Every day, when there was an air raid alert, the civilians would go to shelters, the SS would man their stations in the watchtowers, but I would stay in the workshop the whole time. After a few alerts, my brother and I became more confident and after checking that there was no one around we decided to take the radio sets out of their boxes and turn one on. We were elated when we heard a voice speaking in French. Only we and André Matignon knew about this. By listening to the radio, we were able to learn some news which was spread around the camp like wildfire. The Germans could not figure out how we knew all the news and of course it worried them. Our listening almost cost us our lives. One Sunday morning, during an alert and thinking all of the civilians were in the shelters, my brother and I were listening to the Voice of America. Suddenly, the door flew open and a civilian came in before we could conceal the radio set. He screamed at the top of his voice telling us he knew we would get shot for this. While he was busy yelling, the programming in French ended and was followed by one in German. This took the civilian by surprise and he came closer to the set and listened, expressing "ya, gut" from time to time. Once the program was over, I told him: "If we kaput, so are you, because you also listened to the Voice of America." He put his finger on his forehead saying "I am not crazy. I want the Americans to come quickly and combine forces with the Germans to drive the Russians out." It was not like me, but I shook his hand. It had been a very close call.

Also during the alerts, we took care of mechanical parts. We made small incisions with a metal saw here and there so that they would not show too much. I used bits to puncture electrical cords in order to sabotage them. The holes did not show at all and I would put everything back in their wrappings. Subsequently, explosions could be heard in the distant installations and it made me feel good. During this entire time, our commando was still busy digging a passage for the wiring to reach one of the testing sites. A high power cable was needed for a compressor fed by an 800 horsepower engine. The 4 meter spools of cable happened to be stored near the workshop where I worked. Each cable was about 200 meters long. At first, I did not pay attention to them, then it dawned on me I could inflict on these big cables what I was doing to the small ones and the idea stuck in my mind.

Every day a large number of rockets came on a ratchet train. During an alert, I measured the distance between the plug for my electrical drill and the cable, and made an extension cord that I had kept hidden. In the evening, I would think about my wife who was also somewhere in Germany, my children who would not have forgiven me had I not succeeded, and

Hercule, who often told me an act of sabotage has to be carefully planned. I was so determined that only bullets could have stopped me. If I succeeded, these monster machines would be kept from functioning for at least a week. I also thought about the English royal family, how all this equipment was to be used to destroy the United Kingdom. I thought about the wives and children of the soldiers who had left their countries and who were waiting for the invasion to liberate the countries in Europe that were occupied by Germany. I thought of all those who were in concentration camps in the heart of Germany and elsewhere.

I prepared everything and waited for the next alert. When the time came I sprang into action, plugged in my drill and fitted it with a thick 10 millimeter bit that could do serious damage to the cable. I did not look around me, not even at the watch towers with machine guns ready to shoot in all directions. I could not anticipate which part of the cable would be concealed in the trenches we dug for it. I went to the cable and started working on it. The bit went through the outer protection made of tarred fabric, and then through the metal protection and into the insulation. From my calculations, I should do damage to the cable every 20 meters or so. I drilled it in six different places, and once the job was done, I put everything back into place and filled in the holes with tar. Was the French Resistance going to deliver a big blow right in the middle of Germany? I could only wait and see. It was imperative that I kept my action to myself; I could not even share it with my brother because there would have been retribution against him if my scheme had been discovered.

Once the trench for the cable had been dug, the electrical cable was unrolled and every 2 meters they placed a prisoner. These people were to carry the cable up the mountain and put it in place in the prepared trench. This maneuver claimed the life of a young Frenchman. An SS guard considered the lad was not working hard enough and kicked him. The young man turned around and said a few insulting words. The SS guard must've understood for he shot him in the back. The bullet went right through him. He put his hands on his wound to try to keep the blood from flowing, and yelled "mommy, mommy, mommy" as if she could hear him and come to help him. He then collapsed and it was over for him.

We installed the cable and connected it to the power source. When everything was in place, I was eager to know what would happen. It was not long before I found out. Explosions were heard and in certain places the cable overheated so much we could not touch it. The surge protectors in the transformer all tripped at the same time and made a terrible noise. The engineers stopped the operation and could only admit that the equipment was faulty. They ordered new equipment, but could not get it because there was none available. I asked one of the engineers why the cable had overheated. His answer was "The problem is, we in Germany only employ foreign workers and they sabotage everything." "So the cable was sabotaged while being manufactured?" "Yes, no doubt." This helped me relax. He also explained that he had just finished installing V-1 launching ramps near Caen and had encountered a lot of problems with the electrical circuits that were often sabotaged. As for the cable we were dealing with, the engineer asked us to install electrical fans near the areas that overheated. All of these setbacks delayed things at least one month, and even in middle of the winter, this warmed me. They eventually managed to get the system to work in spite of these obstacles.

Thanks to my radio set, I learned about the landings in Normandy, the liberation of Alençon by General Leclerc, the liberation of Paris and the whole country, and then that of Germany. A few days before the Americans reached our factory, the archives and the scientific documents were carefully put into boxes and placed in a tunnel that was then obstructed by rubble. My brother and I were the only prisoners that witnessed the operation. When everything was done, one of the engineers looked apologetic and said "In order for this secret to be kept, they're going to kill you." I had thought this could happen and was expecting it. An incredible stroke of luck gave us the possibility to go back to the camp. Since the Americans were approaching so fast, the Germans gathered all the POW's and took them back to Buchenwald, forgetting our knowledge. Also at this time, SS guards were deserting the camps. The SS that stayed were often turned against by the prisoners.

I had the opportunity to figure out how the Germans organized things under the Nazi regime. The young people were 100 percent pro Hitler, but not the older generation. Some of these young Hitlerites were rats. In fact, a special office was created in the factory to receive anonymous letters implicating so and so who criticized the regime or because someone saw something suspicious. From time to time some German civilians were sent to concentration camps because of these informers. At the camp they were beaten, their heads were shaved and they were made to wear the striped prisoner's uniform. One of them told me his story. He was at the barber's and like everywhere in the world, in Germany too, people discuss the news. Someone there said "I don't know what is going on in this factory, but there sure is a lot of noise." The civilian answered "I work there and what you are hearing is rockets we are testing." The next day he was arrested and taken to our camp.

The civilians were wary of each other. In our work group, only two of them could not stand us two brothers. One day one of them was pushing large rocks down the mountainside, trying to fell one on my brother below. I warned my brother "Watch out, he wants that big block to fall on you." My brother couldn't completely dodge the rock and suffered a serious leg injury. They almost had to amputate his leg, but fortunately there were doctors among us who took care of him and saved his leg. Another day the second of these two Germans reported on two of my friends and had them punished with 25 slashes with a cane. This angered me and I went to see the head of the workshop and told him about the infamous Eric. This Eric was one of the rats that had already caused a lot of problems for others. They talked with me about him and eventually told me of their decision "He is an S.O.B. We cannot dismiss this civilian unless we have a serious reason, so we are going to set up a trap for him." The next day, this Eric was supposed to check the electrical equipment in an installation that was connected to a liquid air compressor. When Eric opened the electrical box, there was a loud explosion and the whole circuit was destroyed. Eric's superior reported that Eric was responsible for the explosion. For several days the compressor was out of order. Eric was taken away and we never saw him again.

Engineers came and went. Later, when I saw a photograph of Werner von Braun, I remembered him as one of the engineers.

Something funny involving one of the engineers and myself happened. They trusted me enough to send me and an engineer to a garage, escorted by two SS. The head of the garage had just been drafted. One of the senior engineers brought his car to the garage; it was so dirty you could not tell what make it was. It turned out to be a Fiat Gran Sport with red leather seats. What a car! When the garage owner asked me to clean it, the engineer and I worked on it the entire morning. When the owner came to pick it up, he was very impressed "Only French people can do such a good job; my car has never been so beautiful." And I was thinking: "If only you knew what French people are capable of doing in your secret factory!" He took out his wallet and wanted to give us deutschemarks. We refused because we could not use them. What we wanted was bread. He got upset and said "There is no bread in my pockets." He then gave us a cigar, but I remarked that smoking was forbidden, so he called over the two SS guards and told them we could smoke our cigars. The man grabbed us by our arms, pulled us outside the garage and asked us to sit on a rock while he lit our two cigars. This was the one and only time I smoked a cigar while a prisoner in a concentration camp. We couldn't move before we finished smoking them and we heard some prisoners who saw us say loud enough for us to hear "Churchill was here".

I often congratulated myself for being on the side of those who fought for freedom. Dictatorships are the worst governments that can happen.

The order given to our captors was that the allies should find no one alive in the camps. We were to be either killed or moved elsewhere. They decided to move us. At first we walked, then took a train to the camp of Dachau and next to the camp of Allach. There we climbed aboard a flat car on the way to Ratisbonne. When the train was crossing the Danube on a very high bridge, it was stopped. The engine was unhooked and we stayed there all afternoon. The bridge had been attacked by American bombers who had dropped 1000 kilo bombs, but the bridge was left intact. We could hear planes roaring everywhere. Fighters were protecting the bombers and all of these planes were flying over the bridge. They flew as low as 50 meters above us. The pilots would put their aircraft on their sides and we could see them making signs at us. We raised our arms and shook our hats to answer them. Our lives were in their hands. I told my brother Roger and all my friends "I think we are going to take a dip in the river; these bombers' mission must be to destroy the bridge and who knows if our presence will deter them." The bombers probably did take our presence into account because no bombs hit the bridge. That evening the locomotive was again hooked onto our train and we traveled over 20 kilometers, often stopping because of damage to the tracks. Early the next morning the train stopped at a station and we realized we were in Austria. The SS major escorting us asked for two volunteers. I asked my brother Roger to follow me. He thought I was going crazy because we had agreed we would never volunteer. Something told me it was the right thing to do and I convinced my brother to follow me. The major asked us to pull a cart on which he had placed a bag weighing 100 kilos that had been in their car. He instructed us to leave the station, cross the street and go through a door on which we would read "KINO". It was a former movie theater used as a hospital. A nun made the sign of the cross when she saw us and asked the SS "Who are these men?", pointing at us. At the time we weighed about 90 pounds. "They are political prisoners. Please give us bread in exchange for this bag of flour and prepare a hot meal for us." The nun accepted on condition that we, too, would have some bread. Another nun

Father Pannetier with U.S. Airman Chonskie

brought a large pot of sweet coffee and I think each of us drank two liters. She then gave us loaves of bread and I think they saved us because the whole trip ended up lasting 7 days without our ever being fed. Once again a miracle allowed us to finish this trip in better condition than a lot of our companions.

The nuns and the

priests had a well-deserved reputation. Our allies told the aviators that if they were compelled to land on our soil, to seek out religious people for help. This is how Father Pannetier, the priest of the Sablé hospital, sheltered the survivor of a Flying Fortress that was downed in Sarthe. The airman's name was Edward Chonskie of The Mugger. He kept him for several weeks before Mr. Raymond Rayer of Le Mans sheltered Chon-skie and two of his comrades until it could be organized to return them to England.

Father Lelièvre never hesitated to help Hercule in spite of a German armored company that camped on the church square. I could mention a lot of other courageous priests who, like us, new the rules of the game and were unfortunately often sent to concentration camps where they died of the bad treatment there.

After several hours in this Austrian station we resumed our "way of the cross", then, 20 km down the track our engine ran out of water. We stopped again and something unfortunate happened to one of our friends. Near Ingolstadt a wrecked train car full of wheat gave us the opportunity to fill our pockets. A Hungarian Jew who was picking up some of these wheat grains carelessly put his hand on the rail exactly when the train lurched forward. His hand was completely crushed. The following day gangrene set in and proceeded up his arm. A young Belgian who was in medical school said he was lost and that the only way to save him was to amputate his arm. The young Hungarian agreed. In the waiting room of the station, without any anesthesia, the young Belgian severed the arm at the shoulder with all of the precautions that were required. Once the operation was over he cut off some of the useless skin to close off the wound and disinfected it with the only thing he had: salt water. This may sound like something I am making up, but there were a lot of witnesses and I would like to name a few: the young surgeon's name was Georges Nimal and the following people were witnesses: Albert

Dupart, AKA Filou, French, Franck Derick, Belgian, Marcel Cornet, Belgian, and Auguste Versaille, Belgian. Some of these people took advantage of the situation and the absence of surveillance to disappear into the forest. Thanks to the help of a French prisoner they happened to meet, they reached the village of Pitenfeld where Franck was killed during a bombardment. The amputee survived the trip. We helped him the best we could. The poor man died a few weeks later, not of his injury, but of typhus.

At the third stop we were made to exit the train and the SS took us to a field. Thinking they could not take us any farther, they decided to kill all of the Russians, but the SS didn't all agree. Some said they should kill the Jews while others said everyone should be killed. We stood there waiting for our fate. Eventually they were unable to agree and the train was able to continue its trip towards Dachau.

The last leg of our trip was chaotic. The train stopped during the middle of the night at a landing strip that had been bombed the day before. Several Russians and Georges Reme, the "King of Escape" (sentenced to more years in prison than he could possibly live) took advantage of the darkness to leave the train. For Georges Reme it was just another escape and he succeeded; but the Russians were caught by the guards and taken back to the train. The SS hit them with the butts of their guns, then, shot them point blank. We carried two of them into our car; their agony lasted a long time. It was our last leg before Dachau-Allach.

In Dachau the station was full of trains carrying prisoners from all parts of Germany. In a lot of cars there was no sign of life as the trip had been too long. Dachau camp could not take us, so we were taken to Allach, a few kilometers from Dachau. To reach this camp, we walked across an avenue and past a BMW engine factory. A large group of civilians came closer; most of them were young and well-dressed and were with their wives. What a macabre sight we must have been, for we were carrying the dead. As I walked near them I asked "Anybody French?" Immediately I heard someone who said with a Parisian accent "This is what you get for causing trouble in France." I thanked him. These were the French STO who wanted to be called "work convicts". A little farther down the street, a Frenchman holding a broom came close to us and I said to him "Nice friends you've got there." And his answer was "They are the same with us; they think they have the right to bully us."

In the infamous camp of Allach there was a typhus epidemic and bodies were stacked up behind the barracks because the crematorium did not work any longer. A large mass grave had been dug by the prisoners and it was full of bodies of German civilians. They were Germans who had been arrested because they had opposed Hitler's decision to continue the war that was destroying their country. They had been arrested in the streets or in their offices and their families never knew what happened to them. They were taken here, shot and pushed into the mass grave where they were covered with lime. It was early April of 1945, but still cold and some snow remained. When we arrived at our barracks, we were ordered to get completely undressed; we were allowed to keep our shoes and were given a blanket that served as our only clothes and our bed. It was only on the 29th of April that the Americans arrived and we were liberated.

A few days after the end of Hitler's Germany on the 8th of May, the country capitulated unconditionally. Hitler's Germany had caused the deaths of 40 million human beings, 15 million of whom perished in concentration camps. Out of 300,000 French deportees only 30,000 were liberated from the camps and all of these were in pitiful condition. As we had anticipated, Hitler committed suicide in 1945. When we returned to France, the radio transmitter from where the famous message was sent was still there and Madame André Dubois gave it to us Auduc brothers in memory of her husband. (While on display many years later, the radio transmitter was stolen and never recovered).

I think we were one of the last camps in Germany to be liberated, due to the epidemic in the camp. In the watchtowers the SS sentinels were replaced by Americans who wanted us to be disinfected and to receive the appropriate shots before being evacuated.

In the camp I was reunited with a few friends: Father Lelièvre and Dr. Richard Grunberg, who, like us, had just arrived with a few other members of their commando. We hugged, we were so happy to see one another. Father Lelièvre also had to endure his "way of the cross"; there were 300 of them who left Kochendorf to go to Dachau and only 17 arrived. The survivors of this commando said that it was thanks to Dr. Grunberg that they were still alive. There were three or four French doctors in this camp and these men fulfilled the most difficult tasks of all the prisoners. I have since read a lot of books and reports on concentration camps and I have not found any that did justice to the doctors there. I feel it is my duty to mention them.

In Buchenwald I worked at the quarry with doctors, Dr. Goude to name one of them. No doctor ever asked his friends to carry a heavy rock for him or to dig a yard of trench for him. In Laura it was the same story. After having worked for 12 hours with their commando, the doctors in the evenings took care of the sick and agonized, doing all they could to keep them from dying, when they had almost nothing to work with. They gave alcohol, salted water or crushed charcoal to those who suffered from dysentery. The doctors asked that they be sent medicine instead of food in their packages. They saved thousands of lives. These men of valor have played a very important role in the Resistance. My thoughts go particularly to three French doctors in Allach. When the camp was liberated they took charge of the "revier" (dispensary). There were thousands of people sick with typhus and dysentery. What could they do? They did not have even the beginnings of what they needed. What an ordeal for them. They gave the little they had to those who could still be saved. For many, there was no hope of survival. Some prisoners, who did not understand, accused the doctors of having let their friends die without care. I can attest that the doctors did everything they could to save people regardless of their nationality.

Dr. Grunberg saved several of those in his network, for instance, Marcel Veau from La Fleche, a 20 year old with typhus, and Mr. Oscar Monéris from Château-du-Loir who had dysentery. Every day I went to the revier where I could see the devotion of these men as they treated the living and the dying.

The camp had been liberated on April 29, 1945, by the Americans who were pushing towards Munich. The medical staff arrived only two weeks later. The typhus epidemic spread so fast that most of the prisoners were infected.

In 1945, some former prisoners filed complaints against doctors they accused of having let their friends die. The French police informed the doctors of the accusations. One of the doctors asked for the names of those who filed the complaint. The former prisoners had been too cowardly to sign their own accusations. They explained they belonged to a political party and it was their party that had talked them into this complaint in order to tarnish the names of bourgeois doctors. Later, the complaint did have an impact on the doctors' careers.

If these doctors are asked what their roles were in the Resistance and how many lives they saved in the camps, they had a very humble answer: "We did our duty and our job". They didn't say more than that. As a witness and inclined to observe things by nature, I understood how miserable these doctors felt when trying to save their friends without being able to do much, as they lacked equipment and medicine.

To Doctor Richard Grunberg I ask: "do you remember when, in 1943, in the prison of Le Mans you were at the side of the first victim of our Sacristain network? Our friend Chancel had refused to talk and had been tortured to death. Later, in Natzweiler, you closed the eyes of General Jules Frère, a former commandant of St. Cyr Military Academy, after doing everything you could to save him. You also did all you could for a young boy who had promised to give you a cherry tree for your property: Jarrier, but this cherry tree was not to be planted."

Dr. Goude, do you remember when we came for you that night in the summer of 1943, to take care of Max, a French Canadian who had parachuted near your beautiful area, Château-du-Loir? His leg had been broken in his landing (Perhaps badly sprained). You don't like to be praised, but you took such good care of him that he fully recovered. Later, this unfortunate young man, a vulnerable radio operator, was captured by the Gestapo and hanged in Buchenwald. ("Max" was John Kenneth Macalister, "Mac", who had been a Rhodes Scholar at Oxford and was studying at the Institute of Corporate Law in Paris when the war started). I would also like to mention an American aviator who bailed out of his plane in flames and was seriously injured when he touched the ground.

His parachute caught fire and accelerated his fall, causing him serious burns. He was taken care of secretly and recovered, then could return to England. If I had the talent of a writer I would have written a book entitled "Doctors Amongst the Prisoners".

You doctors who were not prisoners of war also did your duty. A lot of soldiers, whether in uniform or not, were able to escape from the hospitals where they were being treated, thanks to your help and that of your staffs. In our networks and in the maquis many wounded members were secretly treated and saved by you.

What has become of these doctors? We find them in dispensaries or in induction centers. Every one of them is always ready to help their former prison mates. I'm not trying to defend the cause of doctors', I simply want people to know the truth because some doctors have been unjustly accused when they were doing their duty.

The prisoners of war and those sent to concentration camps felt close to one another. I want to express my admiration for these prisoners. I was not allowed to, but one day I managed to talk to a POW. It was in April in Thuringe. This prisoner told me about the advance of the Allies and said "In spite of being a prisoner of war all of these years, the Germans never managed to take away our pride of being French." I told him that in the concentration camps we would die with this same pride. On our way from Laura to Dachau we met a number of these men who had this pride; when they saw us they would yell "Hold on guys, it will soon be over. They are coming". They would raise their hands and give the "V", Churchill style. On one occasion I feared for one of them who had encouraged us. He wasn't familiar with the SS and didn't know it was verboten to talk to us. Our "guardian angels" aimed at them, but fortunately did not shoot. The men stopped yelling and retreated. They had gotten the message.

After the Germans surrendered, we had to stay in our camp because of the typhus epidemic. The POW's that had been liberated in the area came to see us and asked if some of us were from the same area as themselves. They were going home and wanted to give news to our families. They also threw over the barbed wires anything they thought we could use. It was a very emotional scene to see these French people meeting in the middle of Germany. I will never forget this scene.

Alfred and
Roger Auduc

This staged U. S. photo was taken after their liberation. Pictured are Afred Auduc, Roger Auduc and Marcel Veau of La Fleche.

The disinfection period lasted one month. During this time I informed an American officer that I had something to report. I wanted to inform him of the tunnel where the secret equipment and documents from the missile factory were walled in. He turned a deaf ear and said it was not his responsibility.

Late May and still with my brother, I reached the French border at last. What joy, what emotion, but I was so worried about my family that I had no news of. At the border a security officer asked us to strip to the waist and raise our arms. I protested, but to my surprise he told me that there was a French SS among us who would have a tattoo under his arm. I congratulated myself for having been cautious about talking about my "activities". This SS was found and shot."

CHAPTER 16   Fighting with the FFI   ("FORCES FRANCAISES DE L'INTERIEUR")

The French Forces of the Interior refers to French Resistance fighters who General Charles de Gaulle organized following the Normandy invasion. Some of these were "Johnny come latelies" who behaved like thugs and were resented by the longer-serving Resistance members. For a period, the FFI  operated as light infantry and manned less active areas of the front. They were dressed in civilian clothing, but were identified by their "FFI" insignia on arm bands and vehicles; their weapons were often their own. In October, 1944, FFI units became part of the regular French army.

Jean-Jacques had now returned from Paris to live at his grandmother's farm. He relates how his thoughts were focused on his parents: "I volunteered for the FFI on August 1, 1944, at the age of 13, and became part of the Cérans-Foulletourte unit that was under the command of the Mayor, Monsieur Lalande. I went through ten days of training before being assigned. My job was to transport and supply the machine gun magazines. Two of my uncles who had escaped the Nazis also joined the group. My aim was to liberate my parents who were still in concentration camps.

One day, in the location called "La côte du Bruon", on the RN 23 road, a convoy coming from Le Mans got machine-gunned by the effective American "double tails" (P-47's) which were in charge of the surveillance of the roads. The Germans who were not hurt put the wounded and the dead in a truck and took refuge in the buildings of the military academy in La Flèche. As soon as they had left, we set fire to the remaining trucks and their loads. When the Germans came back to retrieve their equipment, all they found was a stack of useless black metal. They were so upset by these invisible "terrorists" that before leaving, they set the "Hôtel du Croissant" and several houses on fire, no doubt in retribution.

Many French cars had black tarps to protect them from the rain and sun. They looked somewhat like military vehicles, causing many to be machine gunned by American fighters. I knew a woman who lost her legs this way; she recently passed away at age 102.

Over the following days, we took about thirty prisoners who fought as hard as they could so they would fall into the hands of the Americans rather than the FFI's, fearful of the anger of the French.

We put them all together in an outbuilding of the City Hall, but soon realized we should separate the S.S. from the other prisoners. The S.S. were brutally beating the other prisoners, accusing them of treason. One of these young fanatics, who was only 15, was so badly wounded he had to hold his stomach to keep his guts from spilling; he still managed to yell "Heil Hitler" before dying, calling for his mother in his last breath. Former collaborators would throw stones at our prisoners and insult them; what a sad sight!!!

Some veterans of the Wehrmacht showed us pictures of their wives and children, begging us to spare them. We handed them over to General Leclerc's Division.

Again we had to separate one of the prisoners due to the brutality he was receiving from the others. They had beaten him half to death. He was Polish, and his story was very unusual: this nice mailman from Warsaw, who was married and had a daughter he had only seen once, had been drafted into the Polish army. He was soon captured by the German army and forced to join their ranks. He became the driver of an officer, and one day their car was machine-gunned by an American plane; he miraculously escaped unhurt, but the officer was killed. He started walking on the road, he did not even have a weapon, and this is when we arrested him. He wanted to join the Polish army that had been reorganized by the Americans, and asked us to help him. As he was waiting for his conscription, we found civilian clothes for him. While awaiting his fate, he worked on my grandmother's farm. She fed him and treated him like one of the family.

He was a wonderful man. He had witnessed what the Nazis had done in his country, and he thought the occupation in France was almost 'a bed of roses" in comparison! He stayed with us for about a month before leaving for the Polish military camp in Auvours. He was very emotional when he left, saying he could never thank us enough for having saved his life. One week after he left, a soldier in an American uniform knocked on our door. It was the Pole, Hubert Lukasec. He proudly showed us the insignia of his Polish unit which had been formed by the Americans. Lukasec was bringing back my grandfather's clothes. He had walked 35 miles and was so proud to have the opportunity to prove that we had been right to trust him. Unfortunately, a few months after he left, his family informed us that he had been killed in Italy while he was fighting in the "armée de la Liberté" (as the Allies were called).

CHAPTER 17   Captain Floege Becomes One of SOE's Heroes

American Captain Ernest Fred Floege performed in the field as did few other SOE Agents. For someone as active as he was to continually evade the Gestapo, while several of his networks were compromised and informers revealed every piece of information about him, his safe houses and his operations, is exemplary. Furthermore, on his second mission Captain Floege, code named "Paul", displayed a high degree of military skills which emanated from his sound judgment, as his military training was limited. While certain other descriptions of his Resistance activities during 1943 were related previously, they are not as detailed or complete as the account which follows. Here is the SOE report of April 5, 1944, from an interview concerning Captain Floege's first mission, as abridged by the author.

Fred went into the field on the night of June 14th 1943 and landed about 33 km to the south west of Tours. He was accompanied by Francois Rives, aka Olivier, the lieutenant to Sylvestre, who was going to the north of France around Lille. On arrival Fred and Rives and went to Tours, where they contacted Hercule, who was to act as Fred's w/t operator. From there Fred went first to Versailles and a fortnight later to Le Mans to the Hôtel de la Calandre, the location of Hercule's letterbox, where he found Rives, who stayed there for a further fortnight before going to his appointed circuit.

Fred's mission was to make a reconnaissance between Nantes, Laval and Le Mans, to form groups for the reception of parachuted material and to prepare targets for D-Day. He was also given some targets for immediate sabotage, but he was only to attack them if his organization were in smooth working order; his primary mission was the preparation for D-Day.

Fred had lived in Angers before the war and had numerous contacts in the district and was thus easily able to form the nucleus of his organization. He contacted friends of whose loyalty he was absolutely certain and appointed them as leaders in various districts. They in turn recruited a small number of men to form a network. Six district leaders were so appointed and Fred gave them instructions in the use of explosives, which they passed on to their group. Fred also appointed two couriers, one being his son Claude, who was living in Angers and who joined the organization at his own request at the beginning of November, and the other a teacher known as Pierre, whom Fred described as age 24, small, fair haired.

The first parachute drop of material took place two months after Fred's arrival and six further drops were made during the next four months. Fred twice tried to arrange for the reception of agents, but the only man dropped to him was his wire transfer operator André Bouchardon, code named Michel, who arrived on August 19th, 1943.

Fred had his headquarters in Mée, a hamlet 9 km south east of Craon in Mayenne and 12 km southwest of Chateau Gontier. His contact there was a man called Fournier who kept a small grocer's shop and hotel. This was a particularly suitable place for his headquarters as there were no Germans in this district for 30 miles around. Michel, Fred's radio operator, changed his placed of transmission many times and had four or five houses from which he could work. He most frequently transmitted from Mée however and never experienced any difficulties. He never saw any German goniometer trucks in his neighborhood.

During the six months of his first mission in the field, Fred used the cover of being a timber merchant. This cover, he stated, was particularly good as it provided a pretext for his numerous journeys and for his employment of personnel. He was known in the organization as 'Georges' or more officially as Monsieur Tessier.

Fred's organization operated successfully until, by December, it was completely broken up owing to a series of arrests. Fred attributed the start of the trouble to his connection with Hercule and to the consequent fact that they had many contacts in common, but the final breakup was caused by the arrest of his courier, Fred's son. The sequence of events follows.

When Fred first went into the field he had a radio operator specifically attached to him, but this w/t operator had not arrived as yet. He had to send his messages through Hercule who he said was already "blown". He himself had eventually to put Hercule into one of his own safe houses. When his own radio operator arrived in August, he cut all contact with Hercule, but by this time the damage was done and many members of Hercule's organization, who were subsequently arrested, had knowledge of him, thus putting the Gestapo on his trail. He saw Hercule for the last time in September. After that time the latest news that he had of Hercule was that he was on the run after his wife's arrest; he had no definite information that Hercule himself had been arrested.

On November 1st, 1943, Dr. Goude and about 20 to 25 people belonging to the network around Chateau-du-Loir were arrested. Some of them were in contact with Hercule and hence to Fred, owing to his own contact with Hercule. Fred expected repercussions in his organization. He sent a message to London to that effect on November 5th. The arrests of these people caused a great deal of talk in the district, as they were all tortured. Dr. Goude was even tortured in the presence of his wife, but he did not talk.

Towards the end of October several members of Hercule's network in Le Mans were arrested, including his courier and Monsieur and Madame Brault of the Hôtel de la Calandre. As Fred was also known to them, they could give descriptions of him to the Gestapo and thus provide another link in the chain of information leading to him. The first to be arrested was a courier, a young woman. She, no doubt, was coerced to give the Gestapo the address of the letterbox at the Hôtel de la Calandre. Brault and later his wife were also arrested and the latter had information as to Fred's real identity as she had been present when he was hailed by a friend whom he had known in Angers before the war. Fred held the opinion that Madame Brault gave this formation to the Gestapo.

About the same time a butcher belonging to Fred's organization was also arrested. He had been a rescuer of an American airman who had bailed out. He had information about one of Fred's local headquarters and one day he came in a Gestapo car to this place. He also gave the Gestapo information about the first dump formed by Fred of the material he had received.

Although the various arrests mentioned above were contributory factors in giving the Gestapo information about Fred and his subversive activities, the arrest of his courier, Fred's son, was the main cause leading to the breakup of his organization. Fred had information that the Gestapo was on his trail and therefore sent his two couriers to warn his different groups. On Wednesday, December 22nd, he sent his son to one of these groups and learned only later that there was no train going in that direction that day. His son was therefore obliged to stay in a hotel and was probably picked up in a random search of the hotel. This was only conjecture on Fred's part, as he had no definite news about his son. The sad fact became apparent, however, that his son must have talked and given away not only his own father, but all information concerning the whole organization. This is proven by the fact that his son had no incriminating documents on him when he was captured, with the exception of a left luggage slip for a suitcase left by Fred at the station in Angers. The following day Pierre, the second courier, was also arrested. He had gone to warn the group in La Chartre and on his return went to the house of one of Fred's contacts where he was arrested. He made no attempt to resist arrest, immediately dropping his pistol to the floor. Fred believes that he also talked. About 40 to 45 people belonging to networks in various centers were arrested at precisely the same time, proving conclusively that Fred's son had provided information, as he was the only person to know the location of all the groups.

On the evening of December 23rd, the Gestapo arrived at the Fournier house in Mée, expecting to find both Fred and his radio operator, but Fred had left shortly before. Michel was there, however, and was having dinner when the Gestapo burst in. He was sitting at a table when the door opened and the Gestapo yelled "hands up". Michel put his hands up and then one of the Gestapo came behind him, examined the distinctive mark on his face and asked Michel if he was known by "André". Michel acknowledged that he was, whereupon the Gestapo started to put handcuffs on him, but Michel began to resist arrest. He knocked down the man who was handcuffing him and was then attacked by six others and he himself was knocked to the floor. As he still continued to struggle, he was shot as he lay on the floor and received a bullet in his chest. He pretended to be mortally wounded and was put into the back of a car and taken away; one German was in the back of the car beside him and two others were in front. Just before, while he was lying on the floor of the hotel, he had been searched, but his coat was lying open and the contents of the pockets were not examined. In one of his pockets was his revolver, which Fred told him to always carry since the trouble had started in their district. This revolver was not discovered and as Michel was being driven away, he managed to ease it out of his pocket and shoot his captors. He had seven bullets and put two in each of the Germans. The car, now out of control, collapsed into the ditch. The German beside him was still alive and made a feeble effort to grab him, so Michel gave him the seventh bullet to finish him off. It was learned later that two of the Germans were killed outright and that the third was so badly wounded he has probably died afterwards. Michel then left the car, went to a farmer who had on prior occasions hidden some material for his network and asked him to cut off the handcuffs. The farmer was scared, however, and told him to leave, but Michel threatened him and he finally cut the chain between the handcuffs. After spending the night in a barn, Michel went next morning to another farmer who was not as frightened and managed to get the handcuffs off entirely. Michel was now anxious to convey a warning to Fred, so, in spite of this bullet wound, he walked 25 km across country to Mée, a village near Laval, where the hotel proprietor was in his network. He arrived late in the evening of December 24 and remained until Fred himself arrived and found him.

The Gestapo had expected to find Fred at Mée, but he had left shortly before for Angers. The Gestapo must then have further questioned his son, who obviously gave them the address of his father's hiding place in Angers, as they appeared there early on the morning of December 24th. The house, which belonged to Fred's mother-in-law, was in the center of Angers, but was almost like a country house, as it had a large walled garden in front. The Gestapo posted their men on three sides of the home, but not on the fourth, which had a wall about 3 meters high. Fred was out in the garden when they arrived; he heard people running towards the house and saw two or three men running at him. He immediately got out his pistol and raised it ready to shoot, whereupon the men, who did not at first appear to be armed, shouted: "Watch out, he is going to shoot", and ran away. Then they started shooting all around with automatic weapons. Their fire revealed to Fred where they were and he realized that the high wall was not being guarded. He went into the house, ran up to the first floor and managed to jump down to the wall and so escape. Shots were fired at him, but he was not hit. He stated that the men who first ran at him might have had revolvers, but they certainly did not fire to begin with. His mother-in-law was arrested. After his escape Fred went to a friend's. He had been wearing his slippers when the Gestapo surprised him in the garden, and needed to borrow shoes, a hat, a coat and a bicycle. He then went to Mée to warn Michel where he learned that there had been some shooting and some men had been taken away by the Germans. He therefore wanted to warn other members of his organization and went to the hotel where he found Michel.

The organization was thus completely broken up. The people arrested were taken first to Angers and, a fortnight later; some of the less important ones were sent directly to Germany. Fred was not able to obtain any information about the others, who were, so far as he knew, still in the main prison in Angers.

Fred's son had no incriminating documents on him when he was captured, as he had memorized the message he was to deliver. He had however in his notebook the left luggage slip for a suitcase which Fred had left at the Angers station and which he had asked his son to get out. When the trouble started in the district, Fred wished to send a report to London and, at the beginning of December, went to Paris to a letterbox of which the address had been given to him in London. This address was: M. Duquesne in care of 13 rue Marius-Aufan, Levallois, Seine. When Fred first went there, he introduced himself as Albert and asked that his letter might be delivered. Madame Duquesne, who had opened the door to him, agreed to do so. Fred went back about a fortnight later to see if the letter had been sent and was told by Madame Duquesne, who again received him, that he must have made a mistake as they knew nothing about Albert or any letter to be delivered. She returned the letter, which Fred put in his suitcase. On his return to Angers, he left the case at the station, as he did not want to carry it about the town and it was this case which he had asked his son to get out for him. In the letter Fred had reported on the trouble in the district, mentioning Mr. Bault's arrest. He also provided information about a big artillery ammunition dump which the Germans had made near Le Lude in Sarthe. Everything was written in Playfair code, however, and Fred did not think that it could be deciphered by the Germans (Playfair is a cypher using pairs of letters rather than single letters, but which was in use by the Germans who could be expected to break the code). He is sure that the address to which he went was the right one. He was once asked to come in by Madame Duquesne and in an adjoining room saw a young man whom he believed was an agent. It was not Monsieur Duquesne. On each occasion he was received by the wife, whom he described as aged about 30 with brown hair. She always denied knowledge of any courrier. Fred does not connect in any way his visit to this address with the arrest of members of his organization. He was the only person to know the address.

When Fred and Michel met at Mée on the evening of December 24th 1943, they decided that the trouble in the district was so extensive that they had better leave. They found another bicycle for Michel and cycled 70 km the following day, Michel still with a bullet in his chest, to another of their districts to see if the trouble had also reached there. When they arrived, they found that everyone had been arrested and all the material was gone. They then set out for Paris. Fred tried again to contact London through Madame Duquesne, but she said she knew nothing about him, although he had given her more detailed information and said that she probably knew what kind of help he was asking for. She persisted in her statement that she knew nothing and said furthermore that her husband was not there.

After this failure they went to a place in Paris known to Michel and there met someone in a different network who promised to send a message to London, saying, however, that an answer could not be expected for a month. They waited for a month, but no answer was forthcoming. Michel then remembered that one of his fellow students in the w/t training school was in Laval, so they went there and, within an hour, had contacted the w/t operator, whose name is unknown to Fred, who promised to send a message. Thus relations were re-established with London, as, soon afterwards, a reply came asking them to name a new letter box and wait till they were contacted. The same reply asked this network to give them any necessary assistance, but they did not require any, as they were staying in a perfectly safe place in Paris. During this time Fred traveled about in his region to see what remained of his organization, but Michel stayed mostly in Paris recuperating.

Towards the end of February Fred and Michel were contacted by a young woman who gave the password sent by Fred to London. They left Paris on February 24th and were taken to Lyon where they arrived the following day. From Lyon they went to Perpignan and crossed the Pyrenees into Spain. They had two guides and their journey was extremely well organized. Fred expected it to be much more trying. There was not much snow where they crossed, but he had heard of another party, which crossed further west through Andorra and took four days to reach Spain. Some of them got frostbite. Fred and Michel arrived in the United Kingdom at the end of March.

Fred's reconnaissance travels during January and February determined that a group in Laval was intact and thought that it would be useful to get in touch with them, as they had connections in Laval and throughout Mayenne generally. So far as he knew they had no communications with London. They could be contacted through the Postmaster: Harris.

The Gestapo headquarters in Angers was in the Rue de la Prefecture and the Rue Delage, occupying four blocks. No one was allowed to go near. Fred had no information about the officers but he knew that many Gestapo officials and French informers were working there. It was close to the station and, if a bomb were dropped near the station, it would probably hit their headquarters. Fred stated that to his knowledge the Gestapo did not arrest people by chance, but always had information about them. This was the case in Chateau-du-Loir and in connection with Fred himself. If they lost the trail, they do not take further action for a moment, but waited, confident that the required information would eventually reach them.

Fred did not know the real names of any informers, but had heard of one who came to Hercule's house and later to another organization. He looked like a beggar, always badly dressed and unshaven.

Before Fred was on the run, he was never controlled (had his papers checked), but afterwards was controlled about 15 times. He used a bicycle generally and went by train as little as possible, avoiding especially stations like Le Mans. If he had to go by train, he boarded it at a small station. After his escape however, he used the train more frequently and was controlled several times, especially on the trains to Lyon, where he had been on several occasions before his final journey. He was twice controlled in Laval but the Germans did not examine his papers very closely, only looking at his photograph. Controls in general are increasing and they constitute a considerable danger for an inexperienced agent. Le Mans station is particularly dangerous and also Lyon's. Controls on the trains in the west are more rare, but almost inevitable on the line between Paris and the south. Michel was twice controlled. He did not travel much because of the distinctive mark on his face, which made him conspicuous. At some time during his stay in the field Fred obtained new identity papers including an "ausweis" (control paper) for the zone Coterie. These were made for him by a French gendarme named Eude in Conlie, Sarthe. On the whole the French police cooperated with these subversive organizations and the gendarmes were especially helpful. According to what Fred had gathered, the Milice would be liquidated when the Allies landed in France.

Fred found life as an agent in an occupied territory easier than he expected, but he thought that, nevertheless, students should not be given too rosy a picture, lest they neglected the obvious security precautions. The main thing is to appear natural. If an agent is always looking over his shoulder, as if he expected the Gestapo to arrest him at any moment, he will inevitably make himself conspicuous. One point of security was emphasized by Fred, namely, if several agents were dropped together, none of them should mention the name of any other. When he arrived in Le Mans at the Hôtel de la Calandre, Fred found that Rives had told all about him: that an American named Fred, who belonged to the same organization, was coming. Agents who have newly arrived in the field are inclined to talk too much. This is probably due to a very natural, but nonetheless dangerous, wish to show off.

Fred believed that the airfields in his district were not very active, but he mentioned a more active airfield south east of Alençon.

For some time previous to Fred's departure from France there was considerable movement of German troops. In December about 100 trains passed through Le Mans with troops and tanks going towards Russia. Recently Fred had not noticed any special activity. About a week before Fred left France, that is, towards the middle of February of 1944, he went to Vitré and, on his way back, contacted the group in Laval which was still intact. From them he learned that there was what amounted to a complete armored Division in the district around Vitré, about 50 men in each of the small country villages. They are crack troops, including some of the Afrika corps. Their headquarters is in Vitré itself.

Fred was interrogated about different factories and made the following report. The factory at Précigné was active. It was there that the munitions discovered at his dump were taken.

The Junkers factory was working day and night. It is a small factory on the edge of Le Mans, employing about 300 workers. They make and assemble engines, but Fred does not know what type. The roar of the test bench can be heard 20 km away. Fred knows nothing about any underground works at Solemnes. Regarding the Bollée works, Fred believes this is a small but very important factory making piston rings. It is an excellent plant and its products are of first class quality. Before the war, piston rings from this factory were fitted to all the best makes of French cars. Fred does not know where the production is being sent at present, but supposed that it is sent to all engine factories. He knows an organizer in Le Mans who tried, without success however, to blow up the transformers there. The factory in Léon was a large factory before the war; Fred does not think that it is in action now, as he never saw any workmen. He believes that it is used as a storehouse, as it is heavily guarded and there are anti-aircraft guns close to it. The Gnome and Rhone factory at Arnage was badly damaged by the American raids in September (and in July) and was almost out of action for a time. It has started working again however and, at the time Fred left, was almost at full production. The factory of Carel et Fouche is a large factory within the city of Le Mans, about 600 meters to the southwest of the main railroad station. It consists of a long central building, which, being of wood could easily be set on fire, and four other smaller buildings. It is not heavily guarded and does not have a night shift. It produces parts for submarines and airplane wings, especially the frames. No assembly is done there.

Regarding the railroad line from Le Mans to Paris, it is entirely electric and a steam train is used only if the transformer has been blown. Fred only saw a steam train once. Fred had seen no stocks of coal along the railroad line, but had seen considerable stocks in Chartres.

Sabotage around Le Mans had been inconsiderable, but Fred had intended to attack his secondary targets after Christmas, being unable with the breakup of his organization. Fred suggested the following targets in his district. On a siding near Longuefuye, Mayenne, there are some 14 or 15 petrol tank wagons hidden by camouflage. The group in Laval reported that construction was going on at the airport situated about one kilometer west of the main road from Laval to Chateau-Gontier. The airfield is not active at the moment, but it is being enlarged and runways are being constructed. On the southern boundary, close to the side road leading from the main road to the village of St. Pierre, there is a dump of about 200 very heavy bombs, concealed by camouflage. And, in Le Lude there is a large dump of artillery ammunition.

Paul Volunteers for a Second Mission into France

Captain Fred Floege ("Paul") received a critical review following his first mission. On April 4, 1944, his reviewer stated: Intelligence: not outstanding; Candour: inclined to be taciturn; Powers of Observation: not remarkable; Temperament: a serious, rather stolid type, older than the average agent. It was noted, with exclamation mark, that Fred was: American! In spite of this review, Fred volunteered and was accepted for a second mission. One must wonder about the objectivity of the reviewer, for Fred performed quite well on his first mission and remarkably on his second. His next assignment was to replace an agent who had been organizing a maquis, a gorilla group of Resistants living in rugged country in the east of France near Switzerland. This Maquis was relatively small and poorly armed. Captain Floege's mission was to build an organization and arrange parachute drops to supply it for carrying out sabotage. Fred was 45 years old during this mission. He parachuted into the Doubs departement, on May 4, 1944. The specific objectives of his mission were: (1) sabotage of railway objectives (the destruction of railroad lines and locomotives) in preparation for D-Day (June 6, 1944); (2) destruction of communications; (3) guerilla action for D-Day; (4) stop or reduce production in the area's Peugeot plant. His area of action: Belfort-Lure-Montbéliard in the Doubs departement. His report of March 3, 1945, abridged by the author, follows.

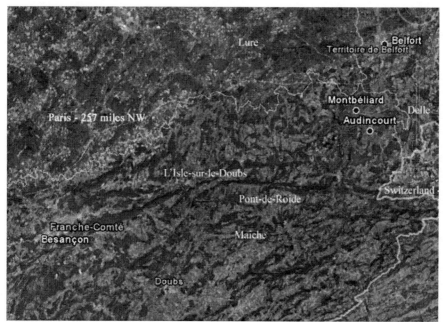

"When Michel (the code name of André Bouchardon, Fred's w/t operator) and I set out for the Belfort region, I had the impression that, judging from the latest developments, we were jumping into a bed of hot coals. We were dropped at 1:30 a.m. near Pont de Roide and received by Lieutenant Joly, the commander of the local Maquis, who had arranged everything perfectly. Things were so well organized that two days later I was able to start my activities.

I started contacting the various groups I was supposed to meet. In the Belfort area there was almost no one left. Many people had been arrested and all the stores of supplies had fallen into German hands. I finally contacted Jean Paul who began to form some new groups. A few days after our arrival I was able to note that the Germans were no more in evidence here than elsewhere.

May 6, 1944 My first outing was almost catastrophic. I was returning from a visit with Michel and had lost time in my tour; it was 10:50 at night by the time I arrived in Montbéliard. Not at all accustomed to the city streets, I started up the main street, but soon realized my mistake. I stopped and began retracing my steps when I saw two Germans on the opposite sidewalk, one in civilian clothes, and the other in uniform, rifle slung over his shoulder. As I was about to get back on my bicycle the civilian cried out "Halte", then both came toward me, the civilian saying in a very bad French "why you go like that and after like that?"-meaning to ask why I had changed direction. I could not, of course, tell him that I was a stranger in the neighborhood and had lost my way, so as hazily as possible I replied, imitating his way of speaking, "Oh, lots to drink; a little 'that way'", pretending to be slightly drunk. The civilian didn't seem very convinced, but the soldier said: "Let him go". Then the civilian motioned that I should move on. When the chain of my bicycle slipped as I started to climb on, the civilian, attempting a witticism, remarked: "Not a little 'that way'; very much 'that way'!"

May 25, 1944 Soon afterwards I contacted Marc in charge of the sabotage party inside the Peugeot Plant (this plant was producing assemblies for the Luftwaffe's Focke-Wulf fighter). As we toured the plant Marc informed me that little effective sabotage had been carried out. My conclusion was that our destruction of the two main transformers would not stop production because twelve individual transformers could immediately supply the largest part of the plant. Marc objected to other plans for sabotage I suggested for fear of German reprisals in case of German deaths. That led me to another plan for interrupting production. We would destroy the railroad lines so that raw materials would be shut off. On May 25 we started the program. After neutralizing the French tunnel guard, the rails within were unscrewed by Lt. Joly's party while my party stopped a train a few miles away. After ordering everyone to leave the train, I launched it and jumped off. Because the rails were insufficiently unscrewed, the train ran through the tunnel; and, at 50 mph the "phantom train" crashed into another train almost in the Montbéliard station. This type of sport became very popular throughout the region. From that day on every time the rail traffic was resumed, sabotage was carried out. When D-Day came the sabotage on the Belfort to Besançon line was such that for ten days not a single train came through. From D-Day on the Peugeot plant became unimportant through lack of material and by the walkout of some 50% of the workers as ordered by Lt. Joly. First the plant's smoke screens were discontinued and then the anti-aircraft guns disappeared and finally the German head manager moved to Longwy.

At the time of the Allied debarkation our Isle sur la Doubs team derailed a train in the Beaune les Dames tunnel, and a few hours later a second piled on top of the first. But, we were constrained in our mission by having very little equipment at our disposal, almost no arms and very few explosives, all in Lt. Joly's hands. This Isle sur le Doubs team was first rate. The chief of the team was nicknamed 'Tito'. A very young man he was: simple, courageous, and tireless. Without explosives to blow up a bridge or tunnel, he improvised using 155 mm artillery shells recuperated from 1940.

It was through Jules Cesar, the lieutenant of Sylvestre, that I had learned that the Belfort group was no longer functioning, the Germans having arrested most of the men and confiscated their material. I told Jules Cesar to try to form a new group, but there, as with the Peugeot plant, the D-Day debarkation intervened.

I went to Lure several times as well, to try to establish a contact. But the men suggested by Lt. Joly flatly stated that they could not participate and had no men at their disposal.

Then by a rather adventurous maneuver I tried to contact a group composed of railroad and postal employees. I sent a letter to the P. T. T. controller in Lure, in which I arranged a rendezvous; then I asked London to broadcast the message "For a surprise. It is a surprise isn't it, Monsieur Controller?" I communicated the exact text of this message to the Controller who unfortunately did not come to the rendezvous point as he was wary because of the many recent arrests at Lure and Belfort. Here as well, the D-Day debarkation cut all my plans short. Fortunately I was later able to contact a team from Aillevillers through one of my men, Boby Dormoy. I supplied this Maquis with arms and explosives received in July. The team did excellent work and neutralized all activity at the Aillevillers depot, a very important center.

On D-Day we were ready in the Montbéliard area, so far as our Maquis groups were concerned, but we did not have the necessary equipment. We started hoping to receive what we needed from a drop during the next moon period. With forty men I established a Maquis in the center of my area near a village called Lomont, which is not the same as the Fort de Lomont. My intention was to attack from there the Belfort – Lure railroad line as well as the other lines in the area and also convoys on the roads. However, I had to wait for a munitions drop, for all I had was four old French Lebel rifles, four Sten guns, two pistols and my carbine. We had no explosives. We waited for 15 days without receiving a drop. Thus on the 6th of June I had many men at my disposal, but nothing to supply them with. I decided to set up with some 40 men in the Banlinot forest while Lt. Joly went into woods near Ecot with about 200 armed men and 400 unarmed. The two fields, which we had designated as "Officer" and "Corporal", were very near my position; the Belfort – Lure line was also within easy reach. Lt. Joly and Tito kept watchful eyes on the Besançon line. Some people awaited the day with impatience, but we always waited for night fall and, with each daybreak, we were a little more discouraged. Michel, my w/t operator, had sent several requests to London, but in the run up to D-Day London must have been preoccupied. According to certain rumors, I had sold out to the Germans, for I kept making promises and the planes I promised never came. I often wondered why my own men did not turn against me. Of the 40, 6 had submachine guns, 4 had revolvers, 3 had rifles and old Lebels and I had my carbine with one charger and 50 cartridges between us, and not a bit of explosives, not even one grenade.

I was nevertheless determined to carry out the order: "Attack all convoys". I ordered each patrol group to attack any German group they felt able to overcome and to confiscate their arms. Three of my men on night patrol on the outskirts of the village of Lomont suddenly found themselves facing five Germans. They opened fire killing three and wounding the other two. One of the wounded probably died in the woods, but the second regained his base and signaled the alert. An attack on the woods and village by 400 to 500 Cossacks forced us to retreat. I was able to gather all my men with no losses, but the Germans took reprisal on the village, killing a man and burning three farms. After this incident I set up a sabotage team between Montbéliard and Belfort. Lt. Joly kept pressing me for arms and ammunition, but to no avail.

The program put into effect by Lt. Joly had been excellent with ample provisions made and the greatest part went off according to schedule. The exception was the post office at Montbéliard where explosives had been poorly placed. The Bavilliers Bridge was blown up and a few hours later a locomotive went hurtling down. Almost all the railway water stations between Belfort and Beaune les Dames were destroyed. All telephone lines were also destroyed, even high tension wires, particularly along the Kemps line.

Attacks on isolated vehicles were carried out. I had placards posted on homes of Germans and collaborationists. Confusion was so great that the Germans did not venture on the highways except in large numbers. Unfortunately, we had to discontinue this sort of activity in view of the return of more Germans from the fronts and our meager armaments.

July 8, 1944 During the 15 days we had been waiting for a drop of arms and ammunition, all that dropped was heavy rain every day. Some of my men, disgusted, returned to their work. I conducted the remnants to the Ecot Maquis under command of Lt. Joly. From the first day on a real friendship had been established between we two and I did my best to get the necessary arms and ammunition. There was no exaggeration when I sent SOS messages to London. What I feared happened on July 8. At 10:00 I was informed that the Ecot Maquis had been attacked in strength at 07:00. Immediately I sent an alarm to all the Maquis in the area with orders to rescue Lt. Joly. At the time I was in command of the Hericourt area. This is what took place a short time before. The commanding officer under Lt. Joly's orders tried to leave his men and take refuge in Switzerland, where he was arrested and returned to the Ecot Maquis. Lt. Joly asked me to take command of that area. I started out with 60 men and all the arms we had, in the direction of Ecot, but half way there we were informed that the action was over. The Maquis had been dispersed with Lt. Joly and 15 of his men killed. The battle had lasted for two and a half hours. This was a terrible loss. Lt. Joly had been the one person I trusted most.

From that day on I was practically put in command by these circumstances. For twelve days it was impossible to find Colonel Morin who was Lt. Joly's direct chief. Nobody knew what to do or how to react against the disastrous effect of the defeat of the Ecot Maquis and the loss of Lt. Joly. One after the other all of the section commanders came to me asking what to do and for help. I took care of them and they remained attached to me.

When finally the Colonel had been found in his hiding place, I had a meeting with him. He designated Monsieur Ponsot as successor to Lt. Joly, but all the section commanders refused and insisted on my nomination. I agreed, because meanwhile I had discovered a lack of organization owing to political reasons. Arms and ammunition had been hidden by order of Colonel Morin at a time when Lt. Joly and I had needed them badly.

Finally an agreement was reached and I was placed in command of the region. Contrary to what the Germans thought and said, the Resistance in the area was not beaten off; rather, a new and powerful movement started.

The Ecot defeat cost us 16 dead, including my friend Lt. Joly, and 29 prisoners had been taken, leaving the men leaderless and scattered. I must mention that, outside of commanding my own small personal groups, I had already been Joly's second in command. All these men who had come to know me returned to me. Without knowing exactly how it happened I found myself practically in charge of the movement. A certain few were not satisfied, but most were.

I regrouped the survivors into small Maquis groups. Those who returned home were heavily cautioned. The Germans issued propaganda material saying that all resistance had been shattered. That was my signal for renewing operations. The German triumph was of short duration. Only a few days after the Ecot defeat, rails were once again being blown and I had the Hericourt Maquis working as far as the Montbéliard station. Three locomotives were induced to jump the track. The garage where the Germans equipped light Ford trucks with light machine guns was partially burned, as well as 12 vehicles.

July 19, 1944 We finally received the arms and ammunition we had been waiting so long for. We began to organize our forces into sections, companies, battalions, and finally, regiments. Meanwhile, to show the Germans that the

Resistance was still alive, we redoubled our attacks on railway and communications targets plus power supply lines. One could hear every night the roar of some explosion. During one of our last meetings, Lt. Joly told me how much he was disappointed with so much political interference within the Resistance movement. Therefore, I told everyone that from now on I would not hear a word of political speeches and I threw out all those who were at the bottom of it. That is how I unified the two main groups in the area, Liberation and F T P. All the men and even some leaders stood with me, so I started the preparation of a real action. I made a trip to Switzerland with Sylvestre, who I contacted a few weeks before, and fixed details for medical supplies and made arrangements with the Hospital of Porentruy. Then with my executive officer we explored the sector in which we intended to bring the action and another officer took steps to prepare the stores of rations. During all that time the sabotages went on and the favorite of all where the phantom trains, so-called because they ran through the stations without an engineer or anyone else aboard.

The Germans did everything to remedy our renewed activity. Barricades on all highways were set up, automobile and truck patrols were armed and ready to fire and periodic raids were made on the villages. From July 15th to August 15th, I found myself in more than one tight spot. One morning I left my house on my bicycle and started off in the direction of Montbéliard, when I suddenly heard behind me the motor of a car that seemed to be traveling at the same rate of speed as I. When the vehicle, a closed automobile, reached me, I realized that it was the Germans. All the windows were lowered and rifles and submachine guns jutted from all openings except one where a head appeared. My blood ran cold on seeing that one of the occupants was a man we call scarface, "La Balafre". He stared at me and then the car stopped about 20 meters ahead. Did he have an exact description of me and was he going to arrest me? I could still make a quick getaway as it was a winding road, but I decided instead to carry on as if nothing were amiss. I bypassed the car and nobody made a move to stop me. The car started up again and bypassed me without paying any further attention. It had hardly gone 200 meters when a truckload of Germans completely armed passed me. I congratulated myself for not having tried to run off.

August 16, 1944 We started our move toward the Lomont Mountains. I must say here that the only one in favor of my project was the D M R Ligne, so I took the responsibility for the action. There is one thing more I have to say about the period from July 8th to August 15th. A terrible hunt was organized by the Gestapo to identify and arrest all those who had been in the Maquis and had resumed work after the Ecot defeat. They launched all their men and women, promising them important rewards. So we decided to counter the action and almost every day three or four of their dogs fell dead in the street or in their homes. The disorganization was such that we could do almost what we wanted without any disturbance. The body of every one of our victims was immediately searched and their homes investigated so we discovered many lists ready to be given to the Gestapo. Most of the names on these lists where our people.

Not wanting to remain on the scene of the Ecot failure, I made preparations for the taking of a strong position. I took a trip to Switzerland to assure myself of medical cooperation. With the assistance of Hippolyte, Sylvestre and a few others, I amassed food stocks and all I could get in the way of clothing, and we made a list of usable vehicles in the region. I mention only in passing the differences of opinion and discussions I had on the subject with certain incapable and tiresome people such as the so-called Colonel Boulaya and Belin. Finally on August 16th with enough munitions to equip about 1000 men, I started to organize men and material.

We got right to work. Trucks that we had taken from merchants and manufacturers were in operation all night long and sometimes even during the day. The Maquis of Hericourt constituted our most delicate transport operation as it was a convoy of 18 trucks traveling more than 50 km. The convoy was held up at the crucial Voujeaucourt grade crossing where a German sentinel was posted. On the first truck was an Alsatian who got down and reprimanded the guard severely. At the ominous sight of submachine guns on all the cabs, the guard hurriedly opened the gates without knowing what it was all about. Before the Germans could recover from their astonishment we were already installed at Lomont. I went there myself the afternoon of August 21st. On the morning of the 22nd we launched our first attack.

Before getting into the Lomont story, I want to give a few more details on the outcome of the Ecot Maquis. In order to protect the men who had to return to their homes from being denounced by collaborationist, as well as from action on the part of Gestapo agents, we had to undertake a severe purge. We selected a committee and with all documents in hand started a series of trials in the Hericourt, Montbéliard and Audincourt sectors, where three to four men were condemned daily. We extended our sabotage of telephone lines to include minor lines. These two combined actions resulted in completely paralyzing the Gestapo and in this manner we were able to protect our men until the actual time of departure.

The Waffen incident, concerning its chief Paul and three aides, took place at the beginning of August. It was through a certain woman that Paul Maillebuaru managed to get in touch with Mr. Gendheur, chief of the Hericourt Maquis, under pretext of being tired of working for the Germans and wanting to avenge a man named Deschamps. He offered his services to the Maquis. Gendheur, a well-meaning old man, thinking he had a real 'find', explained the situation to me and asked my advice. I told him to arrange a rendezvous with Paul, which he did. I appointed six men to take care of him as soon as he arrived. However, he was not alone, but had brought three of his men along who reached for their revolvers at the command "Hands up". My men carried out my instructions and shot all four.

In those days the atmosphere was pretty tense due to the fact that our preparatory work had become of prime importance. The Germans also sensed the tension and were all the more distraught because of their lack of information. Once again I had a very narrow escape. Despite the precautionary measures I was taking, I found myself confronted by a barricade; turning back was out of the question. I took out my papers and everything seemed to be going well until one of the soldiers in searching my pack came upon my dagger jackknife, part of our parachute equipment. I had taken it with me on my trip to Switzerland because of the dogs. I explained that as I was a wood merchant, the knife was useful to me in the woods. I was nevertheless taken to the officer in charge who began to question me. "What are you doing around here if you live near the channel?" "I'm looking for a place for my family to stay as they are uneasy about staying there because of the fighting that has been going on." "Is your family here?" "No, they are in Paris staying with some friends." "Are you Alsatian?" "No." "Where did you learn German?" "In school. Then I worked for years for the Todt organization." "Wouldn't you have preferred to stay at home to await the liberators?" he said sardonically. "Of course not. I used to supply the Todt organization with large amounts of wood, and the terrorists began to send me threatening letters. So, I came here for reasons of safety." "Yeah yeah" he said and very politely returned my dark glasses that he had taken and went as far as to replace my knife in its case. What won't they do for a collaborator!

As I have said, I almost had to abandon the Belfort sector, first of all because there was so little time before the debarkation, and then I had so little material at my disposal. I contacted the Belfort F. F. I. group, assigned targets to them and promised material, which I am afraid they never received.

August 22, 1944   Our next action was the battle for Lomont and occupation of the Maiche plateau. Every night until the 22nd, we carried arms and supplies, and at the same time we drained all the trucks of the Montbéliard, Sochaux and Hericourt area. I moved myself to a new sector on the afternoon of August 21st. At 7:00 a.m. on the 22nd the Germans opened fire in a surprise attack, before all of our defenses had been put in place. Germans were coming from the village of Pont de Roide to attack us. The attack caught me by surprise as I thought I would have at least that day to arrange our positions. Our automatic rifle post and the line of men were well placed. Seeing this, the Germans set themselves up on a rise facing us called the Tour Carrée. We on the other hand were well situated in a wood. However, I soon realized that our men were becoming panicky. Small groups of them, carbines in hand, tried to get away. I ordered them to return to their quarters to await my orders. Checking to see that all my automatic rifles were well-placed, about 60 of them, I instructed each rifle bearer to fire with purpose: for each bullet fired one German had to fall. Our Bren gunners, who were permanently in position, replied at once (the Bren gun was a British-made light machine gun). The Germans, some 180 meters north of us, were firing continuously.

I then ordered the submachine gun group not to fire until the Germans were within 80 meters. Having thus assured the solidarity of our position I tried to envisage possible German moves and realized what the Germans had in mind. It was this: to machine gun us on one side in order to force us out the other, where more Germans were waiting for us. We could hold up all right against the infantry, but there were also tanks, combat cars and motor drawn anti-aircraft guns to be reckoned with. So, I decided to block with downed trees and stone the three roads leading to our positions. First of all I asked for a volunteer group chief to go with 30 men to fell trees across the Pierrefontaine road, some two miles distance, where the battle had not yet reached. Of my four reserve section chiefs, not one made a move. I could envisage another Ecot disaster, so I had to try to instill new resolve in them. They were not lacking in courage, but confidence in themselves and in their chief. I passed on the orders to my assistant officer and addressed the men personally: "I want 30 volunteers to come with me." Sgt. Thiebault, who had come from the First French Regiment to join us, volunteered with his 10 men, others following suit. Soon I had my 30 men armed with two automatic rifles, submachine guns and rifles. We had gone half the distance when I discovered there were only 15 men with one automatic rifle remaining with us. Just before reaching our destination I ran into a light truck bringing men to join us. I asked if they had seen any Germans on the way and they had not. I gave them the axes and saws we had brought to start chopping down trees while we kept watch. We had arrived without seeing a soul. This made me certain that the Germans hadn't yet penetrated this part. We went as far as the turn to begin placing my men, when from the bend in the road hardly 100 meters away there was automatic rifle fire. I was literally sprayed with bullets but not touched. Our one automatic rifle was in place, but the Hindu in charge trembled so that he could not fire. Sgt. Thiebault seized the gun and covered us with furious fire. I arranged my men under cover and the battle began through a small clearing. The Germans had four automatic rifles, but I silenced two. I saw a big fellow gesticulating like a demon, so I aimed at him and the next day I found out the most dangerous Feldwebel of the Gestapo, la Balafre, 'Scarface', had been killed on that very spot by a bullet right in his heart. A few feet from me a young fellow groaned and toppled over. The sergeant told me his five chargers were empty (a 'charger' is British parlance for an ammunition clip), others as well where out of rounds. The encounter had lasted 15 minutes when I decided to battle in retreat, which I covered with the few remaining men who still had ammunition. Results of this engagement for us: one dead, one wounded. The next day I learned that the Germans too had retreated at the same time. It was the moment to say: "And the battle ended for want of men". We regained our camp without incident, bringing our one wounded. We had hidden the body of our one dead and went back that night to find him. It was 11:00PM and the Pont de Roide battle was still going on. News that we had earlier left the battlefield spread around the camp like wildfire, and I realized that I had poured salt on the wound. Fortunately there was no more panic as all were willing to follow the example of the colonel, for I was always 'colonel', I couldn't seem to make them understand that I was not a colonel. I finally had to settle for 'commandant'.

As the others saw us come back they regained confidence and the counterattack began. The arrival of Captain Sicand and his 81 SAS paratroopers (Operation Abel) redoubled the morale of our men. About noon the enemy was chased from his position and for two hours everything was quiet. About 14:00 hours the battle recommenced as the Germans emerged from the direction of Pont de Roide and from Pierrefontaine as well, and a furious battle took place around the Brisepouteau farm. I sent reinforcements, but at the same time four German motor drawn anti-aircraft guns arrived from Noire-Fontaine. I set up the bazookas in such a way as to prevent these guns from hitting our men who were encircling their position. The bazookas were fired only once, for the machines kept a prudent distance away. The Brisepouteau engagement lasted three hours during which time the farm changed hands twice. Our men had to withdraw for want of ammunition and the

Germans occupied the hill facing us once again. Firing continued until nightfall with nothing of significance happening, except that the Germans used large amounts of explosive bullets. Their tanks seemed content to go and come at a safe distance from the camp. Our one bazooka shot disabled one tank to such an extent that it was able to regain Pierrefontaine only with great difficulty. A volley of automatic rifle fire caught another German whose bare torso was unprotected to midriff and he sprawled over the top of his tank. From time to time their armored cars sent a volley of cannon fire in our direction without doing us any damage. With the night came silence; the last shot was fired at exactly 2100 hours. Our day's losses amounted to five dead and 11 wounded. Truckloads of German dead and wounded were being transported all night long through Pont de Roide. According to information, the Germans lost some 50 or 60 dead or wounded.

I had my men rest while I made plans for the following day. I was amazed to learn that at 2200 hours not a German was to be seen on the Pont de Roide or anywhere. I then decided to take advantage of the lull and carry out my plan to occupy all the hilltops surrounding our plateau. I selected reconnaissance groups, but no one was willing to go as far as the fort, so I took a few men and went myself. We all returned without having encountered a single German. I therefore dispatched all the battalion's immediately to their positions, only Capt. Saas deemed the project too hazardous and was reluctant to go. When I threatened to have him arrested he complied, though still not completely convinced.

On the morning of the 24th we expected them again. It was not the Germans who came but a huge line of men who were coming to fight with us. News of our success on the 22nd had spread throughout the valley like wild fire. The Ecot defeat was pardoned and thus began a great movement towards Lomont, not only Germans, but also Frenchmen who came by the hundreds. Large truck loads of supplies came to Montbéliard, Socheau and Audincourt. Enthusiasm grew to such an extent that I had to put a stop to enlistments for fear of a shortage of ammunition and food supplies. In a single day we grew from 1200 men to 2500. I tried to stop this flood by closing all roads but they knew every foot path and the number went up to 3200 men. As the Germans did not show up on August 23rd, I executed the plan to surround the area and occupy the Fort. On the 24th, three trucks loaded with Germans entered the road from Pierrefontaine to the Fort with the intention of occupying it. It was too late and when they saw our barricade and were greeted by our Bren guns they turned back.

My adjutant asked for permission to make a reconnaissance near the Tour Carrée, from which direction fire had let up noticeably. He went off with a lieutenant and 10 men, returning soon with news that the Germans were retreating. I immediately sent Lt. Cassard and his 10 braves with reinforcing numbers from one of Lt. Brand's sections to occupy the position. After a quarter of an hour's fighting the Pont de Roide incline was in our hands.

I set up my Command Post at Montecheroux, a flag pole was erected and the French flag, which is still in my possession, was hoisted. This flag, the first to fly over a liberated village in the Doubs, was made in secret, of parachute silk, by Madame Cuenin. I feel justified in interrupting this battle record to praise Madame Cuenin. Lt. Joly was the first, then I, to install our secret Command Post at her home, I should say at their home, for her husband was as completely devoted to the cause as she. Madame Cuenin is, however, an outstanding personality and any account of resistance activities in the Montbéliard region would be incomplete without her name.

I took advantage of the breathing space the Germans granted us to reorganize my services and form solid battalions. Officers who had heretofore played a rather obscure role presented themselves. From among them I chose the chiefs for my different services; the others I placed in companies with cadre deficiencies; soon the machine was ready to function. At any rate it was the first of September before I found an adjutant on whom I could rely completely: Capt. Mandre. On the 25th there were skirmishes at different points. On the 26th the Germans launched an attack from the direction of Pont de Roide. The section occupying the summit above Pont de Roide was commanded by a worthless officer who was the first to bail. He retreated almost without fighting. I went there myself and asked the battalion chief to have the same section retake the position under a new command. The Germans, whose ranks were rounded out by Poles, didn't put up much resistance.

I then decided to strike a blow at Pont de Roide, working on the principle that the best defensive measure is to attack. Captain Secot (also given as "Sicand") of the S. A. S. (the French Special Air Service), who had just come to us, and I decided to mop up Pont de Roide. His men were to cross the Doubs River and attack the Germans on the left bank, while my best troops, my volunteer corps, were to take the right bank with mortar fire support to be furnished by the SAS. At H-Hour the different groups set out, aided by sure men. The mortar that we had placed strategically opened fire. I was near a captain who seemed to be having trouble directing his fire because he had no smoke shells. The Capt. approached the mortar and a discussion took place between him and one of his men. I heard the captain say: "We will see about that later". We went back to our observation posts. The next shell hit the target right in the middle. Then the captain ordered four more shells to be fired and not one of them hit the target, although the explosion of the first was much louder than that of the four following. Suddenly clots of earth flew all around us. I turned to look and there was nothing left of the mortar or its operators. Only a few steps away a horrible trauma had taken place. The mortar had exploded. Three men were disemboweled and one whose skull was blown off lay there. The fourth dragged himself along for a few feet, groaning: "Ah, les vaches, ah, les vaches", and collapsed. What could have happened? The Captain suggested a defect in the shell as several had been damaged when parachuted. It is also possible that the gunner was upset by the discussion he had with this Capt. and had put the shell in backwards, for the mortar had exploded at its base.

This was not to be the only unhappy occurrence of the day. The SAS group that had crossed the Doubs encountered a group of Germans on their way to meet us. An engagement took place and the group was held up. However, at the appointed hour my volunteer corps attacked from the north and east. The engagement lasted only an hour, but was most severe. From my vantage point I could see my men and had them supported by an automatic rifle dominating the bridge. These men chased the Germans from the right bank and the automatic rifle sprayed them as they crossed the bridge. By nightfall we were masters of the right bank. Deeming the position precarious I had my men evacuate. We hadn't accomplished our aim, but neither had the Germans, for they too had come to attack us. At any rate, the Germans did not come back to establish themselves on the right bank.

It was after this operation that I received that ever famous telegram from London: "Is it true that you attacked Pont de Roide without orders?" Orders from whom, I would like to know. We were engaged with the enemy and no one other than me or my officers could have known what steps to take. It would not have been Boulaya, that solicitor who was anything but a soldier, hidden somewhere in Besançon, or that caricature of a colonel, Belin, an exact reproduction of the officers who had caused the fall of 1940. Why, I kicked him out at Montecheroux and what did he do but set himself up at Pont de Roide where he caused us a lot of trouble. I had taken a responsibility upon myself and I was determined to see it through without interference. If things hadn't come to a head as they did I would have had Belin arrested and maybe even shot. He stayed with my correspondent at Pont de Roide and intercepted all information coming from Montbéliard and Belfort, modifying it as he saw fit or including false reports hoping to confuse me. Fortunately my agents refused to give him any information and saw that it all reached the proper hands. One of these I mention in particular was a girl aged 19 who even refused to give messages to my second Battalion officer, but insisted on bringing them directly to me, wherever I was. How valuable are such people in comparison with such types as Belin or Boulaya with all their underhanded tricks.

During the following nights we received a good deal of parachute drops, though not so many as we needed, but it helped a lot. Every day the road from St. Hippolyte to Pont de Roide was the theater of a massacre of German convoys. They finally avoided using that road and decided to evacuate the plateau Maiche. On September 1st, we extended our occupation to the whole plateau Maiche and put a barricade at Le Col des Pins, with 500 men reinforced by the local resistance people. All the roads were blocked.

August 28, 1944   The Germans attacked again, coming from Pont de Roide. We countered them and, assisted by a 3 inch mortar, our men entered Pont de Roide and by dusk half of the town was ours. I ordered them back because it was impossible for us to hold such a position against very strong attacks.

September 1, 1944   I received an order from Boulaya to send a force to occupy the bridge of l'Isle-sur-le-Doubs. I ordered the expedition and set 280 of my best unit in spite of the fact that I had not any feeling in favor of such an adventure. It was a disaster. Our men came to the bridge, but the Germans had no difficulty in getting the necessary reinforcements, because the flood of their retreating forces passed through this town. A few hours later our men were about to be encircled. They owe their escape to reinforcements I decided to send them a few hours after their departure. We lost eight killed and 15 wounded.

In the meantime the men of the Fourth Battalion were not wasting any time. It took them scarcely a moment to liquidate a patrol of five customs officials near Vanfray. This caused the Germans some concern, so they had all their frontier posts as far as Morteau moved to Maiche or St. Hippolyte. The customs officials at St. Hippolyte had a car, a vehicle and a sidecar at their disposal and by means of these vehicles decided to take all their personnel to Montbéliard. Bad luck overtook them 5 km out as they found themselves confronted by my men of the Second Battalion. Automatic rifles, submachine guns and rifles dealt them a mean blow. Those who managed to escape fire got away across the Doubs or surrendered. Not a pane of glass was left in their vehicles, but surprisingly enough, they managed to get them back to their camp. To release the eighty customs people held up at Maiche, the Germans sent five combat cars and a panzer tank which intimidated my men to such an extent that they let them pass.

The Germans evacuated Maiche on August 30th. On the second of September I occupied with a battalion and a few local units all of the plateau of Maiche as far as Col des Pins. Parachute drops were received almost every night. Independent of the material and men received, these drops had a double effect: first of all the enthusiasm of the men was augmented; second, we foiled the Germans who thought that the support we were getting was much more considerable than it actually was.

I learned later that the Germans were in absolute terror of our sector and would say for the benefit of all hearers: "Oh terrorists nich gut!" We had under our control the whole of an immense production region and several electricity centers as well as the bridge of St. Hippolyte. The bridge at Pont de

Roide was under unrelenting fire from our automatic rifles located on the heights dominating it. Our automatic rifles fired on sight by day and at irregular intervals by night. One day the Germans had the audacity to set up a 105 mm cannon at the end of the bridge on the right bank. A group of my men approached it and put it out of commission with a British made Gammon grenade. Since the Germans made no more advances, we decided to advance. An attack, led by a group of parachutists under orders from Le Puy along with Tito's volunteer corps, against the frontier post of Dannemarie was without result. However, the Germans evacuated Dannemarie the next day without going near Villars-les-Blamont, our most exposed point, guarded by the Third Battalion under orders of Captain Harnich, the best of my battalion chiefs. He took part with a small group on the attack on Dannemarie; his men patrolled miles ahead of our lines; and, it was thanks to his well-made plans and discipline that the victory of September 6 was achieved. Villars-les-Blamont was our communication post with Switzerland. Yes, we had ambulances. The first day a doctor arrived with three. The next day came a surgeon from Paris with nurses and all his material. On the third day Doctor Robin, a surgeon from the Montbéliard hospital, arrived together with his nurses and equipment. At this same time came Doctor Petrogain, who took care of Jules Cesar, and Dr. Didier. I had nothing to worry about on the medical question.

After Dannemarie we attacked Autecheaux with the S. A. S. together with my volunteer corps. The surprise element was successful and the S. A. S. demolished two combat cars and several vehicles with Gammon grenades. The Germans fled to Ecurcey. My parachutists did not find this type of warfare to their liking, so Capt. Sicot decided to attack the Germans retreating to Clerval and to occupy the bridges. I reinforced him with my best men, the Tito group of 40. Confronted by a mass of motorized and armored units coming up the road, he had to relinquish his foothold and abandon the bridges after a moment's occupation. That same day I launched an attack with occupation of the bridges of l'Isle sur le Doubs as our objective. In spite of our 300 man unit, the attack was also repulsed by armored cars. We lost eight men at Clerval plus 15 dead and wounded at l'Isle sur le Doubs. These were the only two operations that I carried out by order of "Colonel" Boulaya.

September 5, 1944   I was informed this morning that French troops had reached Morteau, our southernmost point. I immediately went to meet them and contacted Colonel de Linares at Le Russy. I took him to Maiche where they spent the night.

September 6, 1944   On the morning of the sixth there was quiet along the whole line. About 1300 hours I was informed that some 15 German halftrack vehicles were moving toward Villars-les-Blamont. I sent reinforcements immediately and warned Colonel de Linares at St. Hippolyte. He sent us a 105 mm battery, a tank destroyer, and a few anti-tank guns. In the meanwhile the Germans began the attack. The 7th Company of the 3rd Battalion who held that position under command of Sylvestre let them approach within 100 meters and then opened fire with Bren guns and bazookas. The driver and the leading officer were killed and their armored car turned into a ditch. Another was badly damaged and the rest turned back and regrouped near a cemetery a mile away. They were about to start a new attack when the artillery of the First Army corps who had just reached us took them under their fire. For a change we provided the surprise. Two armored cars were disabled and the others ran like hell.

"This will be the dramatic end of me", said Sylvestre, who was in command of one of Harnich's battalions. His inseparable companion Jules Cesar had just been killed in the engagement and Sylvestre was deeply affected. Before anyone could stop him he grabbed some grenades and with two others left his shelter and ran in the direction of the armored cars saying "I've got to destroy them". In the shelter of a mound of earth he was all right, but when he reached the top he and one of his companions were mowed down by a volley of submachine gun fire. At that moment our artillery opened fire on the cemetery and the armored cars all fled.

The 7th Company recuperated the first armored car which had not suffered any real damage. After the arrival of the regular army we cooperated in two other attacks. One carried us as far as Hérimoncourt, but a German counterattack brought us back to our initial position. We held the most advanced positions for five more days. These positions were Lomont, Pont de Roide and Villars-les-Blamont, which were under continuous shellfire. Then the regulars took over and we retired to the rear. Our losses were 28 killed and 78 wounded during these five weeks of action.

These men were simply wonderful; barefooted, with no change of clothing, they stood under rain and bullets sometimes for two and three days without being relieved. The only thing we did not complain about was food. We had plenty of that.

We stayed with the regular troops until the 19th of September and during this time took part in different combats at Glay and Ecurcey. Then we had the privilege of occupying Blamont. After the arrival of the regular troops several generals came to see our position: first, General Duval, then Generals Bethouard, Chevillon, Guillame de Montsabert and then General Delattre de Tassigny, and finally General de Gaulle, who shook my hand and said a few pleasant words. It was General Bethouard who presented me to General de Gaulle on the 23rd of September in Maiche. And it was time, for the maneuver of the two 'gentlemen' who had gone to London had succeeded, and after I returned from the ceremony I found orders calling me to London. The "Belin's" and all the other malcontents whose ranks Marc had joined took advantage of my departure to spread the rumor that I had been recalled because of disciplinary infractions and that I would be taught what it meant to brush aside men of their caliber. A few days after I left they sent word around that I had been shot for treason upon arrival. Before my departure I had my best elements, about 200, transferred to the regular army and delegated my command to Capt. Hippolyte who had seniority. At the last I had 3500 men at my disposition, 3000 of whom were armed. I left for London on September 25, arriving on October 7, 1944.

An SOE interview with French Major de Mandre (Captain Floege was code named "Paul")

Major De Mandre began to work with Paul at the beginning of September. At the time Paul was in command of the Maquis de Lomont headquartered near Montbéliard. De Mandre stated that during the month of August some 3400 men were organized in the Lomont area. By August 22nd, Paul was ready with 600 armed men at Lomont, the balance not yet having been armed. Just at this time the Germans attacked Lomont on the north and west. The attack lasted all day but was unsuccessful, the Germans having left about 500 dead and wounded before retiring. A number of prisoners fell into the Maquis' hands. Maquis losses were not heavy. De Mandre attributes the Maquis' success to the courage and efforts of Paul and to the wisdom of his tactical decisions. During the course of engagement, Paul knocked out a German tank with a bazooka. Subsequent repeated attempts by the Germans at various points met with no success.

As a result of parachute operations, it was now possible to arm larger groups, and five battalions of three companies each were formed. Companies numbered 150 men each, thus bringing the effective total to 2250. With these troops Paul was able to occupy Fort-de-Lomont and the villages of Montecheroux, Chanesalle, Pierrefontaine and Villars-les-Blamont, all in the Doubs Département. Much material was taken from the Germans, including arms, ammunition and vehicles.

On September 2nd, 1944, Paul decided to occupy the Maiche plateau. His forces started out from Montecheroux and occupied in turn Liebvillers, St. Hippolyte, Maiche and Le Russet up to Fains pass. Barrages were set up around the plateau in the Dessoubre valley. At that time the Germans were falling back from Lyon, Besançon and Val d'Ahon towards Belfort. All of their armored attacks were repulsed.

On September 3rd, 1944, the Maquis took the town of Dannemarie, northeast of Lomont, an action whose success was due largely to Paul's leadership. On September 5th, while attacking D'Autechaux, Paul's forces destroyed five German tanks and some two score troops. At the same time, on orders from higher headquarters, over Paul's protest, an operation was begun against the l'Isle sur le Doubs. Lack of firepower forced the Maquis to fall back after suffering losses.

On September 6th, after regular French troops had occupied the Maiche plateau, an operation made very easy due to work already done by Paul's forces, the Germans launched an important attack against Lomont accompanied by tanks. The main thrust was directed against the Villars-les-Blamont sector but Paul's force, with Paul himself in the most crucial places, forced them to abandon the attack, after they had suffered heavy losses in armor and men. One tank was captured intact and used against the Germans later.

Due to actions of Paul's forces, French army regulars were able to invest Fort de Lomont without a single loss. This, incidentally, is frankly stated by the French C.O. in a letter to Paul.

From then on, Paul's battalions fought with French regulars. At Ecrucey on September 13th, Paul reached the objective given him, but the regular troops did not, and in the German counter attack that resulted, Paul had to fall back. At about the same time, the Maquis was trying to hold a bridgehead at

Pont de Roide but due to lack of artillery support had to give up positions on the left bank of the Doubs and the Germans blew up the bridge. The Maquis continued, however, firmly to hold the right bank and did so until the end of September. Paul was recalled in the latter part of September. After Paul's departure the battalions took the name 'Regiment de Lomont' and took part in all engagements up to and including the capture of Mulhouse. The regiment was taken into the Ciens D.I.C. of the French 1st Army Corps.

Paul was cited by General Bethouart in an Order of the Day on the occasion of the capture of Montbéliard.

From General Chevillon, Chief of Staff, First Army Corps to Captain Ernest Floege, September 10, 1944:

"I tried to see you while passing through Montebeliard to express my personal congratulations as well as those of the Commanding General (Bethouart) on the magnificent work you accomplished before the arrival of the regular troops, and particularly on the occupation of the Lomont Mountain, which spared us the necessity of attack. I would be obliged to you if on this occasion you would furnish me the names of your subordinates who especially distinguished themselves in the course of these operations, in order that I may grant them an award without delay.

Also it seems fitting to me to anticipate a well-earned rest for your troops. This rest will allow for reorganization and re-equipment, so that other missions may subsequently be assigned to them. I have just given orders necessary for the regrouping of your battalions in the region east of St. Hippolyte, the exact location to be determined in agreement with Colonel de Linares."

When Capt. Floege was ordered to return to London, he was just arranging plans with General Duval and General

Guillaume for actions for his men to infiltrate into the German lines.

Captain Floege made this farewell address to the men of his Maquis of Lomont on September 13, 1944 (by this time the Maquis had become part of the F. F. I., the Free French Forces): "We had been living, rather, we had been perishing scarcely a month under the heels of our oppressor, when each of you went to Lomont, since become famous, with the firm resolve to avenge all the harm that had been done, to inflict upon our oppressors the same ignoble treatment with which they have ground us down, and to bring the heat of our vengeance to within the boundaries of their own country. This fine spirit gave life to the defenders of Lomont, on the 22nd of August at Pierrefontaine and the Tour Carrée, and later at the Pont de Roide, route Saint Hippolyte and Villars. However, the relative peace we have been enjoying since then seems to have lessened this desire for vengeance. If in the short period of a month our ardor can cool to such an extent, it would seem well to look to the sincerity of our sentiments.

I realize that the precarious conditions under which we live are largely responsible for this. On the other hand I have noticed while you cannot be surpassed in defense tactics, offensive tactics leave something to be desired.

During an interview I had with General Bethouard, commandant of the Army Corps, he made the following proposal which, I hasten to tell you, I accepted.

1. He wants the F. F. I. battalions to retain their special character and to remain a 'corps d'elité' in the corps of the army and to continue to be, as they have been, the living expression of revolt by the French people against the oppressor.
2. These battalions will be assigned to a division which will administer them in exactly the same manner as the other troops, with American equipment, mess facilities, pay and all supplies.

3. In this manner the F. F. I. will enjoy the same rights as are accorded the Army.

4. Length of service will be taken into consideration and the high command proposes to choose cadre from among our young men for the post-war French army. And, let me assure you that F. F. I. of your fighting caliber will be most in demand for the restoration of France. The High Command will delegate non-coms to improve and supervise training and instruction.

5. Every F. F. I. soldier who declares himself to be in agreement with these principles must pledge fidelity until the end of the war with Germany. Consequently I ask all company commanders to prepare lists of names of men who are willing to adhere to this list of principles. These lists must be in my hands on the 15th of September at the latest.

It is to be understood that these battalions will remain under my command, as well as the men who do not choose to take part in chasing the enemy to within his own territory.

I know that you are proud to belong to the Lomont forces and that you will be equally as proud to be distinguished from other troops by the inscription on your left sleeve: "F. F. I. forces of Lomont". I want to point out General Bethouard's promise that we will be among the troops to enter Audincourt, Montbéliard and Hericourt."

CHAPTER 18   Joyful Anticipation Turns To Anguish

After Germany's surrender, Jean-Jacques could not wait until his parents returned and his family could rebuild their lives. He remembers: "I was staying with my grandmother in Cérans-Foulletourte with my 6 year old brother when the Red Cross told us that our parents had been liberated by the Americans and were alive, but would not be home before a time in quarantine since they were afflicted with typhus and dysentery. They had to gradually learn to eat again: eating normal food after all the deprivations they had gone through could be fatal. Our father stayed in the former house of a Nazi dignitary near Lake Constance, and our mother was very ill in a hospital in Holland.

At last, on June 1, 1945, the mayor of our village let us know that our town's deportees would arrive in Le Mans at about 3:00 PM. I had been looking forward to this since the landing of the allies in Normandy: I was excited and yet so apprehensive. I had in mind this image of our father and mother hand in hand, coming towards us and embracing us lovingly. This is not what happened. Dad came home first, with my uncle Roger. Another uncle, Florent Beaury, who had married my father's sister, had been euthanized in the Mauthausen concentration camp on February 25, 1944. He had also been in our Hercule Sacristain Buckmaster network and was arrested one week after Alfred and Renée, November 11, Armistice Day, the same day as was Father Lelièvre.

I waited on the Le Mans platform for the train that would make my life whole again. It had been 19 months since my parents were arrested. I don't know how I survived without them. Physically, it had been punishing as I was often hungry and cold to my bones. Emotionally it had been terrifying, with the Gestapo often only a step behind, knowing how they would torture me. Not only had I lost my parents' nurturing, I anguished their fates imprisoned in concentration camps. Suddenly, the train stopped before us. Slowly and laboriously a crowd of prisoners of war got off, and only a few deportees. All were surrounded by their families who were asking them questions they did not care to answer. At last I could get close enough to see, but I could not recognize my father, then I was petrified with horror. In front of me stood a human skeleton: about five foot ten and 175 pounds when he left, a cowering 95 pounds now, his head shaven, his face swollen with seeping boils, his eyes set deeply in his head, he was gasping for air, his open mouth showing two rotten teeth where he once had such beautiful white teeth. Dad was wearing what seemed to be an oversize coat and striped pants.

He did not seem to recognize me at first; when he did, there was not a glimmer of excitement or happiness in his eyes; he only looked on. He kept asking if Renée had returned and he refused to attend the official reception. He wanted to see his house at 2 rue du Tourniquet. When we arrived there, we found the Gestapo's seals were still on the front door. We walked in and were shocked at what we saw: our house had been entirely ransacked, those beasts had torn up the wooden floors and smashed the furniture with an axe, holes had been dug in the walls in search of documents we might have hidden, our family pictures were torn beyond repair. Even our clothes had been torn to pieces and scattered all over the place. This showed that the Gestapo had tried to find the addresses of the members of our network. What a sad and depressing sight for people in my parents' conditions. Dad sat down on a wobbly chair, his head in his hands. I was filled with horror when I saw his fingers: they hardly looked like fingers any more as they were crooked, swollen and their nails were missing. These savages had smashed them with a hammer as he was being questioned at rue des Fontaines. These hands, for 19 months, had had to work in temperatures as low as -22 degrees F."

Alfred Auduc also remembers: "Back in Le Mans, we had a warm welcome from the townspeople and I was finally reunited with my wife. Unfortunately, my brother-in-law had not returned. Captain Floege was waiting for me, wearing his formal American uniform. He had always eluded the Gestapo. He was back from Germany where he had searched for us in Buchenwald. I told him about the sealed tunnel which held the technical documents for the V-2. He immediately went to Paris to inform the American high command. The next day we were supposed to fly on location, but at the last minute we learned that the area was now occupied by the Russians. I was disappointed. My mission would have been carried out had I been able to show them this factory. I would have liked to show them the tunnel and explain why there were fans here and there. The Americans were also very disappointed."

Jean-Jacques continues: "Our Mom, Renée, came back with a sanitary convoy later in June of 1945. The SS had sold her to Bayer Chemical for 170 Deutschemarks (about $255 at the time), for gynecological experiments. **(Note 18-1)** Bayer would inoculate diseases, then, try out drugs to test their effectiveness. Bayer would operate on these women or even amputate them without using anesthetics. 95% of them ended up in the cremation ovens at the end of these experiments. When Renée's body could take no more experiments, she was sent to work in a Skoda factory which produced ammunition and bombs. Gun powder hung heavily in the factory's air and Renée suffered burnt lungs that changed her breathing into rasping. When her camp was liberated by the Americans in April of 1945, she also had contracted typhus and dysentery, like most of the survivors. She was taken to a hospital close by, then to another one in Holland and stayed there for 40 days. Renée returned to Le Mans still very weak and in very poor health. Through these horrors her strong temperament remained undaunted.

For one week she refused to see us; she wanted to use this time to make herself more presentable. She wished to hide her condition using a coiffure, clothes and make up in order not to scare us. When she arrived home, very ill, she found her elder son had changed a lot. To honor her, I had bought a new suit as I had learned to be independent and take initiatives. I wore it to show myself at my best when she first came back. She was so taken aback that she burst into tears as she realized she had left a child and was reunited with a young man who did not need her as much anymore.

The family and some neighbors lent us some furniture so we could "start over". Mom had to take Penicillin, which was just beginning to be used in medical science, but the treatment was still very involved, the usual treatment being one shot every three hours, day and night. It was exhausting just to follow the treatment! Renée had to walk to the doctor's house for her shots. The doctor who administered these injections had lost his son to disease in a concentration camp, so he was dedicated to helping Renée. I would walk with her to the doctor's. Renée was finally able to recover to a modest state of health. But, she was to survive only a few years due to the ill treatments of the camps. With all her physical problems, her doctor in Holland incomprehensibly recommended her having another child, for at the time it was believed a woman's system was at its healthiest just after delivering. She gave birth to Marie-Josette on November 4, 1948, but bearing and birthing another child exhausted Renée, who succumbed 5 months later on April 2, 1949.

In spite of my little brother having returned home from his grandmother's, our family was never able to function as before. A cleaning lady would come a few hours a day, but it was not enough and we had to find someone who could stay with us and take care of the five of us. It took three months to find the right person. Considering that my mother and father were very ill, for that period of time I became my little baby sister's surrogate mother. This was not an easy task for an eighteen year old boy. At the time you had to wash and boil the diapers, hang them so they would dry, and everything was held together with safety pins. My sister would wriggle so much, more often than not she undid everything I had just done, and I had to start all over again. I also had to feed her every three hours, and it took forever for her to drink, for she was not a strong baby. If I patted her back a little too strongly for her burp, she would reject everything she had just drunk. Nestle milk was good and sweet; I would finish her boxes, putting on more weight than my sister did.

On Sundays, I had to stay home instead of dating girls like my friends did.

After three months, we found Madame Charlotte Cartier, who we hired away from people that were abusing her and paying her little wages. She committed herself to bringing up our little sister like her own daughter, and I am sure she saved her life. Also without his mother to a serious extent, my little brother Michel, at age four, owed his survival to our kind grandmother who brought him up and protected him.

When her children were arrested, grandmother fled and hid in the forest with her grandson. Later, they were sheltered by farmers who were friends of hers. This brave 66 year old woman had opened her little farm house to the head of our Resistance Network, André Dubois, a.k.a. Hercule, when he had returned from London. She risked her life by allowing her house to become his main radio transmitting location. She sheltered these allied aviators: David Butcher, Albert Carrol and John Zioance, as well as Captain Floege who was the head of the U.S. Sacristain Network. All the parachuted loads that we received were sorted out on her farm: weapons, sabotage equipment and food supplies. In preparation for the allied landing that we understood was planned for 1943, the weapons the paratroopers and Resistants would need were stored in a quarry that was on her property.

She had no money, and to this day we still wonder how she managed to take care of us during the 19 months of my parents' absence and to find the resources to send a package to them every month while they were prisoners in Germany. We learned that the priest of the village gave her moral support, and also financial support within the limits of his meager possibilities.

After the war, Grandmother Marie was rewarded the **"Croix de Guerre"** (*Cross of War*) **with palms (with distinction)**, and received a letter of commendation from General Eisenhower.

I thought we would be able to resume our family life, just like before. **How wrong I was.** Our parents were so traumatized they were unable to live the lives they had before their deportation: there had been too much suffering, too many deaths in our resistance network (64 died, most in the concentration camps, out of 104 members in our network). I, too, had changed, had gotten used to fending for myself."

The Auduc's Struggle to Restart Their Lives

After the end of the war, in 1946, Colonel Buckmaster called for Jean-Jacques to visit him in England. Jean-Jacques had just enough money to purchase passage on a boat, so off he went. On the boat, he travelled with a young lady about his age who had a strong southern France accent. She told him that her parents would be waiting for her at the dock, but Jean-Jacques did not understand this until she explained that she was English but had learned her French in the south of France. Colonel Buckmaster took Jean-Jacques on a tour of the BBC studios, and he was able to see the studio from which General de Gaulle had delivered his messages that had rallied the hearts of all patriotic Frenchmen. Colonel Buckmaster, who had returned to a position with the Ford Motor Company, also gave him a tour of the Ford factory. While in England, Jean-Jacques stayed at the home of a British officer. Jean-Jacques returned to France along with his host's son, Rudy de Belgeonne, the man who later was to send him hats. It was a stormy crossing and most passengers became seasick, leaving the dining room during their meals. His friend and he were not sick, so they entered the first class dining room. When challenged by a waiter, they lied saying that a lady had instructed them to go finish her meal. So they dined on lobster and champagne, the first time Jean-Jacques had ever eaten lobster.

Colonel Buckmaster also asked Francoise Dubois to come to London, to let her know of the esteem he felt for her father, André. Colonel Buckmaster wished to meet the people he had relied on during the war.

Alfred's release from concentration camps did not relieve him from their devastating impact. Those who had been imprisoned in the camps could not stand authority, loud noises, anything reminiscent of their incarceration, so they preferred to be alone.

Twenty friends and family members had joined Alfred's network and died. Other families were left struggling to survive while their fathers and husbands were in concentration camps. Alfred was devastated by this. He related: "I knew I had saved some American, French and even German lives. But, afterwards I wanted to live on a deserted island; only, I had three children and felt the duty to give them a good education. It was thanks to my children that I began to enjoy life again. For their sakes I had to find a job, but I needed peace so I took a job as a forester. The forest was a strong symbol for us. During the war it had been our sanctuary when the Germans had hunted us. And working within the forest's protection we felt safe and calm after the war's storms. I needed equipment for this job and Colonel Buckmaster provided me with a Ford tractor. The head of the water and forest company in the Sarthe and the Orne, as well as the owners of large forest holdings, provided me with contracts. Mr. Robert Airy, who was at the head of the forest cooperative of the Sarthe and was a former POW, helped me with his technical guidance and with financial aid. I have profound gratitude for all of these men. They understood me and made it possible for me to bring up my family that I held so dear."

Aware that Alfred Auduc had recovered somewhat, Colonel Buckmaster requested that he come with his associates to London. Alfred wished to build windmill's after the war but had no resources for doing such. Instead, Alfred, Father Lelièvre and Jean-Jacques travelled to London to meet with Colonel Buckmaster. Under the Marshall Plan, their Departement of the Sarthe could receive three tractors per year, but one had to be a farmer to receive a tractor. However, Colonel Buckmaster, who now worked for Ford Motor Company in England, arranged for a tractor to be given to Alfred, a fully-equipped one worth 97,000 francs. Their new Ford tractor utilized hydraulics. When they were back in France, engineers from Renault heard about the tractor and visited to inspect it. They thought the hydraulics could not work and were amazed by a demonstration of the new tractor. For a while Alfred's and his family members' main source of income came from employing their tractor to assist farmers. But, in time, other farmers also obtained tractors and this source of income dried up. About this time, German war equipment was available to the French, so Alfred obtained a huge tank 8 meters long, one without tracks, which had a 500 HP airplane engine that consumed too much diesel, so Alfred replaced it with truck engine. It arrived on an equally huge Tatra truck, made in Czechoslovakia. Alfred directed students from a local school to convert the tank to a bulldozer. Annie Chervel was a nurse at this school and that's how Jean-Jacques and she met. Annie became Jean-Jacques' first wife when they both were age 22.

The tank, now bulldozer, was so large that it had a steering wheel at each end. The government employed Alfred to use his bulldozer to knock down apple trees because there was overproduction of alcoholic beverages made from apples. As agriculture was expanding rapidly, his giant bulldozer gave him work that he would not otherwise have had. The tank had four axles; the first axle often broke. A McCormick engineer visited, wanted it and swapped Alfred a real bulldozer for the tank.

At this time Alfred was investigated for having made no tax returns for the war years and immediately afterwards. When the auditor arrived, Alfred pulled out his Colt and told him to leave. The auditor contacted the Gendarmes, who came, and were amazed at Alfred's much larger pistol. The Gendarmes tried to confiscate his pistol. Alfred said "No way". The Gendarmes asked if he would drill a hole in the barrel to render it inoperative. Alfred said he would. One should not waste time looking for the hole. Years later Alfred's pistol and Hercule's radio transmitter were lent for an exhibit in Angers. One evening the two historic items disappeared. A few years later, Alfred remarried and his new wife threw away two boxes of Alfred's Resistance memorabilia. What a shameful waste of history!

This was also the period when Jean-Jacques took correspondence courses in forestry, earning a degree. He wished to specialize in reforestation projects.

Jean-Jacques's Military Service: "Unfit to serve??!!"

A law had been passed for those who had fought in the Resistance. Their time fighting was to be taken into account against the 18 months of their military service requirement. Consequently, very few men had to do military service and the law was canceled. Jean-Jacques explains: "When I was called up with my class, in spite of all my efforts with the administration, and of the fact I was a war orphan due to my mother's death, I was told that first I had to go where I was drafted, and there they would consider my request to be exempted. I was drafted in Amiens, in the 406th Artillery Regiment. On my arrival there, I tried to explain to the unfriendly warrant officer my unique situation: I should have had the rank of a non-commissioned officer in the army and I had been awarded the Croix de Guerre (*Cross of War*). He would not even look at the documents I showed him, and said "Sure, and my sister is Maréchal de France (*Field Marshal*)". Instead, he immediately branded me as a <u>"rebellious"</u> recruit who needed to be disciplined.

At the time, in 1951, our military training started with one month inside the barracks. During this period, we received all the required vaccination shots, and we learned all the military ranks, how to salute, march, and hold old 1918 model Lebel rifles at attention. We were also given the wrong sizes of old mismatched uniforms. I was 1m59 tall (5 feet 6 inches), and had an overcoat that would have been the right size for someone 1m80 (6 feet). It would drag behind me like a train, and everyone would call me "The Marquis". Moreover, my boots were size 43 *(11)*, while my feet were size was 41 *(9)*. This created a problem when I had to stand to attention, because my "feet" were rarely straight, and our instructor would yell at me for it.

One night, as I was walking near the gate, I saw a note inviting the officers to the opening of a new theater house for "half price entrance fee". Taking advantage of a moment of distraction on the part of the guard, I went to the new theater house, wearing my ludicrous uniform. As soon as I got there and before I entered, a Captain became so aggravated that he was all over me, pointing out that the drafted soldiers were confined to the barracks. I explained to him that I was a non-commissioned officer and opened my overcoat so he could see the decorations I had made a point of wearing. He was completely taken aback by my story and asked what my name and serial number were. He swore he would settle the situation the next day with the Colonel. He paid for my entrance ticket and made me promise to enter the theater house only after the lights were off, and leave before the end of the movie in order to avoid the embarrassment of having civilians see me in an outfit that was a disgrace for the army.

The next day, my favorite warrant officer came to me and yelled: "AUDUC, you are wanted at the Colonel's office; expect a court martial". The Colonel looked at my train, my oversized hat and my strange way of standing to attention with complete astonishment. The Captain was next to him. I produced my documents and at last had a chance to explain myself. They had never seen anyone newly drafted that already had the rank of non-commissioned officer, and what's more, that was decorated with the Croix de Guerre. The Colonel, pulling himself together, asked me: "Why did you not say anything when you were first drafted?" I answered that "*He* would not listen to me", as I was looking at the warrant officer. The man was placed under arrest for two weeks without pay.

The Colonel warmly congratulated me and wished to introduce me (wearing my decorations) to the General who was to come for an inspection a few days later. In exchange for a furlough, I readily accepted.

The Colonel signed an order for the tailor to make two custom-made outfits for me. He promised to use his influence with the Army Minister to release me as soon as possible, understanding that my father was still very weak and needed me for his little tree planting business. Aware it could take several months, he signed me in at a school in Beauvais, and I used this time to take, and pass, the "Inter - arms" Degree. At last I was authorized to wear my non-commissioned officer stripes. Three long months later I was released from my military obligations."

War scars participants deeply and permanently. Post traumatic syndrome is just a recent term for a long recognized war-inflicted condition. For 18 months, Jean-Jacques was denied his parents love and support, sufficient sustenance, shelter from the cold, security and companionship. He yearned to be a child again upon his parents return from concentration camps. Instead he became the family's caregiver prior to his 14 birthday, depended upon by his father, his mother, his young brother and eventually his baby sister. But this was not the last time essences of his life seemed to be brutally taken from him.

He was married to Annie for just 18 years when she passed away in 1971, the same age, 41, as had his mother, leaving him with their two sons. Now struggling terribly, Jean-Jacques sank into his armchair and considered that he had three options: drink to forget as did so many others; end his sad life, as he loaded his pistol and set it on the table next to his chair; or, go on with his life, and to do this he needed a new companion. He understood that a new wife must have sensitivity for understanding him, with his nightmares and heavy thoughts. He wished to find someone whom life also had scarred so the two would understand and support each other. His cleaning lady at the time was a mother of six who had divorced her husband due to his abuse. Her name was Paulette. Full of fear, she had left her husband, but could not abandon her children. When she returned to them, her enraged husband tied her to a chair in their kitchen, opened the oven and turned on the gas, unlit. One of Paulette's children discovered her, rescuing her from certain death. Perhaps Paulette had the empathy to understand Jean-Jacques. But, a problem arose. His two sons would not accept that their former cleaning lady was to be their step-mother and this refusal to accept Paulette never ceased. They failed to appreciate their father's need for understanding and companionship.

Even Jean-Jacques physical scars are forever present. As late as March 6, 1989, his doctor, Dr. Derveaux from Le Mans, diagnosed that Jean-Jacques suffered from previous malnutrition which manifested in his current digestive problems.

It is unusual for life to offer only sadness and Jean-Jacques has had a good share of happiness. He spent 40 years in peaceful existence as a forester, which he loved, and adored the wild animals he often encountered. His 30 years with Paulette have been filled with happiness. "Messages in Handlebars", which is being translated into French, assures that his family's story, and what it teaches about the price of liberty, will not be forgotten. If only you could see the twinkle in his eyes and hear his keen, ever present wit, you would be assured that this heroic lad has triumphed over every adversity to live a rich and joyful life.

Colonel Buckmaster's Remarks on the Views of the French after the War

Excerpts from Col. Buckmaster's book <u>They Fought Alone</u>: "It has been customary, since the war, to blame the Maquis (Resistance) for every misfortune and hardship that France has now to undergo. It was almost an unpopular thing in France in 1952 to have fought for France's liberation in 1940 to 1945. And if one fought and perhaps died in company with a British soldier, it is now considered almost unpardonable. None of the 'best people' did it. Of course, they were not collaborationist nor supporters of Petain, just the best type that waited to see what would happen. I wonder what, in fact, would have happened if all these brave men and women who continually risked life and property to save our liaison officers had waited on the fence?

A rather similar and equally unfounded prejudice also exists in France today (1959). It is that the members of the French Resistance groups where nearly all communist or, at any rate, that the communist groups such as the FTP Franc-tireurs et Partisans and the Front National where the only groups to do any effective work. This theory is strongly advanced by communist propaganda, but I can say with authority that, so far as the groups were concerned who worked with British liaison officers, we were only interested in their patriotism and their ability to carry out such tasks, and not at all in their political opinions.

In all, during the period March 1941 into July 1944, we recruited over 460 male and 40 female officers for work in the field. It has always seemed to me surprising that there were so many British or Dominion subjects, whose French was faultless, willing and anxious to undertake such supremely dangerous work. And they were in no way conspicuous; the last thing we wanted in them was eccentricity. We denied them glamour, in their own interest; we made them look as homely and unremarkable as we could. In the words of one of them, they were 'just ordinary people, not particularly brave'.

As the war progressed and supplies improved, we were able to send out by parachute to our operators a fair quantity of radio transmitters, cunningly camouflaged, and they were bidden to jettison or abandon sets whose use might seem to them particularly dangerous. The care with which our agents treated their sets was demonstrated to me in no uncertain manner after the war, when, in my travels around the areas where our people had been working, I was handed the jealously guarded suitcases containing transmitters, still in perfect working order, I was assured.

It was evidently essential to relieve, as much as we could, the burden of traffic over the 'clandestine air'. We quickly realized the possibility of using the BBC's French service for sending out previously arranged conventional messages. This system eliminated the need for the intricate coding and decoding which was necessary in sending out Morse messages. There were many occasions on which a prearranged signal, totally meaningless to the enemy, gave an agent the clue for which he was waiting.

The simplest example was the use of a harmless sounding phrase on the French program of the BBC, to confirm, as arranged with the agent, that a parachute operation was scheduled for that night. It was possible to send over the air from Bush House studios at 7:30 p.m. such a message. The message could be of nonsense, but would mean to the initiated reception committee approximately this: the aircraft which you ask for, parachuting stores as arranged and on such and such a field, is scheduled for tonight. If there is no setback in the weather, if the pilot finds the field, you should see the containers floating down to you in x hours from now. A further message on the 9:15 program confirmed the operation again (or, by the absence of such message, intimated to the listeners that for some reason or other the operation had been scrubbed). In winter, when aircraft frequently left their bases before 9:00 p.m., the message at 9:15 literally meant that the load was on its way and constituted an imperative order to the reception committee to get out to the chosen field with all haste.

When it came to choosing conventional messages for subsequent use on the BBC, the boys and girls were surprisingly enterprising. Quotations from the classics alternated with jest, sometimes in dubious taste, so devious that we feared to propose them to the austere authorities of Bush House."

Note 18-1 Although the two following documents, given as evidence at the Nuremberg trials, did not relate directly to Renée Auduc, there had to have been similar ones issued on her behalf:

"Report for the SS Institute of Hygene
To: Head of Service, D III, Oranienburg
From: the Waffen SS doctor at Place Weimar
Weimar-Buchenwald, January 8, 1944

Subject: memo on a series of experiments

The following experiments are presently carried out at the concentration camp of Buchenwald:

on 12 prisoners, control of blood preservation

on 15 prisoners, trials on the immunization against gas gangrene

on 3 prisoners, trials on burns made by rubber phosphorus incendiary bombs

on 10 to 14 prisoners, transmission of typhoid fever.

The experiments all take place at the typhus trial location: Block 46."

Also note: One of the first Nazi concentration camps was Oranienburg in 1933. In 1935 it was replaced by the Sachsenhausen concentration camp which continued to operate until the end of the Nazi regime; 100,000 people were killed in Sachsenhausen before the liberation of the camp by the Soviet Red Army in 1945.

Oranienburg was also the center of Nazi Germany's nuclear energy project According to military historian Antony Beevor, the launching of the Battle for Berlin by Stalin was motivated by his desire to acquire that facility. It has also been claimed that the pre-emptive destruction of these facilities by the USAAF Eighth Air Force on March 15, 1945, was done to prevent it from falling into Soviet hands.

Here is a letter from Dr. Carl Clauberg which was later produced as evidence at the Nuremberg trials:

"To: Himmler

After carrying out experiments that were qualified as the most criminal ones on ten women, "The method is quite satisfactory", "a trained doctor will probably be able to sterilize several hundred and up to one thousand women per day."

Correspondences between the Bayer Company and the Commandant of the Auschwitz concentration camp:

"We would appreciate, Sir, if you would put at our disposal a certain number of women for the experiments we want to carry out for a new narcotic...

"We have received your answer. The price of 200 marks per woman seems to be overpriced. We can only offer 170 marks for each. If you agree, we will pick them up. We need about 150 women."

"We have received your agreement. Please prepare 150 women, if possible the healthiest you have. We will pick them up as soon as you notify us."

"We have received the 150 women you sent. They are obviously underfed, but we have established that they will do. We will keep you informed about the experiments."

"The experiments are now achieved. All the women have died. We will soon send you an order for another shipment." From the archives of the Nuremberg trials: NI (71-84).

Additional note: Carl Clauberg was born in 1898 in Wupperhof, Rhine Province, into a family of craftsmen. During World War I, he served as an infantryman. After the war he studied medicine and eventually reached the rank of chief doctor in the University gynaecological clinic in Kiel. He joined the Nazi party in 1933 and later on was appointed professor for gynaecology at the University of Konigsberg. He received the rank of SS Gruppenfuhrer of the Reserve.

In 1942 he approached Heinrich Himmler and asked him for an opportunity to sterilize women en masse for his experiments. Himmler agreed and Clauberg moved to Auschwitz concentration camp in December of 1942. Part of Block number 10 in the main camp became his laboratory. Clauberg looked for an easy and cheap way to sterilize women. He injected liquid acid into their uterus - without anaesthesia. These women suffered terrible pain. Most of his test subjects were Jewish or Roma women who suffered permanent damage and serious infections. Damaged ovaries were then removed and sent to Berlin for additional research. Sometimes his male and female subjects were bombarded with X-rays. Some of the subjects died because of the tests and others were killed so they could be autopsied. Men's testicles were removed and sent to Breslau for examination. Estimates of those who survived but were sterilized are around 700.

When the Red Army approached the camp, Clauberg moved to Ravensbrück concentration camp to continue his experiments. Soviet troops captured him there in 1945.

After the war in 1948, Clauberg was put on trial in the Soviet Union and received a sentence of 23 years. Seven years later he was released due to an arrangement of exchange of POW's between the Soviet Union and West Germany. He was returned to West Germany, where he boasted of his "scientific achievements". After groups of survivors protested, Clauberg was soon arrested in 1955 and was put on trial. He died of a cardiac arrest in his cell before the trial could start.

CHAPTER 19   Resistance Members Write Their Painful Memoires

L'abbé Julien Lelièvre was arrested November 11, 1943, at 3:00PM in his office. First imprisoned in Angers, he endured 'muscular interrogations'. In January, 1944, he was sent to the prison in Compiègne, then to Buchenwald, block 21. He administered to prisoners there, an instance of humanity in a world of brutality, while working in a factory. After almost a year, all priests were sent to Dachau because the Nazis feared them. Julien administered to the dying of all religions. Understandably, the horrors he witnessed had changed him when he was liberated in 1945. Where, he asked, was the spirituality, the dignity in mankind?

Dr. Richard Grunberg, Alfred Auduc and l'abbé Lelièvre agreed to write their memoirs while at Dachau. Father Lelièvre explained: "My thoughts before starting my memoirs: In Buchenwald camp there was an area for roll call. For that purpose we had to stay for hours on end just waiting. We would have lengthy conversations and it was during one of those that the title for my book was chosen. Our discussions sometimes would drift; sometimes we talked with only a few words; sometimes with passion; always with the glow of the crematoriums nearby. One day, which had been rather uneventful, we started talking about writing our memoirs when we returned home.

"What's the point?" "Nobody will believe us", that's what most people said. "And yet, it will be our duty to inform our countrymen on what is going on here. Everybody must know". "What about you, priest? What are you going to come up with?" "Oh, I don't think I can produce much, but maybe I could write memoirs that would be called "A village priest as just another camp prisoner".

It was just a joke because our return home was far from certain and I didn't feel I would be a good writer. Moreover, I wasn't sure that people in France cared to hear about our suffering. Men in general are focused on their own problems and easily forget other people's. I was ready to talk, I was determined to explain to everyone every time I had the opportunity, but what would be the use of writing? Actually, in 1945, I did tell my story to a lot of people.

Then I thought of the old adage "spoken words disappear, but what is written stays". In 1945, I was talking with one of our famous veterans who told me "You need to write about everything you saw, Father, otherwise people will forget". This also encouraged me to write. I was already feeling that people were going back to their everyday routine and were tiring of all the stories about the horrors of concentration camps. I then thought that, if people were tired of listening, perhaps they would still be interested in reading and our written words will remain when the dust covers all these memories. All the witnesses of these horrors will soon disappear, their lives having been so shortened by their terrible ordeal. Their souls must remain.

Now is the best time for me to write my stories. It is not a novel or the food of our imaginations. No one to my knowledge has ever put any romance in the description of life in concentration camps; how could they?

It is not about anyone's life in particular, for behind our tattoos, we had lost any expression of personality. It is not a propaganda book exalting the role of a priest. It is a simple story that wants to show that a priest was also among the prisoners and that he too served his country and his brothers, just like the farmers, the workers, the teachers, the students, the soldiers, the diplomats and so many others.

"My Parish in Prison" wants to show that there were men from different social backgrounds who did not hesitate to fulfill their ideals in spite of all that was done to ruin them.

"My Parish in Prison" wants to show that French people, even in extremely difficult circumstances, were ready to fight the

Nazi ideology that left such a scar on the German people and most people in the occupied countries."

Preface by Alfred Auduc:

"In 1945, my friend, Father Lelièvre told me "We should write our memoirs; we don't need to be writers to tell our story. We discussed the titles for our stories. He told me there were books such as "My parish Among the Poor" and "My parish Among the Rich" and that his title would be "My Parish in Prison". As for me, it would be "Memories of an Agent of the Hercule Sacristain Buckmaster Network."

Early in November of 1958, Father Lelièvre was quite ill and exhausted. He told me "I don't have the energy to keep writing, so I am giving you what I have written. Do what you think is best with it." He added "The concentration camps have taught me a lot about the men of the 20th century and their civilization."

On November 11, 1958, Father Lelièvre agreed to say mass in Savigne Lévesque to honor those who died during World War I and World War II. It was to be his last mass. He gave his last sermon and pronounced his last words that were so much like him "Always try to do better". At the end of the service he fell into the arms of his friends. God had called him. November 11, 1958, was the anniversary of his capture in 1943. I had lost yet another of my best friends. I made it my duty to print "My Parish in Prison" together with my memoirs."

"My Parish in Prison" by L'abbé Julien Lelièvre

Chapter 1   The cell.

Adjusting to my role as a priest in a concentration camp.

In Colonel Rémy's book, (**Note 9-3**) we can read how extremely difficult it was for the agents of Free France in a country that was entirely subdued and occupied. We must bear in mind how frightened the people in France felt when the German troops invaded their country. These troops were remarkably powerful and disciplined and arrived after a debacle like no other in the history of our country.

In this context the first missions of the Resistance networks were understandably very slow to be organized. Those who were "contacted" to join the networks showed a lot of caution and hesitation.

In a city the place that opens its doors to everyone including strangers is the presbytery. Its religious affiliation reassured people to knock at the door. All kinds of people sought aid there: those who were hungry, people needing help, travelers, also people who were seeking peace of mind, and even people who wanted answers to their problems. The agents of Free France also knew they would be welcome there and often were helped by monks and priests.

This is how, particularly in 1943 and 1944, a lot of convents and presbyteries became naturally involved in helping those the Gestapo were after, those who worked with radio transmitters for the Allies' intelligence services, those who wanted to escape the STO or those who wanted to cross a border to join the French Free Forces.

Our way of 'serving' was quite humble, but not less dangerous because the Gestapo was always watching us. A lot of our fellow citizens did not give the Gestapo much importance, convinced that their lack of imagination made them less dangerous. No doubt those who thought that had never dealt with this organization that was so clairvoyant and powerful that even the army of the great Reich feared it. The Gestapo was constantly watching and sooner or later they would find a network, its organization, or its communications. Again Colonel Rémy explained in one of his books how a network meets its demise. His book will certainly help the history of our time. Moreover, in this counterespionage job the Gestapo was often aided by men and women who were French only in name; their behavior was so despicable they did not deserve to be called French.

One ordinary day or maybe one night a few men were at your door, wearing civilian clothes and would say "German police. You are under arrest." A priest could be called in the middle of the night to assist someone ill; he would hurry to get ready thinking he was going to comfort the soul of the person. But, he would return home only two years later, if ever. The Gestapo had invented this scheme that did not cause unwanted disturbance. Another priest might find his house surrounded, searched from top to bottom, entirely ransacked and, after having been briefly questioned and beaten, he might be taken to prison and join those he had previously harbored. Yet another was made to remove his religious habit that is not to the liking of these men and pushed into an automobile that would take him to prison.

Each arrest was different; generally speaking they would take place very quietly. This was in strong contrast with how much the Gestapo liked to paste on the walls the lists of those who had been shot. It seems that, in 1943, they were concerned primarily about the extension of the French Resistance. A member of the Gestapo one day said as he was questioning someone: "Everyone's involved, including women and priests".

How awful it was to feel handcuffs on your wrists, to leave your family without knowing your destination, not knowing how much these people knew about your activities and not knowing what they were going to do to you. During these long hours of anxiety you would think about a system of defense because, of course, you don't know what charges would be brought against you. "You're all the same, you've never done anything wrong" was what I heard from a big guy who was pushing me out of my office on November 11, 1943, at 3:00PM.

The arrival at the prison is probably the same for everyone. After questions about your identity, everything you own is taken away from you. A priest would only have with him his

Book of Prayers and his rosary. He would receive a lot of sarcasm. He would be exhibited as someone dangerous, an enemy of the Great Reich, a thief and a terrorist. The Gestapo hated priests because they thought priests had a lot of authority over their parish.

They didn't want the prisoners to communicate between themselves, so the last one to arrive was put into solitary confinement. Nothing looks more like a cell than another cell; nothing looks more like a prison than another prison, and yet each prisoner sees it differently. I don't have much to say about my first impressions when I arrived at the prison of Pré-Pigeon in Angers. It was a dark night and they didn't keep a light on for long. I only remember the table near the wall, a wooden stool and a straw mattress in the corner. The next morning I could look at things more carefully; I could see words and calendars written with someone's fingernails. Your first goal is to keep track of time, so you write down the days of the week and of the month. Every evening you cross the end of the day. The important dates in your life in prison are questionings, condemnations and sometimes executions. Looking at what other people had written was a subject of meditation for me.

Meditation was my main occupation in my cell. It must not be the only one and you have to create a daily schedule. During the two years of 1943 and 1944, those who went through this experience all said that the rules they imposed on their daily lives had been essential. Here was my schedule: every morning the guards would open the bolts and we knew it was time to wake up and get up immediately. The man who then gave us our herbal tea was not friendly, but at least it was a human face to see. The unsweetened hot drink helped us to wake up and it was the beginning of a new day. I prayed on my knees on the hard floor and this daily prayer would become my best support throughout my day. I then said mass, by memory of course, and the only sacrifice I could offer was my own in unity with God. Cleanliness was critical. I would do a little exercise, clean my cell, hunt the fleas and that would take up part of my morning. Lunch was limited and always the same: stale bread and boiled carrots, but it, too, filled up a little of our time. I would break lunch into what I called soup, vegetables, dessert and the bread would come last because I would use it to clean up my bowl well enough to use it as a mirror. This was the moment when we talked with prisoners in other cells, and news would spread. The news was always excellent: the Russian army is advancing well, the landing will happen soon, etc. During these conversations we also talked about how we were questioned, but we did so cautiously because some guards might become suspicious. We climbed onto tables and stools in order to peer out our windows and used our bowls as mirrors while conversing. Our conversations stopped when the sentinels fired near our windows. The evenings lasted longer than the mornings and again I would try to keep myself busy. I would say my rosary using my fingers. I would whittle using a piece of glass, clean my cell again, hunt for fleas again and walk until the guards put me back into my cell. Eventually our days would not feel too boring.

Suddenly, you are taken to a room where you are questioned. It is brutal and they behave like beasts while questioning you. It is painful for me to mention some of their techniques: the tub full of water, the fingernails they pull out, the electric shocks, the beatings, all of these things that are beyond imagination. The pain they gave us is still not as excruciating as the fright we felt before. We were so frightened to let some information slip out of our mouths that we were even frightened about any message a few seconds of silence would convey. We were that frightened about compromising someone during these interrogations.

It was all about self-control: controlling your eyes, your nerves, the expressions on your face. You had to choose an appearance and never get away from it. All this sounds easy, but the first time it happens to you it is extremely difficult. The members of the Gestapo may have had slow minds, but they specialized in this kind of job. They were accustomed to observing their victims and even if sometimes they accepted to be misled, it was never for long. However, they were not able to solve many cases, so much so that after 1943, they could not condemn anyone and simply considered all who worked against them as prisoners for security reasons.

A cell is not the best place to pray. A lot of priests had to adjust to an entirely new life there. Some of the cells had three or four prisoners. This gave the priests the opportunity to talk with a lot of other people and learn to know and understand them. Looking back, they will tell you that their experiences in prison helped them in their religious missions. The men that shared a priest's cell also learned to know the priest better and realized that he was someone who was able to share and understand other people's concerns. It changed the image of the priests being limited to their religious worlds and being somewhat selfish. Everyone in prison is on the same level and the priest became a friend, someone respectful of other people's freedom and silence, someone able to discuss all kinds of subjects, someone as clever as anyone in a situation of necessity. A priest was also someone who you could confide in.

The priest could adapt to this life in prison more readily than could others. First of all, they did not have their own family to worry about; secondly, their lives were already simple. The priest was usually educated and could take part in a variety of conversations. He naturally became the person that gathered everyone; the friend you don't want to be separated from.

I saw some priests in the prison of Compiègne, which was sadly an excellent preparation for the concentration camps. I witnessed their generosity and their eagerness to help their brothers whenever they could, without limiting their help to the religious realm.

Chapter 2   Compiègne Prison

It was already a camp and there was a form of concentration, but this compared poorly with what was awaiting us. Actually, Compiègne in January, 1944, was almost welcome after our interrogation prison in Angers. We had more room, we could talk more and the rules were a little less strict. Compiègne could be compared with a prisoner of war camp: roll call in the morning and evening, chores and cooking. The priests had the possibility to say mass and everyone was allowed to attend. We also had a library, meetings, conferences and some entertainment. After the silence and anxiety in the cells and the fright from the questioning, it was a much better existence. Of course, there were the barbed wires and watchtowers, but it was much better than four walls. In Compiègne men would stay sometimes as long as several months, giving them time to think and often they felt the need to talk to a priest. Nobody knew how much time they had and the priest had to hear a lot of confessions and make himself as available as one could. This became the basis of his mission in the concentration camps. In Compiègne, block 2 was the presbytery and that is where the priests received people. It was also where we presented debates and classes on theology that could last for hours. We didn't know what the next day would bring us, but we had the feeling that difficult times were in store for us and we tried to prepare ourselves for them.

I do not keep bad memories of Compiègne and I believe a lot of other prisoners felt that way too. Deep friendships started there and we priests learned to understand better those we were to seek to survive with. Such was not in our liturgy; it came from what our hearts taught to us in keeping with the word of the gospel: "love one another".

The prisoners who had wives and children did not know what had happened to them. Some of them knew their wives had been arrested and tortured and might even be near them in another part of the camp. The most profound pain was the uncertainty about what had happened at home since their capture. This is certainly why the subject of the family came up in our meetings more than we ever heard before. When we asked our friends to make a list of subjects they would like to discuss, family was at the top of the list. These men needed to talk about their memories and what they had never talked about with their families: the education of the children and resolving their families' problems. We needed to understand that their lives in the Resistance with its brutality and its clandestine activities did not allow much of a family life. They were eager to give their family more time. For us priests this was an indication of who they really were and for them it was a revelation. It was obvious for us that we should not only reach out to individuals, but also to their families. They would have long conversations about these subjects with or without the priests, each man looking at his particular situation. The fact that they didn't know what the future had in store for them led them to resolutions about what their lives should be. They wanted it to be different from the past; they wished to be better fathers and husbands.

There were a lot of things they did not understand about Christian religion, about the Old and the New Testaments, about the Church and the role of the priest. At the time the Catholic Church was trying to reach the younger generations and was not attempting as much to reach those who had a family. Life as it was and maybe as it still is does not encourage discussing and solving important problems. Religion for most people was not about life, but about what came afterwards.

*** Like an unfinished symphony, this is where "My Parish in Prison" was interrupted by the Father's exhaustion. ***

When Father Lelièvre went to London after the war, he was invited to the BBC where he asked to meet the French announcers. One of his friends recorded his words: "My friend Fred Auduc, after a commemoration ceremony honoring those who had belonged to the Hercule Buckmaster network, told me: Father, I am taking you to London. I want you to meet our boss, Colonel Buckmaster, for he is a charming man. I'm going to write to Peter de Belgeonne about our visit. We will see him and then we will visit the BBC."

If you knew Fred, you would know that when he has a project in mind he never gives up. His plan intimidated me, but the idea of meeting Colonel Buckmaster, who I had heard about since 1943, was very attractive. So, on Monday I saw the "Boss" and he is exactly like I thought he would be. More sensitive than he appears, attached to his former 'soldiers without uniforms', willing to help them rekindle the flame of their memories. On his request the BBC opened the doors of the French section for us and we were able to relive with one of its members the exalting hours of 1943. We now had seen the studios that we imagined so often. It was such an emotional moment. Only someone who has been involved, who has suffered and who has survived that difficult time could understand our emotions.

I should have told you about our visit in London or in Oxford or at the Ford factory or in Cambridge. It might have been more interesting to you, but what we wanted most was to visit "the Boss" and see the BBC. Please understand that as a former member of the Combatant French Forces, I felt strongly about paying homage to my leader and about thanking the BBC. The BBC had helped us so much during the occupation. They helped us carry on the fight in France and in concentration camps for the defense of the human being and freedom throughout the world."

"Ici Londres" were the first words of each of General de Gaulle's broadcasts and followed the first four beats of Beethoven's Fifth Symphony: "Ta Ta Ta Tum" (which is also the letter "V" in Morse code, a Churchillian "V" for 'victory', of course).

In imitation of General de Gaulle's program, Alfred Auduc finished this passage with: "Ici Londres, vous venez d'entendre l'Abbé Julien Lelièvre." "This is London; you have just heard Father Julien Lelièvre."

In early November of 1958, Julien Lelièvre handed the ten pages of his unfinished memoirs to Alfred Auduc saying he was too tired to finish them. On November 11, the fifteenth anniversary of his arrest, he agreed to say mass for those who had perished during the two world wars. As he stepped away from the podium, he fell into the arms of his friends and passed away. His last words were: "Always strive to do better all the time in every country in the world".

Alfred continued: "Father Lelièvre has left us and is now with his Heavenly Father. His memory will remain etched in the hearts of all the Resistance fighters and friends who knew him. I would like to finish his story with words he cherished: "Always try to do better everywhere in the world." His great ambition was to see all men work for peace. This peace can so often be threatened."

Doctors in concentration camps

Dr. Richard Grunberg was one of many who placed the needs of the sick above themselves while incarcerated in concentration camps. Grunberg was born in Paris in 1912, where his father was a doctor. Richard went to medical school in Toulouse and served in the army as a lieutenant. His father opened an office in Le Mans, where he had a hunting lodge nearby. In 1943, Richard joined the Resistance: "It was out of patriotism, idealism and in defense of our flag and our freedom." In May of 1943, he was requisitioned to serve on the medical commission of the Le Mans STO for the selection of those young men who were to be deported to work in German factories. During this time he had a boarder, Madame Crespel, who worked on his staff. She was the calm person amidst the turmoil and assisted with forging STO documents using stamps fabricated by Renée Auduc. With Madame Crespel's assistance Dr. Grunberg managed to modify a big stack of official forms, which allowed him over the following months to exempt 257 young men from STO.

Richard was a member of Captain Floege's Pascal Sacristain network. He took part in several drops including one on August 20, 1943, where the coded message was: "The waters of Lake Annecy are yellow", one in October with the message: "Jean has a crooked nose" and one on November 11, with the message: "Tell me you love me". Even though the Germans captured some 65 tons of munitions dropped into the Sarthe, much more was put into service by the Resistance.

Dr. Grunberg was arrested by the Gestapo on December 24, 1943, at 6:00AM while still in bed. He was taken to Vert Galand prison in Le Mans where he was being tortured by the Gestapo. Something fortunate happened. A German officer had assigned a Captain Thiator to the office where the STO were being processed. Madame Crespel had noticed that Captain Thiator was a kind man. She convinced Captain Thiator that Dr. Grunberg was an innocent victim. Eventually Captain Thiator promised to make an inquiry and went to Dr. Grunberg's cell to see for himself. He later admitted to Madame Crespel that he had been shocked by what he saw. He said the man who had interrogated Grunberg was a demon and he could not understand why this brute had not been court marshaled. As a consequence the Gestapo was obviously ordered to stop torturing Grunberg, frustrating these brutes that foamed at their mouths. Grunberg was also to be given double portions of carrot soup. Madame Crespel was able to smuggle to him a jar of jam after bribing the guards. Grunberg never saw her again, but was eternally thankful to her. Dr. Grunberg and others that Captain Thiator had prohibited from being tortured testified in favor of Thiator after the war and the French governor acknowledged his actions. Thiator became the first elected mayor of Saarbrucken, Germany, under Allied occupation.

Following his arrest, Dr. Grunberg was deported from Le Mans to several concentration camps. One day in Block 69 in Buchenwald, Grunberg could hear other doctors discussing something indistinguishable. By the time he was within earshot it was almost too late. He heard a handsome young French doctor repeating: "I am a bourgeois, I am Catholic, I am French and I will never do this". It was for Grunberg a revelation and became an inspiration. Later in Kochendorf the Oberscherfurher Buttner ordered the doctors to kill some of the prisoners. Dr. Grunberg relates: "We kept our heads high and refused. We were taken to Buttner who was enraged and although we knew we were facing death, we doctors declared one after the other: "I am a bourgeois, I am Catholic, I am French and I will never kill anyone." Buttner answered: "Then you will be hanged tomorrow." Unfortunately the doctors knew this would be his reaction. All night two of the doctors flipped a coin to decide who would hang the other, as was the custom in the camp. At the crack of dawn Dr. Grunberg was sent to a salt mine and Dr. Mahee was sent elsewhere. French troops had seized Stuttgart during the night, only 30 kilometers from their camp, and the Germans had fled. The doctors were saved.

Buttner was the master killer at several concentration camps, notably at Natzweiler. Even the SS guards were afraid of him. Here is how a man who was wild met a man who could think: Dr. Mahee began 'the rebellion of the hair'. Every five days we were completely head shaven as an act of humiliation. Dr. Mahee suddenly refused to have his head shaved. Buttner, who was inspecting, saw Mahee and raced towards him, yelling. Buttner put his hand on his Mauser at his belt. Nothing happened, only the interpreter received Buttner's wrath. Mahee kept his hair 2 centimeters long and Buttner, after two inspections, refused to see Mahee again. Buttner was later arrested by the Allies and hanged.

Dr. Grunberg was also sent to Mauthausen concentration camp and then finally to Dachau. When he returned to France, he declared: "We were turned in by "C", who gave the Germans the list of names of our network. "C" did not speak under duress, but out of cowardice to try to save his own life. He also handed in seven tons of weapons to the enemy.

The horrors Grunberg encountered as he tried to tend the sick in his concentration camps were to plague him for the remainder of his life. He later served as the mayor of his village. He published his memoirs "French Doctors in Doomed Places" and used the proceeds to help erect the monument to his Pascal Sacristain network in Cérans-Foulletourte.

CHAPTER 20   Reflections of Alfred Auduc

"Captain Floege arranged to meet with the governor of the Sarthe to introduce my wife and me and to describe our activities in the Hercule Sacristain network. The governor congratulated us, but obviously had never heard about us. Other people had claimed Resistance actions that we had carried out. These people were not happy to see us return. We came back only eight months after the liberation of the Sarthe. At the time, some conversations were about "heroes" that we knew had joined the Resistance only in its final hours. We were tired of hearing about Commander X or Colonel Z. One day as I was leaving the prefecture premises with Father Lelièvre, a 'colonel' came to us and introduced himself. He didn't need to do so as we knew who he was and refused to shake hands with him. Father Lelièvre told him "You see, we feel a little uncomfortable about the stripes on your sleeves. Had the war lasted six more months, you might have become a general!" The 'colonel' insisted he wished to congratulate us. Father Lelièvre then told him "You're wasting your time." For some people we were simply unlucky to have been sent to concentration camps and lucky to have returned home. Our being back home was a setback for some people's plans, but for others it was very valuable. For example, Charles Vasseur, the interpreter for the Germans I mentioned before, was in prison as a collaborator. We did whatever was necessary to prove he was not a traitor and wrote a thorough report of all the services he had rendered to the Resistance. He was released.

We kept in touch with the American flyers and their families from the Flying Fortresses that crashed in July of 1943, because I knew where the bodies were of those who had been killed. This is when I learned that those airmen who had survived and became prisoners of war were missing. They had been shot. With my surviving friends, in 1947, we decided to erect two monuments dedicated to the young American airmen, one at the site where the Lakanuki crashed near Poille, the other at the site of The Mugger's crash near Malicorne. Several thousand people including some English and Americans attended the dedication ceremonies.

Our mission was not yet over as we were asked to document the activities of our Hercule Sacristain network. It was a difficult and uncomfortable task that my wife fulfilled until she passed away in 1949. She was only 41 years old and never recovered from her ill treatment in the concentration camps. I want to express my gratitude to the English who helped us document these files. They opened an office in Paris in 1945, to assist the networks. Captain F. W. Hazeldine of the British Army staff and his secretary were particularly helpful. Renée's assignment was to write a folder on every member of our network for an Attestation needed to establish government benefits. These folders were later taken to London.

After returning home Renée and I had some moral satisfaction: we shook hands with General de Gaulle and General Leclerc, we met Colonel Buckmaster in London, we visited the BBC and the room where its messages had been read, we received the U. S. Medal of Freedom from the hand of an American general who told me: "70% of the French do not know about the role of the French Resistance. We think that without the Resistance we would have suffered a million more casualties and the war would have lasted much longer. That France is still a great and free country is due to you."

I was touched by the decision of Mr. Chapalain, governor of Sarthe, the mayor of Le Mans and the city council who gave the names of deported Resistance fighters who sacrificed their lives for their country to some streets in the city. There is now a rue Chanoine Lelièvre, a rue Renée Auduc, and a Hospice which also has the name Renée Auduc. On the front wall of the Hôtel de la Calandre a plaque in memory of Mr. and Mrs. Brault may be seen.

The sight of the children being massacred near the Belgian border, which was the starting point of my fight for liberty, has never left my conscience.

I was devastated by my wife's death in April, 1949. She could not survive the ill treatment of the camps for long. Her code name was Francine and it stuck with her until the end of her life. Among her fellow captives were Madame Genevieve de Gaulle, Madame Michelin and Madame André Dubois. I was also very saddened by the death of our best friends: 20 from our Hercule network and 36 from the Sacristain network. They had agreed to follow me in this clandestine battle for freedom. I felt partially responsible. Another bad memory for me was to have used weapons during the combat, even if it was sometimes in self-defense. And yet, I feel I have saved the lives of Frenchmen, Englishmen, Americans and Germans. In 1940 a military priest told me "If a Catholic becomes involved in a war, his duty is to obey his superiors and defend himself".

I had the opportunity to meet a few members of the Intelligence Service. The last one I saw was about two weeks before I was captured. He needed to see me. He had to go to my address on rue du Tourniquet and needed to take a lot of precautions: first he checked the streets near mine and then cautiously approached my home. From a distance he watched the house and waited until someone left. The first person he saw leaving was the cleaning lady, Madame Buon, who was going to the grocery store. He followed her and pretended he was choosing a few items. He wanted to listen to what she was saying and determine if anything unusual was going on inside the house. He then followed her home. When inside, he checked all the doors and looked for escape routes. Next, he turned to me and said "I have come to warn you; you must leave this house. Take your children to a safe place. If you want to, we can take you and your wife to England, but the job to be done is here in France."

He offered to take us east and asked me if Hercule had given me cyanide pills. Hercule had not because he was afraid they would be used in a moment of panic. These pills would kill a man in less than one minute. He gave me two and told me to conceal them in the lining of our coats. It was October, so the coat idea was plausible. When the Germans captured me, they must have guessed where my pill was because the coat was the first item they took from me. Fifteen minutes later a Gestapo agent brought it back to me with the lining all torn up. He slapped my face and said "No candies. They will be replaced by prunes (French slang for "bullets")." I have always wondered if the English secret agent who had given me the cyanide pills was not in fact a German double agent.

The Intelligence Service was an impressive organization. After our capture, the Gestapo was also after our son, Jean-Jacques. He fled to Paris to stay with relatives. He often had to change abodes because he had no food rations and, above all, people who sheltered him were afraid of retribution. A broom merchant, Mr. Perrin, who lived near the zoo in Vincennes, helped him. No one in the family knew where he was. One day a message was broadcast on the BBC: "Jean-Jacques is comfortable with his friend the broom merchant and is doing well." I must say that the reputation of the Intelligence Service was deserved. Here is another case to prove it. I had indicated to London that the mailbox of our network was in the Hôtel de la Calandre and I had related that Mr. and Mrs. Brault were available day and night for their agents who had parachuted in or were on the run. This hotel was at the corner of rue Gambetta and rue Montoise. The address I had given was rue Montoise. The next day I got a message from London asking me to check the address of the hotel. I contacted my friend Brault who told me the hotel was on rue Gambetta and not rue Montoise. The Intelligence Service knew what they were doing!

Later on when I went to London I asked the French people of the BBC how they had known that Jean-Jacques was staying in Paris with friends. They laughed and said "Don't be surprised by the depth and breadth of what the Intelligence Service knew and did."

During this same stay in London, an officer of the Intelligence Service told me the story of a hobo who had rendered great service to the Admiralty during the war. He was a Belgian from Antwerp and nobody knew how he had escaped to England. The security services took care of him. He wanted to meet agents from the IS (Intelligence Service) and said he could be of great help to them. They took him to their headquarters where he explained that, being from Antwerp, he used to live in the harbor area and was accustomed to asking German sailors on boats for food. The sailors were kind to him and soon let him go wherever he wanted without being suspicious. He must have been a former sailor himself, for he knew much about boats, including submarines. The head of the IS said "There is a plane leaving for Belgium tonight on a mission. We are going to give him a parachute and drop him there." Before he left, they gave him documents of no value and instructed him to take them to an assigned place. An agent on location was informed about the hobo and was asked to take the documents and ask him everything he knew about the German naval ships anchored in Antwerp. Every evening the information was sent to London and soon the Admiralty realized that the information was reliable. This allowed them to learn a lot about the movements of the German navy in the North Sea. It was invaluable information. After the war, they looked for the hobo in Antwerp, but never found him."

Although there were few women in his network, Alfred felt that in other networks credit should be given to women who sometimes undertook missions that only they could carry out. "I think that not enough has been said about this. (The fact that, in networks he knew of, eight women lost their lives serving their country). Not enough was said either about those less than twenty years old who dropped out of schools to serve the Resistance. For example, Jean Royer, from Sablé, at the age of nineteen wanted to be at his father's side. He was captured, sent to a concentration camp, and returned home in very poor health. A young member of my group was not as fortunate. His name was Paul Mechin, about eighteen, and he, too, chose to be at his father's side in the Resistance. He was sent to a concentration camp with his parents. He stayed several months with me and one day he was chosen to leave with a group to an unknown destination. His father died on the way. The SS forced little Paul to dig his father's grave. When this was done, they placed the body of his father in the grave and one of the SS said to Paul "In Germany, we bury manure, but not clothes", then forced Paul to take his father's clothes off. When this was done, Paul spread his arms over his father's body and, weeping, said "I will avenge you". The SS who were there understood what Paul said and shot him like a dog, then put his body next to his father's. How many of our friends had a similar fate?"

Alfred continues: "Even twenty years after the fact, the truth about the Resistance needs to be known. Under the German occupation some French people stayed comfortably at home with their slippers on. They considered themselves more intelligent than others. Some had earned a lot of money by trafficking with the enemy. These same people who wanted to justify this money thought they could spread the rumor that Resistance fighters were given important sums of money by the Americans and that I was one of them. I have a copy of the document that indicates how much I was given and I feel strongly about saying that I did not keep one cent of this sum. My wife used all of it to buy toys and candy for the orphans of our network at Christmas, and unfortunately there were a lot of them.

If the American government had wanted to reward us, we would have chosen to go to America in order to shake the hands of the brave boys who came to our land in order to bring us FREEDOM. Actually we were to meet a few of them as well as other soldiers who risked their lives to save Americans from the claws of the Germans. 'Save' is the appropriate word because some American soldiers who were made prisoners never came back home."

How did he do it? Returning from Dachau in June of 1945, weak, broken and penniless, how did Alfred build one monument to the crew of the Lakanuki and another to the crew of The Mugger by 1948? Sheer willpower is the answer; he was a man not to be denied. But he was not finished. He convinced Dr. Grunberg and l'abbé Lelièvre to join him in writing and publishing their memoirs which are combined in the book: "Memoires d'un Agent des Réseaux". But in 1965, Alfred had been blinded in an automobile accident and had to dictate his memoirs to his daughter Marie-Jo. Enough copies were sold to enable Alfred to erect an impressive memorial to the 64 members of their network who had been executed or otherwise succumbed. Colonel Buckmaster attended the dedication on June 18, 1967, the 27th anniversary of General de Gaulle's address that launched the Resistance.

Colonel Buckmaster dedicated the memorial to the Hercule Sacristain Buckmaster network. To his right are Captain Fred Floege, Claude Floege, two unidentified and Dr. Richard Grunberg.

In 1964, Alfred Auduc went back to the camp of Allach from which he had been liberated and also to Dachau a few kilometers farther. He reported "Nothing remains of the camp of Allach. Because of the typhus epidemic, the Americans burned all of the barracks. The bodies that had been piled behind the barracks had been pushed by bulldozers into mass graves. In Dachau, as I was going through the front gate, I became very emotional. I was thinking of the thousands of human beings who had left this place as smoke from its crematoriums. One area of the camp was being renovated to make it a place for international visitors. Three crematoriums with their sinister equipment (gallows, schlag clubs, etc.) could now be visited.

In that same area there is a life-size statue of a deportee raising his arms towards heaven. A religious building has also been constructed there. On a beautiful lawn a plaque indicates where the SS shot people. In a tidy barrack the archives of the camp may be seen, including books indicating the arrivals of the inmates, their executions and the list of the sinister equipment of the SS: sticks, schlag, weapons, etc.

I was surprised to see how many visitors were there from all nations, even Germany. There were also a lot of students. I asked a German girl what her thoughts were. She answered "After having been here, I would like to change nationality. If my father had been an SS, I would not want to even look at him." As I listened to her I was thinking of the contrast.

Twenty years before, a fifty year old German told me, as he was listening to the roaring of the Allied planes the day before we were to leave the Laura factory "At last, here they come. I have been a martyr for years. I have a son who has no respect for me. He despises me and says I am an accomplice of the cowards who lost The Great War." For this man, as for us, the noise of the Allied guns was the voice of hope. He thought the war should have ended much earlier.

I do not think that all the Germans were responsible. Hitler, like all dictators, governed by the use of force and used an army of criminals; the SS and the Gestapo spread terror in their own country as well as in the occupied countries. But, we deportees were in the hands of Nazi criminals and we have no pity for these monsters. If they were given the opportunity, they would not hesitate to bring new disasters to a world they have already tarnished. Still, I think the new Franco-German alliance is a good thing for future generations.

For the 20th anniversary of the liberation of the concentration camps, I was asked to make a report on the activities of our

Resistance networks named Hercule and Sacristain, better known in England than in France, as the networks were entirely controlled by the English. I chose to write my memoires to honor the memory of a hero of the Resistance: ANDRÉ DUBOIS.

My memoires are not written perfectly as I am blind, the result of a car accident, and I am using a tape recorder. I am grateful to my daughter for having accepted the task of writing all my memories."

Alfred Auduc 1965

Jean-Jacques adds: "My dear father, Alfred, using his own meager funds and raising what else was needed, erected three monuments to commemorate those who served to liberate his beloved country. The largest and most interesting is to his Hercule-Sacristain-Buckmaster network.

The second and third are to those B-17 crews who went down on July 4, 1943, the crews of The Mugger and the Lakanuki (above). I participate in ceremonies at these three sites every year, dressed in my replica of an American uniform and carrying the American flag."

A Touching French Reverence for American Flyers

Countess Jean Armand lost her husband after he saved an airman from The Mugger who parachuted onto their estate, Château de Montabon. Rather than being bitter, Countess Armand empathized with the families of the lost airmen. When the Countess learned that certain American family members were traveling from the U. S. to France to visit the grave of their lost one, her concern was manifested by her actions as shown in her letter of March 18, 1949:

"On July 4, 1943, an American Fortress crashed on my property and two of its occupants died: Lt. R. W. Peterson and Lt. Robert S. O'Connor. Since then we have stayed in touch with several of the survivors and with the families of the victims.

The remains of the two deceased were buried in Le Mans and then transferred to the temporary American cemetery in Saint André du l'Eure (Eure) on July 14, 1945. Lt. Peterson lay in grave #68 and his friend, Lt. O'Connor, who was the pilot of the Fortress, lay in grave #72, on which is engraved "Unknown". I saw the charred remains of Lt. O'Connor; his number was 0.661542. We were very surprised to see the word "Unknown" on his grave; we have all the information about him with us in Malicorne.

Today we learned that their remains are leaving Saint André du l'Eure, but to go where? We are very concerned and would like to know what has become of these two graves, particularly the one in Area H, #72 with the word "Unknown" on it. For us, there is nothing unknown about this grave. Could you tell us who we should contact to insure that Lt. O'Connor's name is inscribed on his grave? At the cemetery in Saint André du l'Eure, the person who looks after these two graves told us that nothing could be done without orders from the Headquarters. These orders seem to take a very long time when you consider that Lt. O'Connor died in 1943, and that we have undisputable proof of his identity.

A member of his family might come to France this year and it would be very difficult for us to tell him what is written on the grave of this brave combatant. I am counting on you, Monsieur, to address this matter and I am willing to come to Granville with all the documents, if it can help you in your research.

With my thanks,   Comtesse Jean Armand"

Countess Armand confided to her friend, Madame Rattier, that her letter (above) had not been answered, which elicited this follow-up letter from Madame Rattier on April 8, 1949:

"Monsieur,

I am writing to you on behalf of Madame le Comtesse Jean Armand.

Last month she wrote to you about Lt. Robert S. O'Connor. On March 21, she learned that her letter that was addressed to "Headquarters 7.756 AGRC, Zone #2, APO 58" had been forwarded to the competent authorities at the headquarters of the American Military Grave Service. This letter gave you all the information that we were able to put together at the time of the tragedy of "The Mugger - Thomas". We both witnessed this tragedy on July 4, 1943, on the property of Madame Armand.

For almost six years now, we have been trying to put an inscription on Lt. O'Connor's grave, which was transferred to the temporary cemetery of Saint André du l'Eure. In spite of the indication "Unknown" on this grave, we have often visited it and taken good care of it. All our efforts so far have been to no avail. Mrs. O'Connor and her two sons have just written to us that they will come on a pilgrimage to this dear grave next July. We would really like to see the inscription modified before this date. Of course, we can guarantee the identity of the pilot since we were there when he was put in his coffin and in spite of the presence of the Germans we followed his remains to the cemetery in Le Mans.

You are asking Madame la Comtesse Armand to send you all of the documents we have. We only have a few personal items considering the fire in the aircraft from which the unfortunate pilot's body was extracted. We have kept these items in order to give them to his family this summer: the metal frame of his wristwatch, the insignia of his regiment (the Wings) which he wore on his jacket as you can see on the photograph I enclose in this letter. We also have a shred of his flannel vest (underwear), a little piece of his burnt parachute, his box of sulfaides, and a few metal pieces of the aircraft. It is not much.

I am also enclosing in my letter a few newspaper clips that will help you understand what happened. These newspaper clips contain the story and the names of the eight survivors of the crew with many details.

Saving them cost Monsieur le Comte Armand his life. He died in a concentration camp like other good French citizens from our village.

We thank you for your help."

These touching examples of French citizens, who had lost so terribly much, wishing to honor those Americans, British and Canadians who liberated their country, have been repeated by many Frenchmen then and ever since. Lt. O'Connor and Lt. Peterson are interred side by side (plot J, row 14, graves 34 and 35) in the American cemetery at Colleville, atop Omaha Beach, with 10,600 of their fallen comrades. This immaculate, beautiful final resting place was given to the United States by General Charles de Gaulle and is now U. S. territory.

Countess Armand dedicated a monument to Lt. Robert O'Connor and Lt. Richard Peterson on her property the 4th day of July, 1948 on the fifth anniversary of the downing of the B-17 The Mugger. Alfred Auduc erected the monument.

A Letter from Alfred Auduc to Edward Chonskie dated December 14, 1945. Chonskie was a survivor from the B-17 The Mugger who stayed with the Auduc's after being rescued.

"Dear Eddie,

Please excuse me for using a typewriter but it will be easier to translate. We learned through Major J. (Jacqueline) Wite that you had made it safely home. How wonderful for us to have heard about you through Jacqueline. With her usual kindness she forwarded your dear letter to us.

Such difficult things happened since the day you came to visit us, but the most important thing is that you could make it safely home as well as Jean and Albert. This means our sacrifices have not been in vain. For you, our first liberators, we were ready to do everything that was necessary to get you home safely.

Our story is very sad. We both got arrested on November 3, 1943. We were tortured, sent to Nazi concentration camps until June of 1945. You know, Eddie, it was hell. We were deprived of food; we did not know what had happened to our dear ones for more than a year. We didn't even know what had become of our two little boys. We had to work twelve hours a day with no food, no clothes. It was indeed a terrible ordeal, but thank God we had the great joy of meeting again after this cruel separation. Thanks to you Americans and the Allies the nightmare ended. Just like you, we had put our lives in line for the cause of freedom in the world.

Here are a few names of French friends who were also captured for having harbored Allies: Abbé Pannetier, whom you stayed with, he was sent to Buchenwald concentration camp. He survived and is back and sends you his friendship; Monsieur and Madame Leproust, who had the butchery store on rue Montoise in Le Mans. Mr. Leproust made it back home, Madame Leproust died in Ravensbrück concentration camp. Our dear friend Chabannes also died in this accursed land of Germany. We have not heard about Monsieur Morant.

You see, my dear Eddie, what a sad story. The Gestapo completely ransacked our home when they arrested us. We have lost everything, but it does not matter. What matters is to have survived (with a much weakened health, of course). Enough of our story, what about you, my dear Eddie? Tell me about you.

Thank you so much for your kind letter. Reading it gave us great happiness. We would like to see you again so much. We wouldn't be able to drive in the Simca anymore because the Krauts stole it from us, with the rest. But, we would still spend pleasant days together. Please send me pictures. I am enclosing a picture of the four of us upon our return. You will see that my dark hair has grown back because the Krauts had completely shaven my head. They did everything they could to demoralize us, but fortunately we had faith and nothing could reach us. We were waiting for your arrival. We were rewarded and God answered our prayer. My little ones, my dear Eddie, are sending you a thousand kisses. You are now a part of our family and we will always be happy to read your letters, or even better to see you again. Tell us about your family. Any news from your brother?

Two true friends from France who will not forget you. Tell everyone that you All have our deepest admiration. The Survivors (Alfred and Renée Auduc)"

Remembrances between the Auduc's and David Butcher's family

David Butcher had to wait 40 years to see his friends in the Sarthe again. In 1983, his brother who lived in Seattle hosted a French student from Rennes. This student was interested in David's story and when he returned to France he had no trouble getting in touch with the Auduc family. From there, the trip across the Atlantic was organized for David and his daughter to join in an emotional reunion. Here is a postcard from David's daughter, Jan Roseman from Brentwood, Missouri in July, 1983:

Dear Jean-Jacques and Paulette,

I cannot find the words to tell you how important it has been for me to have the privilege to meet you at last. All my life, every time my dad talked about what he had experienced during the war, Jean-Jacques was the name that came back so often in the conversation. The time my dad spent with you and your family allowed him to get through the difficult moments the war imposed on so many people. The memory of this 12 year old little boy, much too courageous for his young age, biking through the countryside and doing the job of a man, is something my dad never forgot. In spite of the limited time we spent together at Marie-Jo's, (Jean-Jacques' sister) I can feel that the bond that has existed between our families for the past 40 years is very much alive in my heart and I hope you will always be part of my life in spite of the miles between us.

With all my friendship to you, Jean-Jacques and Paulette, Jan Roseman

A letter from David Butcher to Alfred Auduc dated October 24, 1983:   Hi Alfred,

I was so happy to receive your long letter and the pictures. It brought back so many memories, particularly memories of André Dubois. I remember as if it had happened yesterday. He was killed by the Gestapo after I left; at least that is what I was told.

I remember the day when we went to André's mom's to send a message to London. There was a German base for bombers with two runways. On one of them were the fake wooden planes (ME 109's) and on the other runway were the real planes. André sent the message to London and they bombed and destroyed about 35 ME 109's. This is when Gabriel Chartrand was caught by the Gestapo and I was nearly arrested. The Gestapo took the ID papers of Gabby and you had new ones made for him.

We had an appointment in Chateau-du-Loir where the English were doing weapons drops. I think Dr. Goude, Victor David and the lady who had the bakery were arrested by the Gestapo. This is when I started having doubts about Gabby and never saw him again. I often wondered whether you had seen him again.

I remember having spent some time in a farm nearby. I have pictures of the owner of this farm, but I don't remember his name. I remember having been rabbit hunting with a ferret. We would put the ferret into a warren and a mesh on the other entrances to capture the rabbits. You know, I think I went through your village during my stay in France: I still have an old map that was part of my equipment and Cérans-Foulletourte is circled, so I must have been there with a radio operator or something like that.

I wrote to Dominique. He says he doesn't live far from your place. I suppose he is in Norway for his job. I was really pleased to have this picture of Kenneth Christensen. I knew he was a cowboy and a strong personality.

I don't know if you ever knew how I left your great country. I arrived in Paris just before Christmas, 1943, and left in February towards the south of France. We stayed in a little town about 100 km from Toulouse and then in Toulouse. It was a very risky trip because the train was always full of Germans. Then we headed towards Carcassonne by bus where we stayed in a smuggler's hut at the foot of the Pyrenees. We stayed there about two weeks and then crossed the Pyrenees towards Barcelona in Spain. It was winter and very tough. The Spanish guide and one of the English men had frost bitten feet. I survived OK with just a few spots of frost bite on my feet. We then crossed Spain towards Gibraltar. An English colonel tried to make me say your names, but I did not give in. Consequently, I was detained and then for no obvious reason released.

Fred, I don't know if I can afford to go there because I live on social security, but I will make a special effort and we will see. Maybe by Bastille Day on the 14th of July I will have found a way. The dog that guides you is one of my favorites.

I will finish my letter now. I hope it will find you and your family in good health.

Good night, courage, 'we will beat the Krauts'.
David

Letter from David to Alfred dated November 10, 1983:
Hi Fred,
I decided not to lose contact now that I have found you even if it is just to send you short letters.

Let me try to explain to you who I am. I love flowers: roses, etc. I am very interested in UFO's. I have a small library on the subject. I think I have read every book written on this subject. People tend to think only crazy people are interested in this kind of thing, but I am not crazy. A lot of people don't see farther than the tip of their noses.

I also read the Bible a lot. I am not very religious, but I like to know where I come from and where I am going. It helps me understand the truth on the nature of God.

I am neither a teetotaler nor a drunkard. I drink a little wine or Scotch whiskey from time to time, but I am not interested in getting drunk.

By the way, UFO means "Unidentified Flying Object".

Things have turned out to be a little disappointing for me throughout the years. I had decided to orient my career towards electronics and instead I ended up being a carpenter, which I never liked. I would have been a good farmer because I like working outside a lot: cutting the grass or planting trees and flowers. I had a brother who passed away about four years ago. He owned a little farm in Michigan where I always enjoyed going. His wife kept the property and I still go there from time to time.

I have four children, eleven grandchildren and three great grandchildren (actually ten grandchildren because one of them killed himself last year). It makes quite a nice group when we are all together. It is the beginning of winter and I really don't like the season. Flowers disappear as well as leaves and even a few birds. Here is something else I like a lot: birds. God comes to me on the wings of birds.

Marie, I hope I have read your name properly. About Gabriel Chartrand, if you think it bothers Fred, don't mention it to him. Gabriel was caught by the Gestapo when we were in Tours. He escaped and it is a story in itself. I had suspicions about him and I think that if I cannot talk with him I will take this suspicion to the grave with me. He was seen in France in

1949, but never went to see Madame Monéris or Dr. Goude or Victor David, which always seemed strange to me. ***

Fred, I have a picture of a farm where I stayed when I was in France and I think it is near where you live. I would really appreciate if you would send me your book. My brother, Harry, has a granddaughter who I think has a tape recorder and I will be able to listen to the tape. It will give her less work and I will have your book on the tape.

Well, Fred, this is it for now, until next time. Your good friend, David

*** One of the unfortunate effects of serving in the Resistance was being suspicious of everyone. There is no justification for David Butcher's suspicions concerning Gabriel Chartrand. And, Chartrand did visit those people after the war that David Butcher mentioned in his letter above.

David Butcher was invited to attend a ceremony honoring the crewmen of his B-17 at the crash site in France, but he was a carpenter who had no resources for such an expensive trip. Learning of this, the French who knew him, and of his crewmates, raised the funds to purchase his round trip airfare. During David's 1984 return, he was made an honorary citizen of Poillé-sur-Vègre. Madames Monéris and David were moved to tears by the ceremony at the memorial for the B-17 Lakanuki.

Visits of American families of the downed airmen

When David Butcher passed away on April 19, 2004, in Ferguson, Missouri, his family carried out his wishes to have his ashes spread so they would mingle with those of his downed crewmates of the B-17, the Lakanuki. Grandson Curt Kehoe traveled with Sgt. Butcher's ashes to Poille-sur-Vègre and on September 12, with most of the village in attendance, Curt first poured the ashes over the indention that still remains at the Lakanuki crash site and then he poured what was left around the monument that Alfred Auduc had erected. Jean-Jacques was there, the last remaining member of the Resistance network that had saved and repatriated this brave airman those dark days sixty-one years earlier.

Jean-Jacques Auduc becomes a dear friend

Since its inception, Jean-Jacques Auduc has been a member of the Association des Anciens Combattants Franco-Americains: "Our organization preserves the memories of those Allied soldiers and Resistance members who liberated France in WWII. My particular interest and contribution is making presentations to French students about this important page in their country's history. It means so much that their childhoods have not been disrupted and they breathe the air of freedom that I lost.

It was through this organization that I met Ken and Claire Kirk. Ken is an American from Marietta, Georgia, while Claire is a member of France's old, aristocratic d'Orgeix family. Ken purchased Château RiveSarthe near Malicorne, France in December, 2005. I wished to enlist them in the Anciens Combattants Franco-Americains and was pleased with their eager response. Soon after, Ken invited his high school classmates to join him for a tour of French sites while staying together in his château. He invited my wife, Paulette, and me to join his classmates as they laid flowers in memory of Lt. O'Connor and Lt. Peterson at the memorial to The Mugger, then to speak to this group of 35 at dinner. I know only a few words of English, so Madame Kirk graciously translated my stories and relayed questions and answers. After Paulette and I returned to our home in Le Mans, these generous Americans collected enough money that evening to pay for us to fly to Atlanta, where Ken and Claire met us and took us to their home. These dear classmates then arranged a reception at a beautiful Marietta hotel where 110 people heard my stories. I was presented a U. S. flag which had flown over the U. S.

Capital, a cherished gift from Georgia Congressman Phil Gingrey.

The next day, the Kirk's, Paulette and I joined some 250 Mariettans for Memorial Day services at the Roswell Street Baptist Church, where I met several veterans and officers. The following day was Memorial Day when Paulette and I found ourselves in a convertible, yes on November 11, 2007, which carried a banner on each side reading: "French Resistance fighter who saved American lives". Along the parade route, people saluted us, many shouting out "vive la France" and similar warm greetings. Reaching Marietta's historic, lovely Square, Congressman Gingrey and Mayor Bill Dunaway greeted me. I joined the podium with several other speakers giving Memorial Day messages, again assisted by Madame Kirk, in front of some 400 attendees.

Having only the faintest hope but the largest wish possible of visiting the United States, a country that I admire above all others, my enjoyment of and appreciation for these wonderful Mariettans are boundless. It was a visit that gave me fulfillment and completion of a journey I started 64 years earlier when the rescuing of downed American airmen, our liberators, became my family's main objective.

Today its 2011, and I am the last survivor of those 104 brave resistance fighters who comprised the Hercule-Sacristain-Buckmaster network. My memoirs are dedicated to those 103, for they were my inspiration, my heroes, my companions, my family and my saviors."

Jean-Jacques Auduc   May, 2011

EPILOGUE

Would that there were a "happily ever after" for the brave souls in this history, but war does not allow such fantasies. Only, the human spirit is such that time heals most wounds and those that will not heal may be removed into the deeper recesses of everyday cognizance. Let us rejoice that Nazi tyranny was conquered and those formerly occupied nations of Europe are now free from the aftermath of World War II, even from the stranglehold placed on those behind the Iron Curtain.

Jean-Jacques Auduc has the deep satisfaction in knowing that his family looked eye to eye with the devil and did not blink. His joy is telling his story to the school children of France so that they, too, may know the price of their freedom and of those who fought and died for their country. Jean-Jacques has a deep admiration for Americans and was able to realize one of his dearest wishes when he traveled to Marietta and was honored with a reception, with a special car in a Veteran's Day parade and by delivering his thanks to all Americans in front of a crowd in the Marietta square. He has a dear wife, Paulette, who cares for him gloriously. Jean-Jacques is a joyful man, full of the undaunted spirit which characterized his father and mother. His humor is ever present and his wit can be dry and then sometimes boyish. That 12 year old hero is quite visible through all of his wrinkles.

André Dubois, whose code name was 'Hercule', had not received the British honors he merited until certain recognition was granted recently. SOE Section F agents were commissioned as British officers. The SOE overlooked granting Dubois a commission either during his training in England, as was the custom, or in the field. This omission meant that Dubois did not receive official commemoration in Britain along with his fellow Section F agents. In 2011, however, the Commonwealth War Graves Commission added his name to the Addenda panel of the Brookwood Memorial to the Missing, near Woking, England. Dubois was granted the rank of Lieutenant and the service number 121459. Dubois was worthy of being an honorary civil MBE, the 'honorary' due to his French nationality and the 'civil order' necessary since he had not been taken into the British armed forces. During the war Dubois was recommended for such an MBE, but when his fate was discovered, the regulations did not allow this award to be given posthumously. The official British film of F Section's wartime activities "Now It Can Be Told" depicts a version of Dubois' shoot out and arrest, featuring Marcel Rousset playing the part of Dubois. André Dubois may have perished in front of a firing squad, but his heroic actions sped the defeat of the Nazis. André is survived by his beloved daughter Francine, whom he called "Fan Fan" who still lives in the family's hometown of Tours. Francine, Jean-Jacques, the author and his wife Claire recently attended a ceremony at the Valençay Monument that is dedicated to the 140 SOE agents who gave their lives in the liberation of France. Only three former SOE agents were able to attend as this page of history is being turned.

Francoise Dubois, Andre's beloved 'Fan-Fan', remains friends with her sweetheart from 1946, Philippe de Belgeonne, whose family hosted her along with the Auduc's and Father Lelièvre when they visited with Colonel Buckmaster in London. Her son, Patrick, lives in the United States.

The French remember the Allied sacrifices made to liberate their country; have no doubt. Countless memorials and memorial services abound, today as yesterday. Consider the work of one individual from the Sarthe, Jackie Emery, who has documented all 86 Allied aircraft that went down in his region. He has produced his own memorial to those gallant airmen in the form of an extensive booklet.

Michel Auduc, Jean-Jacques' brother, lives in La Bouguelière, proud of the plaque that memorializes the significant role his home played in the activities of the Resistance. After the war,

Alfred and Roger Auduc refurbished La Bouguelière using wood that had been dried for ten years.

Claude Floege, although in poor health, lives in Angers and for many years has been a member of the Association des Anciens Combattants Franco-Américains. He is cherished by all who know him. The two leaders of the Association are Madame Marie-France Rogers and Jean-Claude Faribault.

Madame Leloup resides on her family's farm and continues to place fresh flowers on the monument to The Mugger, located just outside of Malicorne-sur-Sarthe, her way of paying homage to her parents who rescued a downed American airman, only to pay with their lives.

Jean-Jacques became eighty years old on July 9, 2011. He continues to address students and groups to relate his family's Resistance activities, hoping that listeners will go away with a new appreciation of what freedom costs. Jean-Jacques and

Paulette live a simple life and it would be grand if they might benefit from the proceeds of the sale of this book.

Ken and Claire d'Orgeix Kirk reside at Chàteau Rive-Sarthe, which they use as a base for conducting tours for North Americans around the major tourist sites in northwest France. Their highly acclaimed gourmet tours include the D-

Day landing beaches of Normandy, Monet's gardens at Giverny, Chartres cathedral, the chateaus of the Loire valley, Le Mont St. Michel plus other points of interest. They daily pass by places which are prominent in the story of the Auduc's Resistance network.

Château RiveSarthe and its 11 out-buildings are on a 52 acre park bordering the Sarthe River, some 25 miles southwest of Le Mans.

REFERENCES
"200 Figures de la Résistance et de la Déportation en Sarthe" author: Joseph Estevès 2009
"SOE in France" author: Michael R. D. Foot 1966, revised 2004
SOE files from the Kew National Archives in London
"They Fought Alone"   author: Maurice Buckmaster   1959
The memoires of Jean-Jacques Auduc, Alfred Auduc and Father Julien Lelièvre
Paul McCue provided additional information on André Dubois which he obtained from the research he has done on all 104 fallen Section F agents who have been memorialized on

the Valençay Section F monument. Paul may be reached via his Email address: **paulmmccue@gmail.com**
"The French Resistance" author: Don Lawson 1984

ABOUT THE AUTHOR

The author is immersed in this story both emotionally and geographically. Having purchased Château RiveSarthe near Malicorne, France, in 2005, he lives near the epicenter of the Auduc's Resistance activities. Jean-Jacques Auduc has become a dear friend and his stories have endeared both the author and his wife: Ken and Claire d'Orgeix Kirk. Having had four uncles who served during World War II, one in the 8th Air Force, the author is immersed in the stories of the bombing raid on Le Mans on July 4, 1943. Claire's father commanded a tank squadron in General Leclerc's 2nd Armored Division and his tank, named "Paris", was instrumental in the liberation of Paris. Colonel d'Orgeix, Claire's father, contributed to the book and the film "Is Paris Burning?" The d'Orgeix family has carried the titles of Marquis and Count since the 12th century.
This is the author's first manuscript. He has made good progress on his second, of historical fiction, about the exploits of an American reporter in Paris during and after The Great War. Mr. Kirk has several times been a Guest Columnist for the Marietta Daily Journal.

The author is a modest homo universalis. After being a standout scholar/athlete at Georgia Tech, he earned an MBA from Georgia State University, which offered him a full fellowship to study for a PhD in economics. He declined in order to pursue business and civic interests and has served on the boards of the Marietta/Cobb Museum of Art as Chairman, on the Marietta Board of Education as Vice Chairman, the YMCA, the Marietta Schools Foundation, the Marietta Rotary Club and the Friends of the Strand..

As a Rotarian, Mr. Kirk conceived and administered the Adopt-A-Polio Lab project in conjunction with the CDC to support the worldwide initiative to eradicate poliomyelitis. He was recognized as the U. S. Rotarian who had contributed the most to polio eradication for the three year period ending in 1996. He simultaneously served as Rotary District 6900's chair of World Community Service which was recognized as one of the top ten programs in Rotary worldwide.

His began his business career with Lockheed Aircraft in Marietta, GA and Sunnyvale, CA, when he almost single-handedly designed a state-of-the-art word processor system. Next, he was an international banker who conducted business development in Western Europe. This led to a corporate banking position with Credit Suisse where he managed their Atlanta office.

As real estate was a booming industry in Atlanta at this time, the author joined with his two brothers, Adrian and Mark, to develop residential real estate and build houses. To date, their company has developed some 430 building lots. Concurrently, Mr. Kirk taught finance at Kennesaw State University.

Mr. Kirk opens his Malicorne property for events and has hosted the U. S. Ambassador to France, the U. S. Counsel for Western France, a group from the U. S. Nuclear Regulatory Commission, and, for the 24 Hours of Le Mans Gran Prix races, 120 British fans. From their 52 acre and 11 building property, Ken and Claire conduct gourmet tours for North Americans of many of France's favorite sites.

Mr. Kirk was a national champion and national chairman in Masters track & field.